SOUTHAMPTON

Southampton

Gateway to the British Empire

Edited by
Miles Taylor

I.B. TAURIS

LONDON · NEW YORK

Published in 2007 by I.B.Tauris & Co Ltd
6 Salem Road, London W2 4BU
175 Fifth Avenue, New York NY 10010
www.ibtauris.com

In the United States and Canada distributed by Palgrave Macmillan
a division of St Martin's Press
175 Fifth Avenue, New York NY 10010

ISBN: 978 1 84511 032 1

A full CIP record for this book is available from the British Library
A full CIP record for this book is available from the Library of Congress

Library of Congress Catalog Card: available

Typeset by Jayvee, Trivandrum, India
Printed and bound in India by Replika Press Pvt Ltd

Contents

Illustrations

Contributors

Anne Anderson is lecturer in the History of Art and Design at Southampton Solent University and the co-author (with Mike Bucknole and Sophie Calloway) of *Southampton School and College of Art: A Celebration of 150 Years of Artistic Success* (2005).

Stephanie Barzcewski is Associate Dean and Professor of History at Clemson University, South Carolina. Her *Titanic: A Night Remembered* was published by London and Hambledon in 2004.

Ian Beckett is Professor of History at the University of Northampton. His books include *The Great War* (Longman, 2001) and (as co-editor) *The Oxford History of the British Army* (Oxford University Press, 1996).

Michael Hammond is a senior lecturer in English at the University of Southampton. He is the author of *The Big Show: British Film Culture in the Great War* (Exeter University Press, 2006).

Philip Hoare is the author of biographies of Stephen Tennant and Noel Coward, the historical study, *Wilde's Last Stand: Decadence, Conspiracy and the First World War* (Duckworth, 1997) and *Spike Island: The Memory of a Military Hospital* (Fourth Estate, 2001). His study of the New Forest Shakers, *England's Lost Eden: Adventures in a Victorian Utopia*, was published in 2005 by Fourth Estate. He is currently writing a book on whales and making a film for BBC's *Arena* on the same project.

Bruce Knox is an honorary research associate of the School of Historical Studies, Monash University. He is presently working on a study of Bulwer Lytton and the colonies.

Tony Kushner is Professor of History and Director of the Arts and Humanities Research Council/Parkes Research Centre for the Study of

Jewish/Non-Jewish Relations at the University of Southampton. His recent books include *We Europeans? Mass-Observation, 'Race' and British Identity in the 20th Century* (Ashgate, 2004) and (with Donald Bloxham) *The Holocaust: Critical Historical Approaches* (Manchester University Press, 2004).

Joanna Lewis is a lecturer in Imperial and African History in the Department of International History at the London School of Economics. She is the author of *Empire State-Building: War and Welfare in Kenya, 1925–52* (James Currey, 2002) and is writing a history of the memorialisation of David Livingstone in Britain and Africa.

John Oldfield is senior lecturer in Modern History at the University of Southampton. He is the author of *Popular Politics and British Anti-Slavery: The Mobilisation of Public Opinion against the Slave Trade, 1787–1807* (Manchester University Press, 1995) and the forthcoming *'Chords of Freedom': Commemoration, Ritual and British Transatlantic Slavery* (Manchester University Press, 2007).

Paul Readman is lecturer in Modern British History at King's College London. He is currently completing a book on the late Victorian and Edwardian land question, entitled *Land and Nation in England: Patriotism, National Identity and the Politics of Land, 1880–1914*.

Adrian Smith is senior lecturer in History at the University of Southampton. His books include *Mick Mannock, Fighter Pilot: Myth, Life and Politics* (Palgrave, 2001), *The New Statesman: Portrait of a Political Weekly, 1913–31* (Frank Cass, 1996) and, most recently, *The City of Coventry: A Twentieth Century Icon*, also published by I.B.Tauris.

Miles Taylor is Professor of Modern History at the University of York. His most recent books include *Ernest Jones, Chartism and the Romance of Politics, 1819–69* (Oxford University Press, 2003) and (co-edited with Michael Wolff) *The Victorians since 1901: Histories, Representations and Revisions* (Manchester University Press, 2004).

Preface

When we think of imperial cities, a city such as Southampton seldom springs to mind. From ancient Rome to neo-classical Paris, Berlin and Vienna, through to modern-day New York and Washington, the imperial metropolis conjures up images of bombastic and hybrid design, ornamental and military pomp, ostentatious mercantile wealth and streets teeming with the labouring poor and service classes. Within the British Empire our gaze might turn to Calcutta in the final decades of East India Company rule. Or we might consider Melbourne, Christchurch and Capetown as they grew as outposts of Britishness during the wave of mass emigration in the middle decades of the nineteenth century. And the list might extend to include Hong Kong, Cairo or Nairobi, cities whose urban landscapes tell something of the recent history of the rise and fall of British dominion overseas. Closer to home, the notion of an imperial city is frequently applied to late Victorian London, as parts of South Kensington and the Strand were transformed at the time of Queen Victoria's golden and diamond jubilees. And the great Atlantic port cities of the United Kingdom – Bristol, Glasgow and Liverpool – whose fortunes, as well as those of their hinterlands, were so tied up with slaves and sugar, immigration and emigration and with the transfer of technology to distant colonies, also qualify as imperial cities at different times in the modern era. Further inland, it has even been argued that a city such as Victorian Birmingham – with its pro- and anti-slavery campaigners, and its arms industry – was immersed in the culture of empire as well.

What of Southampton, then? In its heyday it is no exaggeration to say that the British Empire started and ended with the city and port of Southampton. In the nineteenth century, explorers, missionaries, settlers and soldiers left from Southampton docks for dominions far away, just as in the twentieth century the city was the point of arrival for migrant workers, demobbed Tommies and political refugees. Southampton has been a gateway to and from the empire, yet the history of this most imperial of cities has been curiously neglected, not least by its own modern inhabitants. The history of

Southampton as walled city, ancient and modern port, spa town and model municipality has been told and retold many times. However, the most distinctive aspect of its modernity – as conduit to the colonies and dependencies of the United Kingdom – has never been the subject of scholarly analysis. The ways in which we might remember episodes of Southampton's imperial past, as well as the ways in which that past has been forgotten, are the subject of this book.

The idea for a book of essays that explored the history of the city and port of Southampton in the age of imperialism was one of the first projects of the Centre for the Study of Britain and its Empire, newly established in the history department at Southampton in 2002. At a hugely successful day conference held in the spring of that year, many of the chapters in this collection were aired for the first time, and to their number have been added several significant new commissions to bring breadth and take the volume up to date. The book investigates the history of Southampton from the Napoleonic Wars down to the recent redevelopment of the city, through the lens of empire. The essays in the collection look at some of the major imperial celebrities and policy-makers associated with the region such as David Livingstone, Charles Gordon and the Earl of Carnarvon; at Southampton during the principal wars of the modern period; at the popular culture of imperialism in the port and in the city; and at the experience of migrants. But the book is also concerned with the acts of memory associated with the history of Southampton: namely, how the imperial setting of so much of the city's recent past has been blurred by or overlain with other stories and new ways of remembering its heritage. In this way, the book makes a contribution from the perspective of a local and regional case study to recent debates about how 'imperial' were the British and to what extent the culture of imperialism permeated into provincial daily life in the modern era.

This book could not have taken shape without the input and encouragement of many people associated with the Centre for the Study of Britain and its Empire during my directorship in 2002–4. As well as acknowledging my former Southampton colleagues whose essays now feature in this collection, I would like to thank the following for their support and friendship during three eventful and interesting years on the south coast: Christopher Bayly, Bill Brooks, David Cesarani, Beverley Gough, Peter Gray, James Gregory, Cora Kaplan, John Mackenzie, Ros Oates, Mark Roseman, Sujula Singh, Lorna Young and Chris Woolgar. I am particularly grateful to Shirley Matthews for last-minute assistance with editing the volume.

It is also a pleasure to record my gratitude to the following organisations which have provided the commercial sponsorship for the publication of this volume. They are: Associated British Ports (ABP), the Friends of Southampton's Museums, Archives and Galleries (FOSMAG) and the Ordnance Survey.

MILES TAYLOR

York

Figure 1 Map of Southampton and its region, c. 1802, by permission of Hampshire Record Office.

Chapter 1: From spa to garrison town

Southampton during the French Revolutionary and Napoleonic Wars, 1793–1815

John Oldfield

I

As is well known, for much of the quarter century between 1790 and 1815 Britain was at war, first with Revolutionary France (1793–1802) and then with Napoleon (1803–14, 1815). Perhaps just as important, Britain emerged from this prolonged conflict as 'the predominant maritime and imperial power'.[1] Nevertheless, these were difficult years and for many local communities they were the source of considerable social and economic dislocation. Southampton was no exception. It was not just that the French Revolutionary and Napoleonic Wars brought with them the threat of invasion, although that was undoubtedly important. The intensity of the conflict, as well as the presence of troops in and around Southampton, also threatened the town's reputation as a 'healthy, populous' resort; indeed, for long periods during these years Southampton bore 'more the appearance of a garrison town than of a fashionable watering-place'.[2] As we shall see, there is little doubt that the experience of war created strains within the local community. But, crucially, it also created opportunities and, with them, an enlarged sense of Southampton's place in the world and of the town's regional identity.

Southampton's history as a spa town dates from the 1750s when it was 'discovered' by Frederick, Prince of Wales, and then by the Dukes of York, Gloucester and Cumberland. Royal patronage, in turn, stimulated an extensive programme of rebuilding and enlargement. In 1767, the old assembly rooms in the High Street were replaced by what became known as the Long Rooms, near the West Quay. During the following decade, work began on the rebuilding of the Audit House, and provision was made for the better paving, lighting and watching of the town.[3] Approaches and promenades were also enhanced. In

1769, for instance, the path eastward along the shore was planted and became known as the 'Beach'. Coffee houses, circulating libraries and a theatre appeared, as did the town's first newspaper, the *Hampshire Chronicle* (1772), and its first bank (1778). Finally, improvements in travel (better vehicle design and more roads and canals) stimulated trade and touring. By 1803 there was a daily stage coach from Southampton to London, as well as a night coach which left at seven in the evening three nights a week. There were also daily coaches to Bristol and Bath, and stages to Oxford and Portsmouth three times a week.[4]

In these and other ways, Southampton quickly acquired a reputation as a 'genteel and fashionable resort', which was only secondarily regarded as a port. One important barometer of change was the number (and variety) of shops and trades. The town's first *Directory*, published, significantly, immediately after the end of the French Revolutionary Wars, listed 23 tailors, 13 hairdressers, 9 milliners, 8 mantua-makers, 5 watchmakers and 4 perfumers and wigmakers. There was even demand, it seems, for 2 umbrella-makers, a 'Wedgwood, china and glass warehouse', and a working jeweller. Equally revealing is the presence (in 1803) of 9 surgeons, 7 solicitors, 4 music masters and 2 dancing masters. In short, Southampton boasted 'most of the conveniences and agreements of the town, without that perpetual thunder and clouds of smoke, which blind and deafen those who have not quite lost their senses'. The 1803 *Directory* went further. It was hardly possible, it declared, to see any difference between Southampton and 'fashionable places' like Weymouth and Brighton. To the curious it offered 'an improving and wealthy country', to the traveller 'an increasing trade', and to the invalid 'a fair prospect of health'.[5]

Politically, the town was moderate or 'conservative'. The mayor and corporation had petitioned the House of Commons in 1788 against the slave trade, and there appears to have been some local interest in the issue of parliamentary reform, but, like other parts of the country, Southampton rejected the principles of the French Revolution and rushed forward to pledge its loyalty to the King in 1789.[6] The town was also ready to welcome French émigrés, at least in theory. Initially, most of these émigrés were priests, who had fled France following their disavowal of the oath that accompanied the Civil Constitution of the Clergy (12 July 1790). So many landed in Southampton, in fact, that in 1792 local inhabitants began to complain that they were causing a rise in the price of provisions.[7] But it was not only French priests who found their way to Southampton. Nobles and military officers also sought refuge in the town; others, including soldiers and sailors, were later brought in on British transports. Indeed, over the years Southampton would prove a popular recruiting

ground for émigré regiments, while many of the sailors were reportedly distributed among the ships of the British fleet.[8]

The influx of French émigrés clearly placed a strain on Southampton's limited resources, and it was with obvious relief that in May 1793 the Mayor was
able to get rid of all those who came within the scope of the Alien Act.[9] By this
date, of course, the country was already at war with France. Eager to lend
its support, on 30 January the corporation of Southampton had subscribed
50 guineas towards an 'additional bounty to seamen and landmen who shall
enter at his port'; and the following month it had issued another loyal address,
this time expressing the hope that 'every faithful subject, and every lover of his
country, will press forward with virtuous emulation, to support the dignity
of [the] crown, and the honour of the British name'.[10] Over the coming
months, the town began slowly to adjust to the realities of war. In April, for
instance, the *Hampshire Chronicle* reported that 'the press has been serious here
these two days past, the fishermen, colliers, etc. not having been spared'.
Perhaps more revealing still, in June 1793 local publicans lobbied the corporation to 'obtain an order from [the] government for purchasing or erecting barracks [in Southampton] for their immediate easement, as they are at present so
much oppressed by the number of soldiers quartered at their homes, that their
families suffer considerably'.[11]

Yet, in another sense, the war remained somehow distant and unforbidding;
that is, until 1794 when the remnants of the Earl of Moira's ill-fated expedition
to Brittany arrived in Southampton Water. The eight regiments under Moira's
command had already spent much time being shuttled back and forth across
the North Sea, and, in the cramped conditions on board the transports, typhus
fever had spread rapidly through the ranks; in fact, when Moira arrived at
Cowes on the Isle of Wight in January 1794, over 800 of his men, out of a full
complement of over 4,000 rank and file and 561 officers, were listed as 'sick'.[12]
Some of these men were sent directly to the naval hospital at Haslar, but others
were landed in Southampton where the 'great sugar-house' in Gloucester
Square had been hurriedly converted into a military hospital with space for 700
to 1,000 men. Meanwhile, many of those still fit for active service were placed
in barracks fitted up in Chapel, near the river Itchen, where they received
'an allowance of three pints of porter a day, each man, in lieu of a half pint of
rum, with bread and meat, which made them look healthy and strong'.[13]
Welcome as they were, the presence of Moira's troops in Southampton understandably caused considerable anxiety. Conditions in the hospital were openly
acknowledged to be 'alarming' – one report described it as a 'scene of dreadful
mortality' – while rumours of a 'pestilential fever' prevailing among the troops

in barracks at Chapel undoubtedly deterred many would-be visitors to Southampton.[14]

As spring turned to summer, Moira's troops, augmented by new recruits, three regiments brought over from Ireland and a corps formed out of French émigrés, were placed together in a camp on Netley Common (to the east of the river Itchen). Then in June, amid great excitement, the whole force, consisting of 11 battalions, struck their tents and embarked on board the transports for the relief of Ostend. According to the *Hampshire Chronicle*, the men 'went on board with the true spirit of British veterans, their colours displayed, the regimental bands playing "Britons strike home" '.[15] Yet, here again, tensions quickly rose to the surface. Several of the soldiers' wives, it was reported, 'insulted the French émigrés grossly – swore that if they had firelocks they would shoot them; saying, but for them, their husbands need not have been thus hurried away'. It hardly helped matters, either, that prior to the embarkation of Moira's troops, several hundred French sailors were brought on shore from the transports, who had been sent home by Lord Hood for refusing to 'fight for the King of England'. Predictably, as the sailors made their way to the Chapel barracks, further skirmishes occurred, including one incident in which a French officer drew his sword upon an 'English light-horseman', following 'some opprobrious epithets' concerning the 'characteristic features' of their respective countries.[16]

In what was to become a familiar pattern, Moira's troops were quickly replaced by a roughly equivalent number of regular and militia regiments. Indeed, by August 1794 there were already six detachments of cavalry encamped at Netley, as well as several infantry regiments; in all, over 3,000 men, not to mention wives and children.[17] The comings and goings continued over the summer. In September, five regiments left the camp at Netley to strengthen the defences of the Channel Islands; others subsequently embarked for the West Indies, Gibraltar and the continent. By mid-October only four foot regiments remained at Netley, the 78th, 90th, 96th and 98th, and later that same month the camp broke up, following a 'grand review of horse and foot on Shoreland Common'. Some of these troops appear to have been moved into Southampton, where they swelled an already significant military presence. In fact, several regiments spent the winter of 1794 quartered in Southampton, among them the 108th, whose officers gave a ball at the Star Inn in November, which, by all accounts, was 'brilliantly attended'.[18]

The new year brought with it another flurry of activity. As early as March, it was rumoured that an encampment was again expected, and by the end of July, 11 regiments were under canvas, this time on Nursling Common (3 miles north-west of the town centre). Some months later, this force had grown to 17 regiments, or roughly 10,000 rank and file and 600 officers, while other regiments seemingly were quartered at Netley.[19] The sense of excitement was palpable. Lord John Manners, who visited Southampton in August 1795, wrote that 'as soon as we got into the town nothing but red coats and military were to be seen on all sides'. Interestingly, Manners was also treated to a tour of the camp, which he described as being in a 'very pleasant situation' on 'dry and healthy soil'. He was less impressed by the condition of some of the troops, however. 'Although there were nine regiments on the ground', he noted, 'they did not make up above 6000 men in all, as some were very weak.'[20] Disease proved a constant hazard, particularly when such large numbers were crowded together. Between August and October 1795, no less than eight men from the camp were buried at St Boniface's Church, Nursling, together with 15 children.[21]

The build-up of troops continued throughout August. By the middle of the month there were above 130 transports in the 'river' (Southampton Water), 'more than ever was seen here at a time', and within a week there were half as many again. At last, on 24 August, four of the regiments, under Major-General Doyle, embarked for the little islands of Hedic and Houat, south of Quiberon, where, earlier in the year, 3,500 French émigrés had been routed by republican forces. The remaining regiments finally left Southampton in October 1795, as part of Abercrombie's expedition to the West Indies, but not before they had been inspected by the Prince of Wales, the Duke of York and 'principal officers' in a grand review on Nursling Common that lasted from nine in the morning until five in the afternoon.[22] 'There never was seen, by the oldest men living, so much hurry and bustle as this town has experienced for the last two days', the *Hampshire Chronicle* reported on 3 October, 'boats full of troops going on board the transports, and others returning from them, together with near 200 sail of vessels moored off the quay'.[23]

No sooner had this force departed, however, than several more transports came up the river, this time filled with Hessian and Hanoverian troops, who were quartered in barracks for the winter.[24] Then, in December, Doyle's troops returned to Southampton, having spent several weeks of sickness and semi-starvation on the Île d'Yeu. For locals, the desperate condition of Doyle's four regiments must have brought back painful memories of Moira's abortive expedition in 1794. The official monthly returns indicate that in January 1796 over 400 of his men were listed as 'sick', out of a total of about 3,000. In addition, Doyle brought back with him a group of 'loyal emigrants', of whom 40 were again 'sick'.[25] As if this were not enough, the flow of troops in and out of the town continued. In March, for instance, five regiments marched into Southampton to embark on board the transports for the West Indies, followed by two emigrant regiments, one commanded by the Duke of Choiseul, the other by the Count D'Hompach. By the early summer, however, the town was at last returning to something like normality. The hospital in Gloucester Square was finally removed in July 1796, and Southampton and its inhabitants were 'left once more to the tranquillity and quiet so conducive to the health and pleasure of our visitors'.[26]

For the moment, at least, attention turned to the threat of invasion. Already a supplementary or additional militia had been established in 1796, and, following the collapse of Britain's allies, volunteer units were also hurriedly organised throughout the country. With the support of the corporation and local gentry, four volunteer regiments were raised in Southampton between 1797 and 1798: the Southampton Volunteer Cavalry, commanded by Major William Smith, collector of customs; and three corps of infantry – the Southampton Volunteers, the Portswood Green Volunteers and a corps of Associated Householders.[27] Like the militia, these units were drilled and disciplined not by regular officers but by 'well-intentioned gentlemen of respectable county families'. For this reason, there was always a certain social cachet attached to being a member of a volunteer 'regiment'; and, to judge from local newspapers, Southampton's volunteers certainly enjoyed themselves. But there was also a serious purpose behind the balls and dinners. Like the militia, volunteer units were required to do varying periods of serious training each year; in return, the Government provided arms, pay and freedom from militia service. Moreover, under the Duke of York, who took over the Command-in-Chief at home in 1795, they were also provided with the support of an advisory body of field officers, who, besides inspecting volunteer regiments, offered their commanders advice and encouragement.[28]

Over the next two or three years, these volunteer units would become a familiar sight in Southampton. In other respects, however, the town remained relatively quiet and undisturbed; certainly, there was little of the excitement that had characterised the early part of the war. But then, in 1799, Southampton suddenly found itself at the centre of another military build-up. The first transports arrived in the 'river' in May 1799, and by July the town was 'crowded with the successive arrivals of the 25th, 69th, and 9th regiments from Cowes, the 35th and 79th from Lymington, and the 55th from Guernsey'. More troops followed, including the 2nd Queen's regiment from Ireland and 'the remainder of the Guards'; in all, probably 10,000 men squeezed themselves into the camp on Shirley Common.[29] The *Hampshire Chronicle* reported on 15 July that 'this place is very crowded and very gay. Every lodging-room in the town is occupied, and the trading part of the community look to a profitable season'. A week later, the whole force was on its way to Yarmouth, where it embarked for the Netherlands. But no sooner had the encampment broken up than the 46th Regiment of foot and a division of the North Devon militia arrived in Southampton, where they joined the 18th Regiment of light dragoons, who had been in the barracks since early May.[30]

Almost exactly a year later, another expedition began to assemble in Southampton, this time on Netley Common. The 52nd 'took the ground' in May, followed in June and July by the 9th, 13th, 54th and 79th Regiments. Eyewitness accounts from this period are rare, but years later Harriet Lewin, whose family lived nearby at Pear Tree Green, recalled 'the general aspect of the tents, the music of the military band playing before the Commanding Officer's tent, and the women in pits dug out of the ground, cooking and washing linen, etc.'[31] Ultimately, the men encamped at Netley (with the exception of the 13th Regiment) would form part of Abercrombie's successful expedition to Egypt, where he defeated the French at Alexandria, but at the time the destination of the troops was kept a 'profound secret', much to the frustration of the local press, the transports sailed from Southampton in August under sealed orders.[32] By this date, of course, local inhabitants were accustomed to the bustle surrounding the departure of these military expeditions. Nevertheless, 'the distress of the poor women, who were not allowed to embark with their husbands', obviously made a deep impression on some observers. One of the women, it was reported, was so overcome with grief that she threw herself into the river and was drowned.[33]

Abercrombie's success, followed by Nelson's victory at Copenhagen in April 1801, signalled the end of the French Revolutionary Wars. Peace preliminaries were concluded in October, to be turned into a definite peace treaty at Amiens on 27 March 1802, bringing to a close what for Southampton had been a difficult and testing period. For over five years the town had been at the centre of a series of complex troop movements, involving thousands of men and officers, that had brought the conflict home to its inhabitants in a dramatic and sometimes alarming way. Particularly worrying, not least to local businesses, was the threat of disease. As we have seen, troops regularly disembarked in Southampton in poor health and, in many cases, carrying typhus fever. Lord John Manners reported in 1795 that one regiment at Nursling had just arrived from Jersey, 'where they had buried 250 men of fever'. Clearly, the risk of infection was high; according to one recent estimate, the death rate in Southampton in 1794 and 1795 was roughly twice the national average. Southampton survived these challenges. Yet, as the bullish tone of the 1803

Directory suggests, the French wars undoubtedly dented the town's reputation as a 'healthy, populous, and genteel place of resort', even if they do not appear to have done it any lasting damage.[34]

II

As it turned out, the peace of Amiens proved to be short-lived. By May 1803, Britain was once again at war with France, opening another prolonged struggle that only finally came to an end with Wellington's victory at Waterloo. Immediately, thoughts turned to the threat of invasion. In Southampton, as in other parts of the country, the local volunteer units, with the exception of the Southampton Volunteer Cavalry, had been 'disembodied' in 1802, when they had 'delivered up their arms, to be forwarded to the depot at Portsmouth'.[35] Hurriedly, they were re-embodied, this time in the form of a single corps, the Loyal Southampton Volunteers, under the command of Captain Josias Jackson, a retired West Indian planter. 'The spirit and alacrity with which the Volunteers enter in this town, at once evinces the zeal and energy of a free people', noted the *Hampshire Chronicle* in August 1803, 'and we have no doubt but that a numerous and effective force will soon by ready to resist any attempt of invasion that may be made by our implacable foe on this coast'. Once again, the Corporation contributed 100 guineas towards the training and equipment of the Volunteers and, suitably 'accoutred', early in October they marched to the Audit House where they took the oath of allegiance.[36]

Similar units were also organised at Ringwood and Fareham, which not only drilled together on occasion but also shared and swapped garrison duty. In May 1804, for instance, all three units were in Southampton, when they mounted a 'sham fight' on Pear Tree Green, and the Loyal Ringwood Volunteers were in Southampton again in 1805 and 1806. From time to time, the Loyal Southampton Volunteers were also augmented by the South Hampshire Regiment of Yeomanry Cavalry, commanded by George Henry Rose, one of Southampton's two members of parliament.[37] Understandably, these comings and goings excited considerable local interest. But whereas the inhabitants of Southampton were inclined to view the influx of regular troops with a degree of distrust and suspicion, their response to the Volunteers was, on the whole, positive. Interestingly, the departure of the Loyal Fareham Volunteers in May 1804 was regarded by some as a matter of regret, 'not merely for their steadiness and good behaviour since they have been here, but from the pleasure which has been hitherto derived by viewing this excellent corps perform its different manoeuvres'.[38]

If there were important continuities between the Revolutionary and Napoleonic Wars, however, there were also important differences. The most glaring of these was the absence of the sort of large-scale military build-ups – the camps and the embarkations and disembarkations – that had characterised the earlier period. Throughout the Napoleonic Wars, there was always at least one regiment, or part of a regiment, of horse or foot stationed in Southampton, and others regularly passed through the town, either en route to Portsmouth or, occasionally, to the Continent.[39] But there were never any large numbers of regular troops quartered in Southampton, not least because successive secretaries of war favoured concentrating Britain's forces at Portsmouth and East Kent.[40] For this reason, the war took on a very different relevance and meaning for the town's inhabitants, especially after 1805 when Nelson's victory at Trafalgar finally removed the threat of invasion. Priorities changed and, with that, Southampton began to regain something of its former reputation as a fashionable 'watering-place'. Capturing the mood, the *Hampshire Chronicle* reported in July 1809 that the town was 'full of gaiety, being thronged with company of the first rank and fashion. The principal inns are crowded, and it is expected there will be a very full season'. Even between 1812 and 1815, when Britain was also at war with the USA, Southampton continued 'full of company'.[41]

If anything, the Napoleonic Wars' most dramatic and far-reaching effect was on the town's shipbuilding industry. Southampton, of course, had long been associated with shipbuilding. In the words of an Admiralty survey of the south coast from Devon to Land's End, Southampton Water, with its 'good and even soundings sufficiently deep for any ship', afforded everything to be desired 'for sustaining and preserving the greatest naval strength in the world'.[42] It was these natural advantages that attracted many London shipbuilders to the area. During the 1740s, for instance, Henry Bird, a famous London shipbuilder, took over George Rowcliffe's yard at Northam, on the river Itchen; and at about the same period, Robert Carter, also from London, was building for the Crown at Chapel. By the late eighteenth century, Southampton's shipbuilding industry was concentrated in the hands of two local shipbuilders: Thomas Raymond at Northam and George Parsons at Bursledon, on the river Hamble. In addition, there was a highly successful shipyard at Buckler's Hard near Beaulieu, which produced 30 ships of the line between 1745 and 1790, including the *Agamemnon* (1781), which formed part of Nelson's fleet at Trafalgar, and the *Illustrious* (1789).[43]

The outbreak of war in 1793 and again in 1803 brought with it new opportunities for local shipbuilders. Put simply, the demand for ships of all types – ships of the line, frigates, sloops, brigantines and corvettes – could only by met by contracting large amounts of work to private shipbuilders. George Parsons at Bursledon, to take one example, produced 12 ships for the Navy, among them several sloops and a much larger number of frigates, between 1793 and 1807, at which point he appears to have moved to Warsash.[44] More remarkable still is the story of Thomas Guillaume, who in 1805 owned a yard at West Quay in Southampton and who that same year bought the yard at Northam, which for some time had been 'unemployed'. Over the next six years, Guillaume built 13 ships for the Navy, most of them brigantines. Indeed, such was his efficiency and reliability that he regularly completed contracts within the specified period of time, sometimes by as much as 26 days; in 1808, he is reported to have completed a brigantine in just seven weeks. By contrast, the yard at Buckler's Hard, admittedly working on a much larger scale, produced five ships of the line between 1805 and 1810, nearly all of which were many months late.[45]

Estimates of this kind are necessarily tentative, but it seems likely that at least 23 naval ships were built in Southampton between 1803 and 1814, not to mention the 11 built at Buckler's Hard.[46] More difficult to determine is the impact of this industry on the local economy. In 1808, the 'cost' of a brigantine was somewhere in the region of 6,000 pounds, that of a frigate closer to 25,000 pounds. Ships of the line were more expensive still. In 1805, the Adams at Buckler's Hard quoted the Admiralty 81,656 pounds to build a two-decker warship with 74 guns. These were impressive sums of money, although this is not quite the same thing as saying that shipbuilding was highly profitable.[47] What we can say with some certainty, however, is that the yards in and about Southampton provided a stimulus to the local economy, both in terms of jobs and wages; in 1805, roughly one-sixth of the cost of a brigantine or frigate was made up of labour. Moreover, shipbuilding also had an impact on the growth of allied trades: timber, tools, iron goods, tar and rope. Small wonder, then, that large crowds of 'respectable' people are reported to have attended the launchings of these ships, or that the industry of men such as Parsons and Guillaume was noted and applauded by the local press.[48]

War, and the prospect of war, helped to sustain Southampton's shipbuilding industry until at least 1813 (after the peace of 1815, the Admiralty decided not to build any more ships in private yards).[49] But, to some extent, the frantic activity in the town's shipyards struck a false note. Mary Russell Mitford could write in 1812 that, to her mind, Southampton had 'an attraction independent even of its scenery, in the total absence of the vulgar hurry of business or the chilling apathy of fashion'. She went on: 'It is, indeed, all life and gaiety: but it

has an airiness, an animation, which might become the capital of Fairyland.'
Mitford undoubtedly exaggerated, but she was not alone in being charmed by
Southampton's seeming 'other-worldliness'. Moy Thomas, who visited the
town in 1810, described it as 'upon the whole' a 'large and respectable Town,
very clean and of a pleasing appearance', adding that 'its contiguity to the Sea,
the beautiful Walks and rides about it, throw a charm around this spot, which
will ever secure to it a high reputation as a Watering place of Elegant and
Fashionable resort'.[50]

Yet, as the regular movement of troops through the town testifies, the war
was an ever-present reality for the inhabitants of Southampton. It was with
understandable relief, therefore, that they welcomed the prospect of peace. The
proclamation announcing the end of hostilities in July 1814 was greeted with a
series of spectacular illuminations. The Custom House was 'most superbly
lighted up', and the Audit House, Town Hall, 'and every Public Office were
equally brilliant'. There were also a large number of 'beautiful and appropriate
transparencies', which reportedly 'surpassed any thing of the kind that has
before been attempted in this town', and, to conclude the evening, a display of
fireworks.[51] The war, it seemed, was over. In September, the military staff in
Southampton were reduced to the peace establishment and, perhaps more
meaningful still, in November the barracks stores were disposed of by public
auction. So quick was the adjustment that Wellington's victory at Waterloo the
following year seems to have caught many local inhabitants unaware. Hurriedly,
the lions of the Bargate, in the centre of the old town, were illuminated and
decorated with laurels, but otherwise the celebrations in Southampton seem to
have been strangely low-key.[52]

III

The experience of war undoubtedly tested the patience and resolve of
Southampton's townspeople. As we have seen, the influx of large numbers of
regular troops, particularly in 1794–6 and again in 1779–1800, changed the face
of the local community. It also brought with it disease and the risk of infection.
Some of these problems, of course, went away. Others, however, proved more
insurmountable. While most of the troops passing through or encamped in the
neighbourhood of Southampton appear to have caused little or no trouble, a
small minority (we do not know how many) were guilty of petty crimes, most
often theft, or else found themselves involved in brawls and skirmishes.
In June 1809, for instance, a party of Irish soldiers quartered in Southampton
'knocked down, with their bludgeons, two watchmen, one of whom is

dangerously ill, in consequence of which four of the ringleaders are committed to prison'.[53] French soldiers were also viewed with obvious suspicion, particularly when, as happened in 1794, they were discovered carrying concealed weapons. Even officers were guilty of transgressions. In July 1795, the *Hampshire Chronicle* reported that a duel had been fought by 'two officers of the army near Netley', adding ominously that 'one of them was so dangerously wounded that his life is despaired of'.[54]

It is also true to say that these years (1793–1815) witnessed a certain degree of economic dislocation. As Temple Patterson argues, the French Revolutionary and Napoleonic Wars 'checked the promising development of [Southampton's] seaborne trade', leaving it 'largely dependent upon its coastwise, Channel Islands and Irish traffic, all of which were also a little diminished'.[55] Disruption of this kind inevitably created scarcities. The corporation was forced to intervene to provide the poor with soup and bread in 1794–5, 1795–6 and, again, in 1799–1800; and, as Roger Wells and others have noted, there were food riots in Southampton in 1799 and 1800. In September 1800, for instance, an 'angry crowd assembled in the Market, seized all the butter and potatoes displayed on the stalls and sold them at reduced prices', prompting the Mayor to call out the Volunteers.[56] Finally, it is generally agreed that the Revolutionary and Napoleonic Wars slowed down the physical development of Southampton and, in particular, the work already under way in the area known as the Polygon, most of which remained incomplete, as well as that in Albion Terrace, which was never finished.[57]

Nevertheless, it is easy to exaggerate the scale of these problems. Whatever critics may have feared, troop movements were accompanied by a regular influx of visitors into Southampton. Similarly, the presence of various militia and volunteer regiments, 'officered by some of the gentry of their respective counties', more than compensated 'for any loss through the outbreak of hostilities'. Indeed, at times the town was so full of fashionable company that 'a great number of respectable inhabitants were induced to fit up their houses for the accommodation of the public'.[58] Many of these same people, of course, patronised the town's shops, circulating libraries and assembly rooms, as, undoubtedly, did many of the officers stationed in Southampton. More to the point, the presence of troops – and the regimental parades, dinners, and balls – added to the colour and excitement of local life. To take an obvious example, in June 1804, Josias Jackson entertained 'a numerous company of fashionables' at his home, Belle Vue, after which the company repaired to the Beach, where Mrs Jackson presented the Loyal Southampton Volunteers with their colours. Not to be outdone, regular units also organised balls and other social functions, vying with each other to put on the most 'brilliant' entertainments.[59]

Southampton's inhabitants also learned to turn the wars to their own advantage. For one thing, troops needed to be fed and clothed, and it comes as no surprise to discover that many local tradesmen entered into contracts for biscuits for the Navy and bread and clothing for the Army. (It also helped that large quantities of Spanish wool were imported into Southampton after 1795.) Similarly, Thomas Skelton, a local bookseller, did a brisk trade supplying the army with stationery and (printed) blank documents.[60] None of this is to deny that the experience of war created dislocation and even, on occasion, distress. But, as the history of local shipbuilding demonstrates, it also brought with it opportunities. Perhaps just as important, Southampton emerged from the French Revolutionary and Napoleonic Wars with its reputation as a 'fashionable watering-place' intact. In fact, it is even conceivable that the Napoleonic Wars, in particular, helped to sustain the vitality (and prosperity) of Southampton at a period when its reputation as a fashionable resort was increasingly being challenged by the Isle of Wight and, to a greater extent, by Brighton and Cheltenham.[61]

Finally, it ought to be said that these years helped to (re-)establish Southampton as an important centre of military operations and, as such, a gateway to an enlarged British empire. If the French Revolutionary and Napoleonic Wars came more closely home to the people of Southampton than any previous wars had done, they also reinforced a sense of the town's local and national significance. Indeed, Sotonians could look back upon both of these wars with a degree of pride and satisfaction and not just because of the valiant efforts of their shipbuilders. Time and time again, the town had roused itself, and some of that same spirit (and enterprise) undoubtedly enabled its inhabitants to negotiate the difficult post-war years with greater self-confidence as well as a clearer sense of their own local identity.

Figure 2 Highclere Castle, Hampshire. Home of the 4th Earl of Carnarvon, by permission of English Heritage.

Chapter 2: The Earl of Carnarvon

Highclere, Hampshire and Empire

Bruce Knox

I

Hampshire's place in the annals of the British Empire is secured by the port cities of Southampton and Portsmouth on its south coast. In the north of the county, however, is the estate and castle of Highclere, property of the earls of Carnarvon. The life and career of Henry Howard Molyneux Herbert (1831–90), the fourth Earl, adds another and quite different dimension to Hampshire's record, for this Lord Carnarvon was not only a devoted man of the county but was one of the two or three most distinguished holders of the office of Secretary of State for the Colonies. Having served a kind of apprenticeship in 1858–9, he proceeded to the cabinet post in 1866–7 and again in 1874–8. Later, in 1885–6, he briefly held the lord lieutenancy of Ireland. As Viceroy, he attempted – amongst other things – to apply the accumulated experience of the colonial empire which had absorbed his energies and enthusiasm more than any other aspect of national business and largely defined his political career over some 34 years.

Geographically, Lord Carnarvon had as much connection with Berkshire as with Hampshire. Highclere is but a couple of miles from the county border; from Newbury in Berkshire, 6 or 7 miles away, came the post; and through Newbury passed the Great Western Railway (closer still at a mere 4 miles). From Newbury station, London (Paddington) was 2¼ hours away.[1] This mattered, for Carnarvon was deeply involved in national as well as county affairs from an early age. He needed to be in London during the week when Parliament was in session and even more when he held office. At the same time, however, he was much attached to Highclere and conscientious in attending to the business of his estate and the county. As often as possible, therefore, he took advantage of the railway to return to the country at least at weekends; and, as time went by, he developed the habit of inviting a variety of people in political, literary and artistic life to join him. Not least, he made a point of inviting visiting colonists or colonial officials. Thus was the Hampshire county magnate enabled to extend the benefits – and perhaps some of the values – of his place in the social pattern of England into the overseas empire.

Carnarvon combined county and empire more usefully perhaps than any other British statesman. Succeeding his father in the earldom in 1849, just before going up to Christ Church, Oxford, he was just eighteen years old. He inherited one of the largest estates in Hampshire, with other property in Somerset, Wiltshire and Nottinghamshire – upwards of 35,000 acres in all. He also inherited the castle which the third Earl had set about rebuilding on a large scale, a work that he continued and, incorporating his own ideas, completed. Here lay the core of his concerns. Before turning to politics, he set out to manage his estates, looking for instruction to his guardians (as they were during his minority), especially Sir William Heathcote, another and even larger Hampshire landowner and MP. His first ten years in the task were encouraging.[2] But not all of Carnarvon's efforts were bent in that direction. The county, he asserted, was 'the unit and centre of social and political organisation' in England, and within its boundaries 'we are, for many purposes, an independent and self-governing community'.[3]

Accordingly, his county received Lord Carnarvon's attention early and late. He was a landlord; he naturally also became a magistrate. In 1860, he became Chairman of the Judicial Committee of the Hants Quarter Sessions. As late as 1887, he accepted the lord lieutenancy. More surprisingly, the following year he was elected to the new County Council. This was the only time in his life that Carnarvon submitted, or needed to submit, to election for public office – to a body moreover created by an Act of Parliament which he had opposed because it superseded traditional county government by petty and quarter sessions. The reason he gave speaks for itself. He accepted nomination because, 'I have spent the greater part of my life in this place, to which I am bound by so many ties of affection and property'.[4] Long before this, however, Carnarvon had expanded his activities into wider fields. His view was that it was possible to serve England's interests, 'whether we form a part of the internal or the external existence of the nation, in parliamentary, in municipal, in military, in civil, in active, in literary life, in agriculture, in commerce, in art and science'.[5] Once he had taken his seat in the House of Lords in 1854 he suited action to words.

It is difficult to overstate Lord Carnarvon's awareness of the responsibilities of his rank and station. He was devoted to 'that reverence for the traditionary past which has characterised and ennobled our race'.[6] Officiating in 1878 at the unveiling of a memorial to Lucius Carey, Second Lord Falkland, one of Charles I's most earnest supporters when it came to a rupture with Parliament in 1641, he praised the qualities he believed properly belonged to 'the ideal of a statesman and the very representative of an hereditary class' [. . .] whose duty and defence it is by the diligent use of the greater leisure vouchsafed to them in a busy age to fit themselves for the varied duties of society and legislation'.[7] Perhaps unsurprisingly, he was extremely alive to 'the many risks and the certain evils of multitudinous rule' and believed that 'history and human nature' were against 'the ultimate triumph of Democracy as a form of Government'.[8] His concern, however, was not to maintain, or indeed to create, artificial privilege. As late as 1885–6, addressing his fellow country gentlemen in the wake of the electoral reforms which he believed gave cause for almost unprecedented anxiety, he professed optimism based on 'the maintenance and representation of classes and interests as of yore', rather than 'the licentious and disordered medley of individual voters' drawn from 'a new and numerous class who live by daily wages'. He was not expressing contempt for the newly enfranchised voters, who, he believed, were not lacking in 'conscience and shrewdness and sense of duty'. But such people were of necessity 'totally ignorant of almost all that has made and directed public opinion'.[9] He warned his fellows that the future of the country and the state could not be secured by succumbing to 'selfish or caste feelings' and that 'the fulfilment of the duties of property is as wise as it is right'.[10] These were decent and high-minded notions, but they might also contain a hint as to why Lord Carnarvon was an indifferent player in the rough and tumble of middle and late nineteenth-century politics, with untoward results for his equally decent and high-minded policies as a cabinet minister.

When he spoke of Lord Falkland's qualities, Carnarvon made it clear that they were as apposite for the nineteenth as for the seventeenth century. Thus, again, when he addressed the country gentlemen, he was able to say that during his career he had seen, 'much of English politics and political parties, to observe the inner working of Governments, and, by personal experience, to know the springs and conditions of Parliamentary and public life'. In fact he did rather more than that. In Parliament from 1854, he attended principally to questions of social reform, and he maintained that concern to the end. County matters also remained with him – not least in the matter of prison reform[11] – though he had many interests, from Freemasonry, to translations from Greek and Latin, to ritualism and the Church, to anti-vivisection, women's franchise and 'fair trade' – as well as the history of Hampshire and Berkshire. The question of party attachment naturally arose. The 22-year-old peer was successfully wooed by Lord Aberdeen just before the outbreak of the Crimean War for support. But Carnarvon's instincts were 'Conservative as well as progressive',[12] so the Derbyite Conservative Party was always a possible home for him. Not that the prospect was very encouraging: in Carnarvon's opinion, in 1857, the Conservatives were 'broken and, masterless', and, as late as mid-February 1858, he threw himself into yet closer involvement with estate management.[13] But Lord Derby formed a minority ministry late that very month, and Carnarvon's political and public life took a momentous turn. Conscious of the party's need for 'new blood', Derby offered Carnarvon the under-secretaryship of state in the Colonial Office. After some characteristic (and, not for the last time for his colleagues, irritating) exhibition of scruples, Carnarvon accepted.

II

The great problem of empire was thus opened to Lord Carnarvon by the business of government between February 1858 and June 1859. Ironically, when offered his post, he doubted whether the Colonial Office would provide 'a sufficiency of work to keep [him] really employed'.[14] His mind had, however, been to some extent prepared. His housemaster at Eton was the Revd. Edward Coleridge, Commissary for the Bishop of Sydney and a founder of St Augustine's College, Canterbury, for training clergy for colonial ministry. Coleridge might well have introduced his boys to the idea that the colonies mattered, for he was specially anxious that 'our fellow subjects in the Colonies will not be deemed less our Brethren [. . .] because they have been induced by the spirit of honest enterprise, or compelled by severe necessity, to settle in a distant part of our Empire'.[15] Still, there is no evidence that Carnarvon took a special interest in the subject during his time in Oxford or immediately after. It is true that in 1853 he embarked at Southampton with Lord Sandon for a tour – to describe such an adventurous journey rather feebly – which took him to Beirut, Damascus and Baghdad, then back again via Constantinople. The expedition might have had some effect, for in the House of Lords in the mid-1850s he thrice drew particular attention to the colonies.[16] But a British possession, Malta, was only incidental in 1853, and his only specifically colonial journeys were to be to Canada in 1883 and to the Cape and Australia in 1887.

Carnarvon in 1858–9 participated in an unusual episode in official and political history. Two secretaries of state successively held office. First was Lord Stanley, Derby's son, about as unlike his father as could be. Conscientious, rather equivocal in his attachment to conservatism and lacking warm feelings for colonial connections,[17] he was, nevertheless, a good choice for the department and for Carnarvon. Stanley had travelled widely, to India as well as to the Mediterranean, the West Indies and North America, had published books on his travels and had been Under-Secretary in the Foreign Office in his father's 1852 ministry; and he was highly intelligent. In perhaps three principal ways he contributed to Carnarvon's development. His insistence on 'clearing the desk' by the end of each day helped instil a strict habit of work – reinforcing Carnarvon's legacy from his tutor in Oxford, the philosopher, historian and theologian, H. L. Mansel.[18] Stanley also wrote exemplary minutes to justify and convey his decisions. He was wary of difficult issues: for instance, the problem of whether or not to abandon the Gold Coast settlements and Labuan; Sir George Grey's wayward behaviour at the Cape; the signs of impending trouble in the Ionian Islands; abuses in the conveyance of Chinese labourers to the West Indies; the need to deal with the gold rush in the Hudson's Bay Company's territory; and he always had cogent reasons for conceding whatever was needed to avoid argument with a self-governing colony. Daringly enough, however, Stanley privately assured the Governor General of Canada, Sir Edmund Head, that the British Government would not object to federation of the North American provinces: a source of embarrassment to his successor. Stanley's third contribution was to restrain any enthusiasm which Carnarvon might have exhibited: he did not encourage his junior to take large decisions.

This phase of Carnarvon's initiation into the government of 'fifty colonies in various stages of civilization and in different parts of the world' lasted only three months. If his diary reflects a certain regret that he had not been considered to be of more consequence, it was far from putting him off, struck as he was 'by the manifold character of the business – the great difference in the subject matter of the several colonies, the large questions of government & principle wh. were constantly involved'.[19] He attended to all the papers which came before him – which was most of everything coming into the office – and wrote numerous minutes. Based often on detailed research, he copied and preserved many for future reference.[20] In June 1858, then, Stanley moved to become President of the Board of Control for India. His replacement in the Colonial Office, Sir Edward Bulwer Lytton, Bart.,[21] must be one of the oddest such appointments ever made. He had no previous official experience. He was 55 years of age. His political career had been that of an independent Radical supporting Whig ministries in the 1830s, losing his seat in 1841 for not sufficiently distancing himself from a ministry that exhibited hostility to the Corn Laws, returning as a Conservative (Protectionist) in 1852 associated with Disraeli. The qualities recommending him to Lord Derby during the next six years were those of a pamphleteer and speaker. But Disraeli was personally close to Lytton, and he was very doubtful about his appointment to the Cabinet.[22] Again, though he deserved well of his new party, Lytton was a known eccentric and an immensely popular novelist whose merits were questioned by sundry reviewers.[23] It required a considerable insight for Derby to judge that they showed an imagination that could contribute practically to the affairs of state. Indeed, Derby's chief consideration might have been the use that Lytton might be in the House of Commons by parading the Conservatives' liberal credentials.

Fortunately for Lord Carnarvon, Derby's insight (if such it was) was sound. To the Cabinet, Lytton proved to be a trouble, not least because he was constantly looking for a peerage, while his health (not helped by his estranged wife's irruption into his political life) was problematic by December 1858. To the department, he was a trial. He had irregular habits of work, was given to moods and enthusiasms and was quite capable of misplacing papers.[24] J. R. Godley of the War Office, who knew much about colonies, thought Lytton was 'literally half mad about his responsibilities, and fancies he is going to reform the whole colonial empire'.[25] If this were all, we could agree with Coral Lansbury, who judged that Lytton was 'a lamentable Colonial Secretary'; or that he was simply incompetent. Yet the novelist-statesman was an important contributor to Lord Carnarvon's onward career.[26] Carnarvon was gratified by Lytton's ready recognition of his advice and frequent acceptance of it. More than that, because of Lytton's failing health, the Parliamentary Under-Secretary exercised a remarkable degree of responsibility. Towards the end of the ministry's life he, not the Secretary of State, signed despatches; well before that, cooperating with the permanent officials, he wrote most of the decisive minutes and drafted important despatches, subject only to the supervision of Lord Derby himself.

III

If Lytton had a particular qualification to be Secretary of State for the Colonies, it is that he was the author of *The Caxtons* (1849). The novel's subtitle was *A Family Picture*, but it could equally well have been 'Class, Race, Colonisation, and the Condition of England'. In the course of a readable tale, Lytton prescribed emigration to the colonies as a major hope for the relief or redemption of those who were in adversity in the overcrowded Old World. Australia provided his specific, and he expounded 'a philosophy of colonising'. This is worth considering a little, for David Cannadine has recently cited *The Caxtons* in support of his view that, '[f]ar from wishing to reject the stratified society of the mother country [. . .] pundits and politicians strenuously recommended its replication in the colonies'.[27] Lytton, he says, 'expressed the hope that an aristocracy would develop in Australia'. That – though it needs to be construed – is so: he mentioned 'monarchy' as well.[28] But it is not at all clear that Lytton urged, let alone strenuously urged, 'replication'. He added the words 'self-developed' and 'of a simpler growth than old societies accept'; and he envisaged an emigration blending '*a certain portion* of the aristocratic with the more democratic element'. This would, he hoped, plant 'all the rudiments of a harmonious state, *analogous* to that in the mother country [. . .] and not left a strange motley chaos of struggling democracy'.[29]

As Secretary of State, the closest Lytton came to trying to establish his 'rudiments' was his organisation of the new colony of British Columbia; and he indeed placed a considerable premium on the emigration of as many *gentlemen* as possible to that reclaimed wilderness.[30] But there is no evidence that (as could be taken to be implied by Cannadine) Lytton or anyone else intended to try to impose social hierarchy on the colonies – i.e., the 'colonies of settlement' – 'dominions' in Cannadine's book. Lytton's far from unique hope was that democracy, known to be aggressively supported in the colonies (especially the Australian one), could be restrained from doing the harm which was assumed would be its consequence in Britain. By the time he took office, the view of those others who formed colonial policy was tolerably realistic. The permanent officials in the Colonial Department had been, to some extent, persuaded that giving honours to colonists might be politic – but not that they should be imposed. Herman Merivale, Permanent Under-Secretary, confessed in March 1858 that,

> the tendency of opinion in the educated classes is in favour of hereditary honours in some of our colonies, to a much greater extent than would have been anticipated by those conversant with them 20 years ago. And I understand that the Queen has expressed herself very favourable to the principle, of conferring baronetcies, in very carefully limited instances.[31]

Lord Carnarvon was aware of this tendency, mainly because he (in preference to the rather forbidding Lord Stanley) was approached by Vesey Leslie Foster-Fitzgerald, late Colonial Secretary of Victoria,[32] with rather extravagant suggestions for giving honours to colonists. Carnarvon referred them to Frederick Elliot, the Assistant Under-Secretary for the Colonies, whose opinion was that the project was 'chimerical and ill-founded'. 'What Pitt aimed at', Elliott wrote,

> and others have wished was the creation of an Aristocracy in the Colonies. This, if it were possible, would very probably be a barrier against license and a bulwark to liberty. But making titles does not make Aristocracies. It is in vain to give hereditary titles where fortunes are ephemeral.

Nearly 70 years after Pitt and the Canada Act of 1791, he accordingly judged such plans to be impracticable because, 'in new countries . . . society itself is essentially democratic'. Carnarvon simply initialled this; Lord Stanley fully agreed with Elliot.[33] Lord Derby, the Prime Minister, had thought through the question while he was Colonial Secretary in the early 1840s. He gave a considered judgement at this later time. In a long letter, whose contents were intended to be made known to the Queen, he stated (amongst other things):

> I confess that I have some doubts as to the policy of introducing hereditary distinctions into the Colonies – or rather of attempting to do so and failing. I should consider it most valuable if it led to Hereditary Property also; but I fear that such an alteration in the State of Society is not to be looked for in any of the possessions of the Crown and Titles without entailed property are of very doubtful advantage.[34]

We ought not to underestimate the information available to officials and politicians superintending colonial affairs, or their common sense.

Bulwer Lytton did, however, initiate an increased, even systematic, distribution of honours to colonists. It was in part inspired by the Queen's wish to 'keep up a strong aristocratic link between the children and the parent',[35] but more by curiously complicated representations of colonial wishes mixed with Lytton's hopes to make a mark as an improver of colonial relations. The impossible idea of setting up social hierarchies in the colonies (they were, in a sense, making their own)[36] was not the object. Rather, it was to gratify colonial desires, to make up for previous neglect, to provide a counter to republican influences and to encourage the sense of unity between all the Queen's subjects. The project – for such it became – was given momentum by the curious and embarrassing case of the Mayor of Melbourne J. T. Smith. This Australian civic dignitary came to England with an Address to the Queen on the occasion of the Princess Royal's marriage, hoping to be knighted. There followed a tangle involving Lytton's and Derby's desire for him to have the honour, a deluge of protests from Melbourne and from Australian colonists in London, plausibly alleging that Smith had made his fortune, at least in part, from bawdy houses (which was not taken as enough reason to refuse him his knighthood) and that his wife had actually been a convict (which was). Lytton insisted that the refusal had to be on the grounds of the absence of any precedent for knighting mayors in colonies and the lack of a definite recommendation from the Governor, who was rebuked.[37] Bureaucracy has its uses for unlikely practitioners.

From this slightly bizarre affair, along with others more ordinary, emerged Lytton's decision to send a circular to all governors declaring the Queen's wish to admit more colonists to honours and making suggestions as to how it might be done. This, he told the Prince, if followed carefully,

> will, I am persuaded, tend to deepen the demarcations between Republicanism and Monarchy, and link (by motives of human nature at once elevated and universal) all who, in Her Majesty's distant possessions are moved to a public career by the desire of honour, to the most conspicuous and munificent prerogative of the Crown.[38]

After all this, the problem was not solved. Arguably, it complicated the business of giving recognition to colonists. It certainly did nothing to establish so much as a seed of aristocracy or social hierarchy (in any traditional sense) in the colonies.

IV

Lord Carnarvon was privy to the honours discussions but was unusually reticent, so we have little idea of his thoughts on the subject. Looking more broadly, however, he was acquainted with Lytton before they came together in office. Carnarvon had been a guest at Knebworth; they had corresponded on fairly abstruse subjects, from eastern poets to clairvoyancy; and Carnarvon had tried to get Lytton's support for a plan he had for an educational franchise.[39] Very likely he had read *The Caxtons*. Advice he gave in April 1858, referring to the suitability of Australia for a gentleman emigrant, bears a remarkable resemblance to one of the most significant passages in *The Caxtons*; and another such similarity occurs in a speech he made as late as 1884. Likewise, in a particularly moving case, Carnarvon had Caxtonesque advice for Lady Winniett, widow of a former governor of the Gold Coast, who was distressed by her son's situation as a shepherd in New South Wales. Carnarvon directed that she should be told not only that the Secretary of State had absolutely no patronage in the colony (the conventional administrative response), but that anyway:

> there is no real degradation in undertaking the duties of a shepherd in the bush, however opposed at first sight it may be to English notions and that on the contrary a very large proportion of those settlers who have eventually been most successful have . . . deliberately preferr[ed] to start from the humblest occupation.[40]

For all that Carnarvon, at this time, found democracy positively 'repulsive', was very conscious of his place in English society and would agree with Lytton as to the value of gentlemen in that or any society, there is nothing which suggests that he thought hierarchy could or should be somehow imposed on a colony. Rather, like Lytton, he hoped for the growth of a 'disposition and temperament' approaching that of the mother country: Canada he thought more likely than the Australian colonies to achieve this on current showing.[41]

We can usefully supplement such London views by bringing in one of Lord Carnarvon's relatives to whom he became particularly close, personally, politically and officially. This was his second cousin and exact contemporary (including in class and in Coleridge's house at Eton), Robert G. W. Herbert. In July 1859, Herbert accepted the post of private secretary to Sir George Bowen, first Governor of the new colony of Queensland: an appointment which might have had something to do with Carnarvon as well as Gladstone. In the crude and unformed politics of Queensland, Herbert became the first Colonial Secretary and Premier. We do not know whether he had read *The Caxtons*. His career there, however, and the views he expressed about the colonies, were not incompatible with Lytton's philosophising.[42] Perhaps they went further. For instance, in 1865, he reassured his mother that 'England will not hold all the men who have to earn their livelihood, and some of us must migrate'. Granted that he was in a peculiarly favourable situation, yet he saw a good deal of young gentlemen of education and family who lacked capital but were unable or unwilling to '*de-fine-gentlemanise*' themselves (as Lytton put it[43]) and had little time for them. 'The aristocracy of England', he wrote,

> emigrating to these colonies, for the reasons which bring them do more harm than convicts do. Many who come out here are in fact transported for their social and family crimes, and sent to penal servitude till they can pay their way home again.[44]

From yet another vantage, the Governor whom Lytton appointed to Queensland assured the author of the validity of 'the advice which Trevanion gives to Pisistratus Caxton, in a work of which you may possibly have heard'.[45]

But it is Herbert's rather than Bowen's experience that matters. After six years in the colony, he returned to England and was at first wanted by Lord Carnarvon (Secretary of State by then) in the Colonial Office as Legal Adviser. Carnarvon then approached him to be Lieutenant Governor of Natal. Herbert took instead an assistant secretaryship in the Board of Trade; thence he proceeded to the Colonial Office in 1870 as Assistant Under-Secretary and succeeded Sir Frederic Rogers as Permanent Under-Secretary in 1871. By the time Carnarvon again became Secretary of State in 1874, his chief adviser was this cousin with whom he had close ties in family matters and in politics.[46]

V

Altogether, we must not dismiss Lytton as a statesman of empire, massively impractical though he could be. Benjamin Jowett spoke at his funeral of Lytton's 'endless activity of mind', and judged that 'the experienced eye' would see in his novels 'the delineation of principles . . . in the background'. Jowett thought that indirectly, 'he is teaching a lesson about human character, about the influence of circumstances, about the mixed nature of men, and conflict of duties'.[47] Gladstone, who for a few months during 1858–9 stood in a special relationship to Lytton, wrote with unaccustomed freedom, 'He may not be exact in business and he may be too flowing in language but . . . his views are broad, his judgment sound and . . . his heart warm to boot'. Carnarvon, though not so certain of his chief's judgement, shared this view,[48] so Lytton was a tolerably proper exemplar. It is of the first importance that he also learnt from Lytton the value of private hospitality as part of his official duty. Lytton was the first Secretary of State to invite visiting colonists to his house for weekend stays, Carnarvon often being included as well as staying separately at Knebworth. Probably such an occasion did much to calm the Canadian delegates in England late in 1858, whose federation and railway plans were not supported. Carnarvon also issued such invitations – to Highclere.[49] This practice he developed further, not least in 1866–7 when his social as well as diplomatic qualities facilitated the completion of, precisely, British North American confederation. Wider yet, Carnarvon found Lytton's view of the Empire generally congenial. There is one caveat. Both supported the establishment of self-government in colonies of 'Englishmen', but Carnarvon could not envisage peaceful or friendly colonial separation, and he looked for a future in which the Empire remained intact whatever the independence of the colonies. Lytton was ambiguous on the subject, consulting as he did latter-day colonial reformers C. B. Adderley and J. R. Godley for guidance in making plans for British Columbia.[50] During that process, in fact, it became clear that Lytton's determination to cast almost the whole cost on the new colony's revenues was at odds with Carnarvon's view (and Herman Merivale's) that the mother country should provide adequate resources to lay the foundation of a civil society.[51]

Lytton nevertheless paid Carnarvon a remarkable tribute in a memorandum for Lord Derby – again disagreeing with his under-secretary, this time on the question of how to deal with Sir James Brooke and Sarawak: 'your Lordship knows the high estimation in which I hold Lord Carnarvon, whose remarkable combination of industry and acuteness will render his minutes invaluable to any or all who may succeed him in the office that he holds'.[52] One of Lytton's most characteristic talents failed to influence Carnarvon: what Gladstone called his 'too flowing' prose. At its best, it flowed eloquently and effectively, but Carnarvon (and in a couple of cases, Derby) had to try to moderate the language of some of his despatches, and Carnarvon's drafts were a distinct contrast to them.[53] Nevertheless, Carnarvon was glad to have served under Lytton and was unequivocal about his 1858–9 experience:

> Of all departments of state I may truly say that I feel grateful to have been brought into connexion with the Colonial Office. All that I had ever heard or known, or imagined before of the colonies was comparatively a dream but the actual contact with colonial questions and eminent colonists . . . made the reality much greater than the original imaginations.[54]

Carnarvon was no longer a neophyte in affairs of state. He did not cease to attend to the local affairs of Hampshire and Highclere: the 1860s indeed saw continued work on the Castle and also his most significant achievements in relation to prison reform. But when Lord Derby undertook yet another minority ministry in July 1866, he offered the colonies to Lytton, who (as Derby expected) declined. The secretaryship of state went instead to Carnarvon who gave every sign of having prepared himself for it. Eight months later, he resigned over the Reform Bill. In the meantime, he had a singular achievement. On 19 February 1867, he moved the second reading of the British North America Bill in the House of Lords with a specially careful and powerful speech. This was preceded by delicate and sometimes difficult negotiations which were more than once eased by the congenial surroundings of Highclere Castle. Thus did Carnarvon bring to fruition a policy begun in Lytton's time for the creation of the Dominion of Canada.[55]

In office in 1866–7, Carnarvon greatly increased the momentum of his career in imperial statesmanship. But his resignation in March 1867 was a serious setback: he believed that he had been making a difference in colonial relations and acknowledged that his resignation meant abandoning 'work that was only half, and that will probably never now be quite finished'.[56] He was shunned by his late colleagues whom he resented for their treatment of him. There could be scarcely any prospect of further office, nor for some months did he value such a prospect.[57] By early 1870, however, the Conservative peers sought the return of Lords Salisbury and Carnarvon to the front bench. This coincided with one of Carnarvon's most impressive parliamentary performances which re-established and consolidated his credentials as a champion of the colonial empire: namely, his speech on colonial relations aimed at forcing some reconsideration of the Liberal Government's policies. It was followed by an extraordinary exhibition of confidence in him by the Canadian Government which authorised him to use its confidential documents in Parliament or privately if he thought he could effect any changes in the Government's policy towards relations with the USA.[58] Serious family affairs, international events and ill-health much restricted him thereafter, though he was anxious enough to be available when the Gladstone Government seemed about to collapse, early in 1873.[59] A few months later, Carnarvon achieved a kind of rapprochement with Disraeli: perhaps Disraeli's imperial sentiments expressed in his famous speeches of April and July 1872 helped. He retained a residual distrust of the leader, but it is clear that Carnarvon would accept office in a Disraeli ministry were he to be offered it, which he was.[60]

VI

Entering his second and more important term of office as Colonial Secretary of State, Carnarvon knew that his appointment was welcomed in the colonies and in England. Before Disraeli's ministry was actually formed, he had a letter from Edward Wilson, proprietor of the *Argus* newspaper of Melbourne, Victoria, who was anxious to secure the Imperial Government's involvement on his party's side in the colony's politics. Thus he wrote to Carnarvon hoping for his appointment to 'a post in which you have always shown so intelligent an interest'. Wilson was rewarded by an assurance of Carnarvon's determination to 'spare no effort to maintain unimpaired that which I prize so highly the integrity of the Empire'. Wilson's flattery was the kind of thing which Carnarvon had, in a sense, cultivated in colonial circles for several years. In this case, on both sides there was perhaps some misunderstanding. Carnarvon's position on the particular issue had always been more complicated than Wilson seems to have realised, while Carnarvon was perhaps just a little too gratified by this and other evidence of good opinion.[61]

A second letter of the same day was from the Permanent Under-Secretary of State for the Colonies saying:

> It would be hardly bearable to have to work with anyone else, with a chance of having you here not availed of. The Department & the Colonies are I am satis-fied unanimous in hoping that you will take charge of their interests. And this is a time at which you can do a specially large amount of good in various ways (socially included).

This communication began, '[m]y dear Carnarvon', and ended, 'Yr affte cousin, R. G. W. Herbert'. It was more than simply encouraging. Herbert knew Carnarvon well, and, in effect, he gently urged his cousin not to let unpleasant past experiences rule him.[62] All in all, Carnarvon might well have been persuaded to a perilous degree that he had an opportunity to achieve great things.

Estimates of the likely fate of the self-governing colonies are here involved. Herbert's Gladstonian predecessor, Rogers, had earlier told Carnarvon that the colonies were already independent, and that '[r]esponsible Government once established the dissolution of the Empire is a matter of time'; nor did he think Britain with its 'republican' polity was in any case capable of sustaining a great empire.[63] Herbert, it is true, had not been much encouraged by his Australian sojourn but was more willing than Rogers to wait and see. He disdained the idea that Disraeli's accession to office meant that Britain 'had entered upon a new imperial epoch'; but he believed that the Empire could not survive without a judicious use of diplomatic and military strength and, mayhap, expansion. In this, he was pretty much at one with his cousin.[64] The great difference between them was that Carnarvon had a temperament and enthusiasms which caused Disraeli to refer to him as 'Twitters'. No such description could apply to the sardonic and sceptical Herbert.[65] Still, it challenges belief to suppose that, during their frequent meetings at Highclere and in London recorded in Carnarvon's diary between 1866 and 1874, the cousins did not consider the colonies. Thus, it seems likely that, for instance, before 1874 Herbert discussed with Lord Carnarvon the idea that South Africa could be rendered secure without British military involvement. The prospect of achieving what no one else had achieved was, however, to lead Carnarvon into something like disaster.

People mattered to Carnarvon, for their conversation, their personalities, their achievements, their experience, their ideas and, occasionally, their advice. This is why Highclere was such an important contributor to Carnarvon's way of serving the Empire. It was a civilised trait marred by a crucial weakness. For it is one thing to welcome the views of other people in forming one's own, but it may well be dangerous to be swayed by congenial views (perhaps couched in flattering terms) tending to risk-taking or even impracticality. Montague Corry, Disraeli's private secretary in the 1874–80 Government, wrote irritably of Carnarvon's 'coterie of Liberal editors who praise him and drink his claret', and Disraeli himself, contemptuous of Carnarvon's stance on the 1876–8 eastern policy, reported scathingly to the Queen about the 'weak enthusiast'. The Liberal Lord Granville gently and more pertinently suggested that Carnarvon should take more time 'to mature his plans so as to bring them to the most favourable issue'.[66]

These views were not wholly without cause. For instance, Carnarvon seized on travel plans of the historian and essayist J. A. Froude (an old friend, and publicist of strong views on the Empire) to send him to the Cape on a 'secret mission' to promote federation – Carnarvon's 'first & urgent consideration'. This was both an interesting idea and a terrible mistake. Lord Blachford (formerly Sir Frederic Rogers) said of Froude: 'I cannot imagine a more unpersuasive person'.[67] Of Froude's performance in South Africa, this was to say the least. Again, imperial defence had long been a prime concern to Carnarvon. When, therefore, Sir Charles Gavan Duffy from Victoria urgently but misleadingly pressed him to consider an elaborate scheme based on Australian possibilities, Carnarvon's enthusiasm was aroused and only slightly dampened by Robert Herbert's dubiety. This was effectively the origin of Carnarvon's attempt to 'return the bearskin' (as Disraeli put it) not only to Canada but to Australia.[68] Both ventures were serious failures in their respective ways.

There is a tinge of tragedy, particularly in relation to South Africa, for the projects promised much, and the discussions at Highclere which helped so much to initiate them were intelligent. There is a tinge also of irony, for another component of Lord Carnarvon's career stems directly from the ideal to which we have seen he subscribed, of the duties owed by a member of 'an hereditary class' to his countrymen, to the Crown and to the State.[69] His wish to conform to this combined, sometimes to a fault, with what might be called his intellectual individualism. His problem lay not in a lack of intelligence or general ability. It was rather that, not without a measure of simple ambition, he aspired to be a statesman without being a mere politician. Carnarvon suffered also from the common intellectual's delusion that rational argument must eventually prevail, whether with his colleagues or with colonists. In the wake of his brief but notable tenure of the Irish viceroyalty, his old friend Lord Salisbury shocked him and brought his political career to a close by excluding him from his 1886 cabinet. A year later, he offered Carnarvon the lord lieutenancy of Hampshire. What might properly have been recognition of perhaps the most deserving of the county's grandees appeared instead to Carnarvon merely 'as a test & evidence of his wish at least to be on friendly terms with me'.[70] When Carnarvon died in 1890, the *Saturday Review* called him 'one of the best types of English noble that our time, or any other, has offered'. But it also noticed in him 'a certain disproportion and want of balance in political judgement'. Likewise, the *Spectator* called him a statesman 'of the old and thorough culture' who had 'arrived at conclusions … for himself', but the paper added that this 'sometimes made him difficult to work with'.[71] Such a mixture of qualities goes far to explain, rightly or wrongly, Salisbury's decision to leave him out of his administration.

Acknowledgement

Quotations from the Royal Archives are used by gracious permission of H. M. the Queen.

Figure 3 The return of David Livingstone's remains, April 1874. Copyright *The Graphic.*

Chapter 3: Southampton and the making of an imperial myth

David Livingstone's remains

Joanna Lewis

I   Death not on the Nile

A confidential telegram sent on the 27 January 1874 by the acting Consul in Zanzibar, Captain William Prideaux, to the Foreign Office in London contained the secret news that the explorer Dr David Livingstone was dead. It was intercepted by a journalist at Aden. Soon the Victorian press ran with the story, and a nation mourned. Livingstone was renowned the world over. Although latterly his explorations had not matched the success of his first travels across Africa in the 1850s, which included the sighting and naming of the Victoria Falls, he nevertheless remained much loved and admired for his persistence and bravery in the field of exploration, and he was also associated with evangelical Christianity and the anti-slavery cause. He had been thought lost for ever in the wilds of central Africa a few years previously but then was famously found in 1871 by Henry Morton Stanley, who led a search party paid for by his employer, the proprietor of the *New York Herald*. Stanley instantly netted himself the biggest media scoop in history, and he simultaneously immortalised this encounter and them both, for his first words, 'Dr Livingstone I presume', became universally acknowledged as the epitome of classic English understatement in a tight spot. Stanley was, of course, Welsh.[1]

Livingstone had been on his third and what was to be his last visit to Africa which began in 1866.[2] It was a desperate mission to find the headwaters of the Nile in central Africa to prove his critics wrong and prove himself and his causes right. It makes for grim reading. His party was always too small; always too few men carrying too few supplies; too often pushed beyond endurance in order that Livingstone's goal at this stage of his life, that of beating his rivals, be achieved. In 1870, one of Livingstone's favourite employees broke away and was apparently cannibalised. Evidence of the spread of slavery – Arab and also African directed – was horrific, with women tied to trees by the neck, left to die when they proved too weak to keep walking. Constant ill health plagued the expedition. At times, Livingstone had to be nursed and had to travel with Arab slave traders in the area. Supplies were stolen, including the medicine chest. Constant trudging through areas in flood, up to the waist in mud and foul-stenching water, took its toll. Livingstone developed foot ulcers which were so painful he could not walk for three months; also lung problems, dysentery and permanent anal bleeding. Falling victim to swamp fever, he began to dream up theories about the source of the Nile which became less based on science and more far-fetched. To the outside world, he was lost, probably dead, until Stanley arrived. After a period of rest and travel together, Stanley gave him more men and supplies, leaving him to continue his efforts to prove that that the river Lualaba was the true source of the Nile – and that he had located the 'Fountains of Herodutus' as identified by Ptolemy. He was mistaken. As his health deteriorated, his growing realisation of both made the pain of each more acute. Slowly he lost the ability to walk, then to see, and, knowing his own death was now inevitable, he passed away. The date was late March 1873, and the place was in a makeshift grass shelter outside Chief Chitambo's village in what is now northern Zambia. His African servants, loyal not just to the end but far beyond, embalmed his body then disguised it as a package so they had a chance of surviving a perilous journey back to the coast to 'return him to his people'. The body arrived in Bagamoyo about nine months later and, after some delib-eration and confusion as to what to do, Livingstone began his final journey home.

The news of his death focused attention on his extraordinary life, which, for many, seemed not to merit such a horrible death. Livingstone the martyr was born. Many newspapers – secular and religious – covered the story and kept embellishing the details. The Gladstone Government feared a hoax. However, the Dean of Westminster Abbey believed it to be true and immediately offered the Abbey as his final resting place. Livingstone was from a poor background and he was a member of a Dissenting church, so the decision was controversial for some; for others, it was a mark of the man's greatness that he would take his place in such an illustrious setting. Throughout February and March, details of the death were circulating in the British press. According to the proprietor of the *New York Herald*, James Gordon Bennett, receiving his material from Stanley, and who was carefully micro-managing a steady 'news' flow, Livingstone had apparently commanded his men to 'build me a hut to die in'; thereupon 'he suffered greatly groaning night and day. On the third day he said

I am very cold'.[3] On the fourth day, he was insensible. Later, the story was further embellished – re-Christianised – to include an account of him dying submissively on his knees in the act of prayer, and, when this was then illustrated, it became one of the enduring images of Livingstone, the Christian martyr, going gently into that good night.

Whatever the veracity of these and other accounts, spellbound readers understood that Livingstone had died with an acute sense of failure, depressed, dejected and unaware even that the outside world knew he was still alive. His very painful and sacrificial death and the compassion shown by his companions became vital elements in his memorialisation and integral to construction of the Livingstone myth which followed. Death really did become him; it transformed him into something quite unique – 'a Protestant saint', as John MacKenzie has put it.[4] And his death plus his funeral have also been subject to more recent attention, most notably in John Wolffe's fascinating *Great Deaths* – a half chapter with General Gordon under the title 'Martyrs of Empire'.[5] I too have argued elsewhere that the manner of his 'pathetic' death, as it was described at the time, deeply upset the Victorians and explains the potency of his afterlife. The Government's provision for his remains and for his family in Britain was shambolic, but the huge outpouring of public grief and sentimentality carried the day. It was provoked by the detailed knowledge of the manner of his death, but drew on a deeper sense of sadness and anxiety felt by the mid-Victorians about their own time and a sentimentality born of guilt towards the spirit of working-class aspiration.[6] As the emotional and charged accounts of what, by any standards, was a remarkable tale were published so hard news came through in late March that his body had gone from Zanzibar to Aden and was now on the final journey home. Livingstone's remains, accompanied by one of his African followers travelling with the body and a former slave, Jacob Wainwright – were now on the *Malwa*, a P&O Company steamship heading for England. It was promising to be something of a major event. And that was how Southampton Town Council perceived it. For the *Malwa* was scheduled to dock at Southampton before London, and, for a number of reasons, the Town Council was adamant that the body should be unloaded first onto English soil at the ship's first port of call.

What this chapter will highlight is the key contribution made by the port of Southampton in the process of commemorating Livingstone. The significance of this ceremony and the details of the event have been somewhat obscured in the vast canon of literature on Livingstone, with the focus being much more upon London and the manufacturing of the 'myth' of Livingstone. However, when the news reached England in late March 1874 that the remains of

Livingstone had been transferred onto a P&O steamship travelling from Bombay to Southampton and London via the Suez Canal, Southampton Town Council was determined to make this a great occasion. Southampton's efforts not only forced London to step up the capital's lacklustre and tardy efforts but their reception also culminated in the nearest thing to a state occasion that Livingstone – the national hero of the moment – was to receive. This was mostly because it suited the local interests at the time to make a big splash. A set of impressive wheels within wheels began to stir into action: specifically, a tightly knit community of businessmen and Freemasons backing the initiative, who ran the council and had the support of the press. The pomp and ceremony were designed to leave nothing to chance or thrift, and, by comparison, exposed the extent of the informality of what was to come in Westminster Abbey. However, even the best-laid Victorian municipal planning could go astray. There was much drama and chaos surrounding the arrival of the remains, and, at times, it seemed as if the solemn preparations might descend into comic opera.

II   The Mayor, the MP and the media

By the 1870s, Southampton was feeling the pinch. Although riding on the back of decades of respectable growth and prosperity from trade and commerce, being a port town surrounded by a fertile hinterland, the ground had felt a little wobbly since the mid-1860s.[7] True, there was some increase in port activity; in 1871, the main quay was extended by 400 feet. However, other south-coast ports as well as London had, on occasion, proved better placed to feed off the juicy fruits of imperial expansion. In 1867, the landing of incoming mail from the West Indies was relocated to Plymouth, now benefiting from an extended railway line. A further downturn in the volume of Southampton's trade was precipitated by the Franco-Prussian War of 1870–1. More seriously, a worrying rumour was circulating in the town early in 1874 about the much-valued P&O Company. With the opening of the Suez Canal in 1869, more cotton goods were being exported to India via this route, and the company had just been granted permission to send its mail through the canal. London was looking more and more attractive as Suez Canal traffic increased.

Sensitive to such ill winds was a network of commercial entrepreneurs in the town. Southampton had just elected a new mayor. Edwin Jones was one of its most successful and well-known businessmen.[8] His retail stores in the town centre were thriving, and he supplied over fifty 'branch' shops in the region. Jones's business would become a public company in 1888, with a capital value of 200,000 pounds at his death in 1896, and later became part of Debenhams. Jones was solidly liberal and destined to be a twice-failed Liberal Party parliamentary candidate. Locally, he found more success. He was Founder and first President of the local Liberal Association. More importantly, from 1870 onwards, he rose rapidly up the greasy pole of the municipal politics and, by 1874, was elected Mayor. It was a good year in other ways too. A widower, he married for the second time, taking a younger bride. The timing was right and the means were there to continue an established tradition of lavish entertaining at Audit House. Aware that his fortune owed a great deal to his customers, in February 1874 he famously organised and paid for a ball to celebrate the marriage of the Duke of Edinburgh, to which he invited 1,600 townspeople. In June, he hosted a party for 12,000 schoolchildren, attended, apparently, by 40,000 people. In 1875, he was re-elected for another term in office.

The extent to which the council was tightly knit into a wider community and primed for action can be gauged from an account of a dinner held at a local hotel on 31 March 1874 to celebrate the 15th anniversary of Lodge Perseverance, a branch of the Order of United Britons' Friendly Society.[9] Jones presided. Also present – some holding office – were other members of the town council and members of the Hampshire Volunteers' Regiment, all of whom were called upon later to play their part in the reception of Livingstone's remains, as we shall see. In addition to his toast to the Mayor, who was praised for being 'one of the most liberal and public spirited mayors the town had ever had', Councillor Weston proposed that even if the major companies pulled out of Southampton, the port would survive; they just needed four more lines of railway. A man named Geddes responded. The attempt to make London a port of departure and arrival for mail-packets would fail, he insisted, 'and the steamers would return to their old love; for after all that would be found to be the best.' It was not to be. In November 1874, the P&O Company relocated to London, and 1875 saw the start of a general trade depression.

Concerned by the threatened loss of the P&O Company, and keen to enhance its reputation within the local community, the town council must surely have salivated at the prospect of the remains of Livingstone touching English soil at Southampton in April 1874.[10] A successful ceremony would be a chance to display civic prowess to an international audience as well as an opportunity to court the P&O Company, all good for re-election prospects. In addition, hundreds of local people flocking into town to witness such an historic event would do no harm to local businesses. The steady trickle of returning war heroes and battleships regularly brought in extra income, and the organisation of receptions for returning heroes – alive or dead – was a local speciality. However, it would be unfair to impute solely selfish motives for what was to become an extremely spirited response. Livingstone had star-quality appeal on his own merit. And it is very likely he had a particularly strong symbolic appeal to men such as Jones and his deputies who probably felt a personal connection to him as much as they recognised that in others (particularly their customers). Although Edwin Jones does not seem to have been remembered as a big churchgoer nor an active supporter of the anti-slavery cause that Livingstone was identified with, Jones could well claim a similar lineage. He too hailed from humble, Dissenting stock: his father was a Welsh coal merchant and railway carrier, and an enthusiastic Congregationalist. Jones also had a rags-to-riches story, starting as a young apprentice and then owning one small shop selling lace and button boots to women. For many years he slept on a makeshift bed on the shop floor. And he believed in self-improvement and the importance of education, his later philanthropic causes being the Young Men's Mutual Improvement Society and the Polytechnic Institute.

Not surprisingly, therefore, the Town Council enthusiastically formed a reception committee on learning that the remains of 'the illustrious African traveller were expected to arrive on the 13th', which was formally agreed to at the first possible council meeting on 1 April 1874.[11] The decision was unanimous and clearly implies a lot of previous behind-the-scenes discussion. And it proved to be crucial. In contrast, plans in London had yet to take shape at this point despite the knowledge that the body was getting closer and the offer of a burial place had been made by the Dean of Westminster Abbey at the beginning of the year. It now seems likely that Southampton's close interest in the affair and keenness to plan a bit of a do was a sharp spur both to the Government and to the Royal Geographical Society (RGS) in London. The RGS had the strongest connection to Livingstone at the time of his death. Livingstone had left the employment of the London Missionary Society as far back as 1857. The success of his first explorations won him a Gold Medal from the RGS. He had become the Queen's 'roving consul' on a salary of 500 pounds per annum, and the Government sponsored his second Zambezi expedition, which was a failure. By the time of the third expedition to prove once and for all the riddle of the Great Lakes region (i.e., the location of the source of the Nile), he was not so lucky, having received a measly one-off payment of 500 pounds from the Government with 'consul' as titular only, and 500 pounds from the RGS.[12]

The RGS did not want to be saddled with the cost, somewhat understandably. There was no great love for Livingstone among the rank-and-file membership, and he had cost them much already in search parties.[13] But the continued lack of any commitment from the Government to pay for the cost of the burial was immediately taken up in the House of Commons by one of Southampton's two MPs, Russell Gurney, according to the *Hampshire Advertiser*, apparently an action agreed to after the committee was set up. Gurney was a considered a 'progressive conservative' at the time (for example, he believed unmarried women should have the right to vote). Its editorial of 4 April credited the joint actions of Gurney and the Council with providing the necessary impetus for a 'fitting recognition' of Livingstone.[14] Other local papers lauded his intervention – widely featured in the national press too – which, according to the *Southampton Times*, prompted 'a somewhat ungracious reply' from the Prime Minister.[15] The Government feared a scam and still baulked from agreeing to pay for a big funeral for a man who stood for humanitarian intervention in Africa. However, on 8 April, the Council of the RGS met and set up a funeral committee. The next day, following an unauthorised report in *The Times* that the Government had given way, the Chancellor formally offered the RGS a 250 pounds grant to organise the event.[16]

However, sections of the local press were not impressed. In London, a 'leading journal' had insisted that it was the intervention of a London business merchant that had quickened the Government. The *Hampshire Advertiser* was having none of it. 'We are inclined to resent this patronizing sort of air' was the line taken by its editor. If it had been a matter of money, Southampton would have taken up the responsibility, the paper continued, but 'as we said last week, the national homage ... should take an Imperial shape'.[17]

So, in contrast to London's preference for handing the body over to his family, with its confusion over responsibility and a reluctance to identify too closely with Livingstone and his missionary causes – for Southampton's great and good, a big ceremony was a simple win-win situation. Similarly, the local press wanted to see a reception and had much to say about the matter. Newspaper coverage of the death had been limited and unremarkable until it became clear by early April that the body of Livingstone would touch English soil first at Southampton. From then on, there was much space taken up with setting out why his life was worth commemorating and why Southampton must do this properly and *be seen* to be doing so. This may be indicative of a general sense of wanting to display Southampton's place in the wider world and to challenge the growing ascendancy of London as *the* Victorian imperial entrepôt.

By early April, local newspapers had moved from giving small notices to the death of Livingstone to offering fulsome commentary and detailed news.

The *Southampton Observer*'s editorial for 4 April 1874 had begun with the melodramatic statement that 'the very same seas that have brought to us in safety from the West Coast of Africa the brave soldiers [from the Asante wars]' will be 'bearing to us as we write, a very different freight . . . from the Eastern Coast of that same continent'. Pleased that the Town Council had seen fit to appoint a special reception committee, there was, however, room for improvement. The council was criticised for the less-than-inclusive composition of that committee. The all-official affair had — according to the paper — left out 'many others who feel an interest in this reception'. Possibly this was a reference in part to local religious and humanitarian representations. Later on, for example, a group of Nonconformist Sunday School teachers approached the committee for permission to join in the procession.

However, the approval rating of the council soon began to move dramatically in the opposite direction. A rumour had circulated that Livingstone's body would not come ashore at Southampton after all, but instead go straight to London, apparently at the request of the family. Further credence was attached to this by the intelligence that the remains had been stored deep in the bowels of the ship and underneath cargo. So, on the Wednesday or Thursday (accounts vary) of the week before the body was scheduled to arrive, the Mayor and Town Clerk travelled up to London and called on the Foreign Office to seek reassurance that Southampton would be the drop-off point. According to the *Hampshire Advertiser*, Lord Teuterdon was unable to give any firm confirmation until Friday, when he sent a telegram containing Lord Derby's confirmation.[18] Thus, Southampton was deemed to have 'once again proved worthy of itself', since the following Monday 'we shall have the melancholy satisfaction of receiving on behalf of our age and our nation, one who belongs, not to our age and nation only, but to the world'.[19]

Yet there were still worries floating around as to what the ceremonials would consist of. 'At the time of writing', fretted the editor of the *Southampton Times*, they had 'not been informed as to what the arrangements will be but they will doubtless be simple and solemn' and in keeping with the man 'whose memory the nation mourns'. By now, the Government had agreed to cover the cost of the funeral expenses in London, but there was no information as to where and when the funeral would take place. Perhaps fearful that the Council would similarly downgrade the event, the paper gave a global perspective for extra impetus: it was announced that America would be honouring Livingstone. The Secretary of the American Geographical Society had telegraphed to ask for details of the event so it could be marked on both sides of the Atlantic simultaneously. Even Africa was dreamily brought in, since the editor confessed how,

We cannot help but wish that some information could be conveyed to those African tribes by whom 'the wonderful white man' has been for 5 and 20 years known and respected. Whether by beating of drums or firing of guns, in some rude way or other . . . the memory of that friend and benefactor of Africans would be honoured.[20]

III   The arrival at Southampton

By Sunday evening, all seemed to be going well. The party of friends and family invited down from London had been entertained on the Saturday with a lavish impromptu dinner, hosted – and presumably paid for – by Edwin Jones at the South-Western Hotel. These included his close relatives, the missionary Robert Moffat (Livingstone's father-in-law), the explorer Henry Morton Stanley, the acclaimed hunter-traveller William Webb from Newstead Abbey, Revd Horace Waller (Anglican devotee of Livingstone and future editor of his diaries) and, from the Admiralty, Sir William Hall, who had come down to oversee the landing of the body. Also present was Arthur Laing, described as a Zanzibar merchant, who had been charged with looking after the body since it left HMS *Vulture* (the naval vessel which had initially borne the remains from the east African coast), but who had sped home via Brindisi to help. Apologies had been received from Sir Bartle Frere, President of the RGS, detained in London due to having to hastily make the funeral arrangements, possibly an enormous understatement, considering the shortage of time now available. A number of churches and chapels on the Sunday had preached special sermons commemorating Livingstone, and a number of the ordained visitors preached sermons at different places of worship. The Council had published an official programme detailing the arrangements for the receipt of the body and the procession. And onlookers travelling in from villages outside the town had already started to arrive the night before.

However, on Monday morning, 'the town awoke to a great universal feeling of depression', as the *Southampton Times* later put it. The weather had changed from 'a soft and spring-like character to something so unfortunately different as to threaten to eclipse the public ceremony', and there was no sign of the *Malwa*. People were left standing around since very early, as 'numbers of persons of all classes and conditions' had assembled to await the arrival of the body. Heavy rain did not stop falling until 11 a.m. The plan had been that when the *Malwa* was sighted out to sea, a telegram would be sent ashore from Hurst Castle and then the news telegraphed to various local railway stations to bring people in. Meanwhile, the townspeople were on the alert for bunting at half-mast, as instructed by the Council. After a couple of hours, the visitors and committee held an emergency meeting at the hotel, where it was decided that a steam-tug (the *Fawn*) would be chartered to take the party onto the *Victor Emmanuel* hospital ship off Netley, where they would wait. Officials were left to read out letters of apology from dignitaries unable to attend. These included the Bishop of Winchester and three local MPs. At 4 p.m., another meeting was held. Now it was agreed that even if the body arrived that day, it must be kept at sea to facilitate the reception. This would now take place the next day, and leaflets were printed announcing the change of plan.

However, Tuesday also came and went the same way, described in the *Southampton Times* as 'another day of watching and waiting; and another day of disappointment'. Apparently, in the storm, one of the *Malwa*'s engines had been flooded with water. But, according to the intelligence received at the *Southampton Observer*, 'the foul state of the *Malwa's* copper' was also to blame. Unfortunately, a telegram sent from Hurst Castle announcing the arrival of a Royal Mail steamship, the *Tagus*, was mistaken for the *Malwa*, which, when combined with a flag flying at half-mast at the South-Western Hotel, sent hundreds of Sotonians down to the quayside in eager expectation. They were to be disappointed. The visiting party was taken off to inspect a troopship for the afternoon whilst journalists began to report on each other. The *Observer* mused how London journalists showed their 'usual ingenuity' in keeping their readers amused, making use of local history in a fairly accurate fashion, apart from one who wrote that it was Southampton which had the honour of receiving Sir Garnet Wolseley on his return from the Gold Coast when, as 'everybody in England knew', that honour went to Portsmouth.[21]

Finally, Wednesday was *the* day. At 6 a.m., the *Malwa* appeared within sight of Hurst Castle despite a heavy gale during the night. Telegrams were sent and flags hoisted half-mast at the Bargate and Audit House. Onlookers began to gather, including young apprentices from the town before they went to work. The P&O tug waited to take a small party of close family and journalists out to meet the ship. According to the *Daily News*, 'there were some stragglers', and it was forced to wait.[22] Two boats had already gone ahead – one carrying health officers to inspect her; the other to collect the mailbags. Suddenly, on nearing the *Malwa* she let out an unexpected belch of thick black smoke which came spurting out of the ship's funnel. The journalist present for the *Southampton Times* described how 'it covered the ship like an enormous pall', and, considering the timing, he felt it to be 'a remarkable incident'. When visible, the ship looked battered from the storms. Once aboard, the reception committee faced another potential hitch. The *Malwa* had now run out of coal through being stuck out at sea in the bad weather. She now had to make for the docks to refuel, and these were very close to the railway station. The reception committee had chartered an Isle of Wight vessel, the *Queen*, the plan being to transport the body to the Royal Pier on this vessel and proceed through the town to the station. Another meeting was held. Not wishing to upset local plans, it was decided that the *Malwa* would be taken to the north quay and berth under the shears. From here, the coffin would be put onto the *Queen*, which would then take it to the Royal Pier.[23]

Where were Livingstone's remains? At least from here on there were no more nasty surprises. The coffin lay in the mailroom and was draped in the ship's company flag. According to the *Advertiser*, 'it was lighted by a couple of sailors with lanterns, and standing around were a couple of Manilla men and Lascars. This was a scene likely to be long remembered'.[24] Satisfied that the necessary solemnities had been given to the body, attention soon switched to the personage of Jacob Wainwright. Detailed descriptions of his appearance and his depiction as an adolescent ran through all papers – national and local. Jacob Wainwright was 'not more than 5 feet in height and wears close woolly hair, his nose is almost flat', whilst his lips were thicker than usual having being struck on the mouth the previous day by a rope.[25] He was not the only passenger to suffer in the storm. One woman unexpectedly gave birth to twins. Wainwright's ordeal was just beginning (perhaps hers too). When the *Malwa* docked, he was made to take off his clothes and to change into something deemed more suitable. He had been wearing, amongst other items, a pea-green jacket and a pair of field glasses slung over his shoulder.

IV   Plain sailing

From then on, events went more to plan. The coffin was hoisted onto the small Isle of Wight steamship, the *Queen* and guyed onto two wooden benches. The P&O Company flag over the coffin was replaced with the Union Flag. A Mrs Philips of Bugle Hall and William Hall boarded the steamer to place 'a magnificent wreath of immortelles' on the coffin.[26] The official reception committee, members of the RGS, and others involved, boarded. Everyone uncovered their heads. By this time, all ships, public buildings and foreign consulates had their flags at half-mast. As planned, the boat proceeded to the Royal Pier where those involved in the procession disembarked and made their way to Audit House, from where the ceremonial procession would begin.

The order of the procession had been clearly choreographed. Precise details had been printed on the leaflets published on the weekend, although in some newspaper accounts, extras do appear. From Audit House, the Mayor and family of Livingstone led the way down to the Royal Pier, preceded by four policemen and the band of the 1st Hampshire Volunteer Engineers, as yet silent. Known as 'Buchan's Band', they had been engaged by the Town Council and wore black frock coats and top hats.[27] They were followed by the sheriff, the two bailiffs, the aldermen, the harbour and pier commissioners, the town councillors, the magistrates, members of the County Council and Sir Fred Perkins, Justice of the Peace, MP. Then came the local clergy. Following them were the representatives attending from the RGS. Then came representatives from the Medical Society and the medical profession, representatives from the American and German consuls, Colonel Lacy (staff officer of the Pensioners), members of the press and the poor law guardians. Behind them came members of the Council of the Hartley Institute, the members of the Southampton School Board, the committee of the town's Literary and Philosophical Society, the Executive Council of the Ancient Order of Foresters, the Royal Navy Reserve and 'representatives of other bodies'. These included 50 Nonconformist school teachers.

As planned, at 11 a.m. the procession reached the Royal Pier and was ready to receive the coffin. It subsequently reformed. In front and first to walk through the town were the Mayor and all the council representatives. Then came the hearse. Following directly behind were the family and friends of Livingstone. According to accounts from those there at the time, the coffin was mounted on a gun carriage and, directly behind, 'strode the tall thin figure of Henry Stanley'. 'It was a great sight', reminisced one onlooker in 1930, 'and has remained vividly on my memory ever since'.[28] Then followed the clergy, the RGS, the doctors and so on, as before. It was quite a formidable and long line-up, with the council dominant, forming a 'long black line'. Numbers were further swelled with naval reserve men marching under their own flag and schoolchildren sponsored by the P&O Company under theirs.[29]

This was a seriously formal and official ceremony. Nothing was lacking. From the detailed newspaper accounts, it seems little expense had been spared with regard to mourning insignia. As the ledger from the funeral company shows, items billed to the mayor included loan of best hearse and horses with plumes, best pall, 31 yards of silk and two pairs of kid gloves, plus nine mourning coats. Due to the delay, the driver, undertakers and horses had been engaged for three days.[30] The driver was possibly William Fugett, the manager of Wallace's Mews in Carlton Place.[31] All officials wore black crêpe on their arms and were decked in their municipal robes. All maces and corporate regalia were also encased in black. The officials, who moved forward to remove the

Union Flag and replace it with a black velvet pall with a white silk fringe, wore black hat bands. The coffin was carried ashore on the shoulders of six men from the council. It appears that local men – symbolically – were given the honour of carrying the coffin. It was placed on a hearse drawn by four horses decked in black plumes. Behind the hearse marched the 1st Hampshire Engineers, their drums draped in black. 'It was an imposing sight', according to the *Hampshire Chronicle*.[32]

Nor was it just top marks in the visual department. The Mayor Jones and the Council had links with churches and with the Order of Foresters and local regiments as well. Hence, they could offer Livingstone most of the trimmings associated with a state ceremony. As the procession left the quayside and moved slowly through the town, the band of the Hampshire Volunteers played 'The Dead March' from Handel's *Saul*. Minute guns were fired from the Platform Battery by the 1st Hampshire Artillery. Bringing up the rear of the procession marched seamen belonging to the Port and the Royal Naval Reserves. Meanwhile, the muffled bells from the Holy Rood rang out. Slowly and solemnly the cortège made its way along the Town Quay, then down Bridge Street, Bernard Street and Oxford Street, finishing up at the Docks Station at half past twelve – a journey which was 1 mile in length.

Along all the streets were onlookers, quite a few in mourning dress and, if accounts are to be believed, many stricken with emotion. According to the *Southampton Observer*, 'the people of Southampton came in their thousands . . . to do such honour as they might to the poor remains of the noble-minded man who died like a true soldier of humanity'.[33] The great majority showed some sign of mourning, no discordant remarks were heard, the scene was imposing, a repressed murmur could be heard alongside 'The Dead March' and muffled bells, and all of this 'affected the spectator strangely'.[34] According to the *Faversham Gazette*, along the route, 'every balcony crowded, every window occupied, save where the blinds were drawn down, not a shop could be seen without closed shutters'.[35] As the procession moved along, at the corner of Bridge Street there was a rush of people; again, at the railway station the crowd swelled. The police held people back while the horses were detached from the hearse, which was then placed on a truck and attached to a special train courtesy of the South Western Company. It steamed out of the station at 1 p.m., stopped at Basingstoke and arrived at Waterloo at around 3 p.m.

In line with reporting styles of the day, newspaper coverage did not extend to interviews or quotes from ordinary people who had come to pay their respects. So it is difficult to gauge exactly why people were there and what they were feeling. One exception was the unscheduled addition to the procession just as it left the pier gates. Many papers reported on the other 'negro' in the ceremony. The man's name was John Thomas, whom the *Southampton Observer* described as 'a black and well known in the town as one that can speak seven languages'. A Mr Dodman had paid for a horse-drawn cab to join the procession. Thomas was 'mounted on the box, and held in his hand a large white banner, edged with back fringe and crape, bearing in large black letters the words "In memory of Dr Livingstone, the friend of the African"'.[36] According to the *Faversham Gazette*, it read 'Livingstone, friend of the slave'. Perhaps the popular image of Africans at this time was that they were all slaves or ex-slaves.

V   The verdict

As the body made its way up to London, those involved in planning and executing Southampton's reception for the arrival of Livingstone's remains must have felt that the ceremony could not have gone better. A few would have been grateful and relieved that it had actually taken place at all. The Town Council efforts won them new friends and a place of honour in the funeral procession in Westminster Abbey. At the end of the ceremony in Southampton, the Mayor and Council were presented with a letter of thanks from the family and friends of Livingstone.[37] The RGS later acknowledged Southampton's splendid efforts. And, nearly forty years later, the event was written into local history as being one of Southampton's 'best conducted receptions'.[38] All memory of the blips and bumps were forgotten.

Many newspapers at the time would have concurred. In the days after the remains had left the town, accounts of the morning's events began to be published in local and national newspapers (if published after 18 April, they prefaced long descriptions of the internment at the Abbey). Tributes came thick and fast for the Mayor, Town Council and the Reception Committee. The *Southampton Observer* praised everyone, including the Chief Constable, Breary, for the way in which 'everything was carried out in a liberal and satisfactory manner' virtually everyone, every building and every mourning activity in the city was reported upon favourably, as the reception had passed off. 'Public houses had even suspended business', and it was not enough to describe 'Mrs Quilter of the Royal George' as being closed but she was 'quite closed'.[39] The editorial for the *Southampton Times* similarly reported how 'the multitude respectfully raised their hats'; 'Mr Dyson, the courteous station-master' had made the necessary arrangements. Even the train displayed the correct solemnity: it 'quietly pulled out of the station'.[40]

Coverage of any funeral brings out a more forgiving side in commentators. But what seems to be happening here, in addition, is a local press wanting to emphasise Southampton as a civilised urban centre, in the context of a metropolitan snobbery towards the provinces whose towns were looked down upon for being untamed, unsophisticated. *The Times*, for example, reported that the event had been particularly remarkable because it had contained a feature 'rarely seen in any English town great or small', namely the absence of crowd violence. Southampton had, the paper informed its readers, 'not known such a magnificent gathering' with 'a crowd that showed itself not only amenable to the orders of a mere handful of police [. . .] but also heartily co-operated with them'.[41] The fact that there were lots of soldiers on parade and guns going off seems not to have been considered a factor in this demure behaviour, and the compliment was simply re-reported in the local press.

What for some must have been a point of unspoken satisfaction was the way in which the signs of mourning and reception arrangements for the remains in London looked so poor in comparison to those of Southampton. 'The contrast was striking', noted the *Hampshire Chronicle*. Apparently, there were only five or six people on the platform at Waterloo when the train pulled in, and two of these were railway employees. The only sign of an event taking place was six policemen put on duty outside the station, and just three mourning carriages followed the hearse, plus two 'with no signs of mourning at all'. It was clear, the paper believed, that Londoners regarded Southampton's reception as the event of the day and were focused more on Saturday's burial. But, since time of the arrival of the train had been known throughout London since noon, the paper's inevitable conclusion was that it 'might have been marked with more ceremony'.[42]

Yet, not everybody watching events unfold in Southampton was satisfied. The editorial for 18 April in the *Southampton Observer* ended on a stern note of mid-Victorian political correctness. Surely, the editor opined, 'it would have been more appropriate to the life and works of the man, had his body been interred on the shores of one of the mighty rivers or in the depths of some interminable forest in the country of that Africa "whose people he loved so well" '.[43] Clearly, there was no pleasing some people.

And finally, there was at least one Sotonian for whom the events would always conjure up even more mixed emotions. Six weeks later, the Finance Committee of the Town Council considered a claim for compensation sent to them from a local man called Paskins.[44] His sailing boat had been moored in the dock for cleaning in its usual spot. He had not been warned that the platform guns would be fired. The *Julia* had been damaged by the gunfire incurring him costs of 9 pounds 5 shillings and 6 pence (covering repairs and loss of earnings). It was unanimously agreed by the Committee that he should not be reimbursed by the Town Council Corporation. So he wrote again, asking them to reconsider, appearing before the Committee on 11 June.[45] It was agreed the guns had been fired: the old guns with a 3-pound charge, the artillery guns with a 5-pound cartridge. But the committee stuck steadfastly to its previous decision. If only he had been a member of the Order of United Britons.

Acknowledgements

I am grateful to a number of people for helping me complete this work: the patient staff at the public libraries I visited in Southampton and Winchester; my sister and brother-in-law for their hospitality in Winchester; Genevieve Bailey for kindly sending me a photocopy of the funeral parlour's ledger; Professor Andrew Porter for inviting me to give a paper on the death of Livingstone to the Imperial History seminar at the Institute of Historical Research in 2003 and to the audience for their helpful comments; and, finally, Dr Giacomo Macola who, in Zambia in July 2004, gave me the will to finally write this up upon my return.

Figure 4 Hubert von Herkhomer, self-portrait, 1911. Copyright Mike Bucknole, Logan/ Bucknole Collection, Southampton.

Chapter 4: All roads lead to London …
or elsewhere

The Southampton School of Art, 1855–1984

Anne Anderson

Southampton – a provincial town in England, devoid of all art, present or traditional.[1]

Introduction

Although Southampton Institute boasts the John Everett Millais building and gallery, where the centenary of the artist's death was commemorated in 1996, Southampton is not readily identified with a famous artist.[2] Southampton's artistic record is hardly known, even locally. Yet the new Southampton College of Art and Printing School was opened by Roy Hattersley, MP, on 17 March 1974, at a cost of 'about 720,000 pounds', the modern successor to the School of Art founded in 1855.[3] The Art School's

> establishment was the outcome of an artistic revival which followed the Great Exhibition, the Prince Consort being at the head of the movement, from which flowed the setting up of the Schools of Art all over England. Southampton was one of the first places to respond to the Prince Consort's appeal, though it is a fact [. . .] that Andover led the way in Hampshire.[4]

The original location of the Art School was the Royal Victoria Assembly Rooms at the end of Portland Terrace, overlooking West Bay towards Hythe and the New Forest. But, despite the early provision of such a vital amenity to aspiring artists, Southampton never developed a 'school' of artists. One looks in vain for the equivalent of the 'Glasgow Boys' or the Birmingham Group, which developed around their municipal art schools in the 1880s.[5] Southampton did not respond to the great blossoming of the decorative arts in the later Victorian era – one can detect no local response to the Arts and Crafts Movement or Art Nouveau, as can be seen in Glasgow, Birmingham or Liverpool.

Yet, during its early years, the School of Art promised a great future to the 'local boys' passing through its portals, even though critical and worldly success would not be achieved locally. As the *Southampton and District Pictorial* noted, 'chiefly because of the association with [. . .] local boys Herkomer and Edward John Gregory, both in later years Royal Academicians', Southampton School of Art was held in 'very high esteem [. . .] throughout artistic England' in 1912.[6] But Southampton did not have the resources, either cultural or financial, to sustain a 'school' of its own; as Hubert von Herkomer himself noted, the city was 'devoid of all art, present or traditional', perhaps until the opening of the Southampton City Art Gallery in 1939. The Civic Centre, encompassing a city hall, law courts and art gallery, was completed just in time to be bombed in the Second World War. Given the apparent wealth of the city, the extremely late founding of the municipal art gallery seems incongruous.

1   The 'trappings of civilisation': provincial art galleries

Southampton did not develop the trappings of a great Victorian or Edwardian city despite the wealth being generated by the shipping industry, especially in the early 20th century from the transatlantic passenger trade. Compare Southampton with Bristol, Liverpool or Glasgow, the most important ports along the western coast of Britain, looking towards America and the West Indies, and the cultural impoverishment of the city becomes clear. The majority of industrial and mercantile cities were graced with a municipal museum and art gallery by the 1880s; it was a matter of civic pride to provide museums as 'palaces for the people'. As Lambourne notes, such amenities were seen as an important educational resource, even as an escape route to higher things for the intelligent artisan.[7] Similarly, a grand library was essential, the ethos of self-education being paramount to the Victorians. Such institutions were a means of establishing municipal identity, the great civic centres of Leeds, Manchester and Liverpool offering the benefits of civilisation. American cities often went one better with an opera house and city orchestra.[8]

The process of civilising society and educating the artist began with the founding of the National Gallery in 1824, which moved to Trafalgar Square in 1838. The passing of the Museums Act in 1849 devolved gallery provision to town councils, although some cities lagged behind in their response. Salford was the first municipal authority to establish a library, museum and art gallery in 1849. Birmingham Art Gallery, which opened its doors in 1867, relied on bequests; Sir John Middlemore, J. H. Nettlefold and Sir William Kenrick formed its core holdings. Opening on a Sunday, although controversial, boosted visiting figures. Gallery-going was a popular Victorian leisure pursuit, appealing across the classes as a means of 'improvement'. Within a year of opening in 1886, the new Birmingham Art Gallery attracted 1.165 million people, at a time when the population of the city was only half a million.

Intense rivalry between Liverpool and Manchester, or Leeds and Bradford, ensured local support for grandiose building schemes. Liverpool, Southampton's mercantile rival, where wealth had been generated since the 18th century from shipping and trade, acquired a completely new civic centre built beyond the confines of the original metropolis. St George's Hall, described by Norman Shaw as 'one of the greatest edifices of the world', rose up like a shining neo-classical beacon proclaiming Liverpool's wealth and status in 1854.[9] The William Brown Library and Museum, with its impressive reading room, followed in 1860, and the Walker Art Gallery, which today houses the city's magnificent collection of sculpture and paintings, many of them by eminent Pre-Raphaelite artists, opened in 1887. All this civic aggrandisement was largely made possible by individual patronage. Andrew Barclay Walker, a Liverpool brewer, alderman and mayor, gave his city 20,000 pounds for a new art gallery to commemorate his term of office, whilst William Brown, a local merchant, endowed the library and museum. Beneficence resulted from the rapid economic and social expansion of the middle classes.

Local patriotism led the 'new breed of philanthropic captains of industry' to provide 'all the trappings of civilisation', but not, apparently, in Southampton.[10] The city had its 'great and good', but the money generated by the shipping industry does not appear to have been spent on a programme of urban improvement. Samuel Cunard (1787–1865), the 'Merchant Prince of the Oceans', born in Halifax, Nova Scotia, founded the British and North American Royal Mail Steam Packet Company in 1840. This was shortened to the Cunard Steamship Company in 1878. Lavish headquarters were built in Liverpool (1916), a grand Italianate palazzo that still graces the Mersey waterfront. The White Star Line, founded in Liverpool in 1845 by Henry Threlfall Wilson and John Pilkington, was Cunard's competitor in the transatlantic passenger business. Following bankruptcy, the White Star Line was sold to Thomas Henry Ismay in 1868, whose fortune amounted to 1.25 million pounds at his death in 1899. The wealth generated by the shipping lines apparently served to benefit Liverpool and its environs rather than Southampton. So the city was rarely beautified and enriched by wealthy local benefactors, although Henry Robinson Hartley was a notable exception. A descendant of two generations of Southampton wine merchants, Hartley bequeathed nearly the whole of his estate, amounting to more than 100,000 pounds, to the Corporation of Southampton in 1850. This vast sum of money was to be employed

> in such manner as [might] best promote the study and advancement of the sciences of natural history, astronomy, antiquities, classical and oriental literature, such as by forming a public library, botanic gardens, observatory, and collections of objects in connection with the above sciences.[11]

Rather understandably, his family contested the will, and it was not until 1862 that the Prime Minister, the third Viscount Palmerston, was able to open the newly completed Hartley Institution, with its library, museum and lecture halls.[12] But the city had to wait a further 77 years for its art gallery, the provision of which was largely made possible by the beneficence of Robert Chipperfield (1817–1911), a pharmacist who had moved to Southampton in 1842. Chipperfield's will provided for the construction of an art gallery and school and also established a trust fund for the purchase of works of art:

> My aim shall be the furtherance and encouragement of the Art in the town of my adoption [...] to build an art gallery which shall be free to the public [...] and also establish a Southampton School of Art which shall be worthy of the name.[13]

2   Provincial art schools

As Chipperfield's bequest indicates, the art gallery and art school often went hand in hand, as copying the old masters remained a vital part of the artist's education throughout the 19th century. But the municipal art schools, when first envisaged in 1837, were not charged with producing painters and sculptors but better industrial designers and workers. Throughout the Victorian era, there was an ongoing concern for the education of the 'intelligent artisan class'.[14] Arguments were largely couched in economic terms, with competitor nations such as France and Germany seeming to benefit from a more skilled workforce. This led to the founding of regional art schools that were, in effect, 'schools of design', whose purpose was improve Britain's industrial output. In 1852, Sir Henry Cole was put in charge of the newly formed Department of Practical Art to administer the schools, which now mushroomed all over the British Isles. By 1860, the number of schools had risen from 20 to 80 and the pupils from 3,200 to 85,000. In 1894, the schools, which numbered 285, instructed 150,000 students. The National Art Training School at South Kensington, the heart of the system, became the Royal College of Art in 1896.

However, the bias towards the fine arts increased to such an extent that in 1888 more than three-quarters of the 426 students studying at the National Art Training School were fine artists.[15] This shift was partly caused by the boom in the contemporary art market, as many aspiring painters hoped to follow in the lucrative footsteps of Millais, and by the higher social status accorded to the fine artists. Those who aimed high would seek further tuition, at the National Art Training School, the Royal Academy (RA) schools or the more progressive Slade School of Fine Art, founded in 1871.

Southampton was not the first school of art to open in Hampshire, evidently being beaten by Andover, but it did produce, during its first years, several eminent artists. But 'Southampton's Boys', as they came to be known, did not find a local elite to sustain them. Southampton's amenities, such as they were, provided a starting point for a successful career which had to be forged in London. In order to assess Southampton's position, we need to understand the workings of the contemporary art establishment, particularly the role of London.

3   The Victorian art world and its institutions

The provincial artist had to contend with the RA, which hosted the largest annual show of contemporary art, with between 1,000 and 2,000 exhibits covering its vast walls. Getting a work hung at the RA Summer Exhibition was an achievement, as the Council, exclusively composed of members of the RA, selected the works. In other words, it was a closed shop. In 1875, 4,638 works were submitted, of which 561 were accepted, 995 marked doubtful and 3,082 rejected. Academicians and associates had the right to exhibit up to eight works automatically. The RA, conservative by nature, was an obstacle to the reception of more progressive styles coming from Paris, which was seen as the centre of the modern art world. There was resistance to modern subject matter, scenes of contemporary life being tolerable when there was a narrative or moralistic element. The loose, rapid, brushwork associated with the emergence of French realism and impressionism was equated with loose morals and firmly suppressed by the old guard, practitioners of detail and finish: 'the Academy began to be seen as the bulwark of orthodox mediocrity, increasingly hostile to innovation and opposed to modern creative art'.[16] The RA's stranglehold was becoming intolerable, resulting in a number of breakaway groups. The founding of the Dudley Gallery in 1865 and the Grosvenor Gallery in 1877 would go some way to assuaging those with a taste for more aesthetic and daring works. However, the RA remained a powerful establishment. The new art galleries opening in the midlands and the north, plus those being founded in the colonies, made frequent purchases from the summer exhibitions, 'which were regarded as a benchmark of orthodox attainment'.[17]

The artists who submitted works to the RA Summer Exhibition dreamed of painting the picture of the year, the pressing crowd held back by a rail and, the ultimate accolade, a policeman. Such a success would help their progression to Associate Royal Academician and finally to election as Royal Academician, thus guaranteeing financial success in the elite. The financial rewards of becoming an RA could be very great indeed. Although posthumous fame may have eluded them, the most successful Victorian artists, such as Sir John Everett Millais (1829–96) were rewarded with a knighthood and lavish studio accommodation. Millais enjoyed popular acclaim, his works, in print form, gracing many middle-class drawing rooms. Admired, even idolised, many wanted to follow in his footsteps.[18]

A pattern of advancement can be easily discerned. Training at a provincial art school would lead on to the RA schools, which were free, or the National Art Training School at South Kensington. Progressive early works would often attract critical attention and gain a loyal following. Relations, friends and fellow artists could be very supportive during these early years. The more adventurous patrons, especially those from the artist's home town, would offer commissions. A breakthrough would be achieved with a well-received painting, which resulted in election as Associate Royal Academician. The artist could now strive for the elite, for the most part London-based artists, or provincial success, which, although second division, might be more easily attained. Local success, however, could only be sustained if there were sufficient patrons and exhibiting institutions like those which could be found in Liverpool and Glasgow. Both cities successfully developed their own local schools.[19] From mid-century, the provincial art schools also provided a locus for aspiring artists. Here they would meet to discuss the new trends from Paris and the state of the market in London. Lasting friendships would be formed. Again, local patrons were necessary to support a regional school or group, as seen in Glasgow and Birmingham in the 1880s and 1890s. Ironically, prior to the founding of the Southampton School of Art, prominent local artists such as William Shayer (1787–1879), born on Lower East Street, Southampton, and Frederick Lee Bridell (1830–63), 'the man called Southampton's greatest painter', did not have to look far for financial support.[20]

4   Artistic success in Southampton: Shayer, Bridell and Hicks

Of the prominent artists associated with Southampton before the School was established, William Shayer is perhaps the best known. Shayer produced meticulous, highly finished paintings of attractive rural subjects; he had a tendency to repeat certain successful formulas. Rather sentimental, and certainly picturesque, they provided reassuring images, which are today encountered on greeting cards and calendars. Shayer, the son of a publican, was a self-taught artist who began his career as a heraldic painter for a coachbuilder in Chichester. The coach-painting trade seems to have provided the early training for many British artists – for example, Thomas Sydney Cooper, John Crome, Thomas Daniell, John Martin, Clarkson Stanfield and Alexander Nasmyth. While continuing his occupation of heraldic painter, Shayer began his career as a landscape artist. Michael Hoy, a prominent Southampton merchant and landowner, recognised his talent as an artist and greatly encouraged him: 'with the munificence of a true patron of art [he] employed Mr Shayer until his rooms were almost covered with his works and thus gave this native artist the means and the heart to prosecute his toilsome way'.[21]

Shayer developed a successful pictorial formula, his work falling into two categories: woodland scenes populated with Gypsies, animals and cheerful rustics and coastal scenes based around small boats, fishermen and their families. Shayer's popular success rested on the Society of British Artists, Suffolk Street, London, where he exhibited 338 works, and the opening of the Hampshire Picture Gallery on Southampton's High Street in 1827. The proprietor of this latter establishment was Henry Buchan, a significant local figure who helped develop Southampton into a major port.[22] Buchan certainly created an attractive space in which to display and sell contemporary art:

> The Gallery consists of three compartments:- an ante-room, in which drawings, fine engravings, and a few pictures are placed; an entrance gallery, where highly finished cabinet pictures can be seen in a powerful light, and so close as to permit their high finishing to be examined; and the principal gallery.[23]

Artists who enjoyed national reputations, including Edward William Cooke, William Collins, John Frederick Herring, Sr., Alexander Nasmyth and David Roberts, regularly exhibited. Shayer's work was so popular that he moved next door to maximise his potential, but by 1843 he resided at Bladon Lodge in Shirley, where he remained until his death 36 years later, the attraction being 'the beautiful skies that are typically to be seen in that locality'.[24]

London-based artist Thomas Sydney Cooper, who specialised in painting cows and sheep, urged Shayer to move to London and take his place in the art world: 'These invitations Shayer resolutely declined, he was content with his life, could sell his works as fast as he painted them and preferred to go his own way'.[25] One of his reasons for staying was his proximity to his subject matter. He painted mostly in the New Forest, an area that has attracted artists through the ages; Lucy Kemp-Welsh (1869–1958), the illustrator of *Black Beauty*, would be drawn to the forest's ponies and Gypsies. But 'his reluctance to leave Hampshire for London [. . .] was certainly detrimental to his career, for his fame would have been far more widespread if he had not cut himself off from the publicity that London would have provided'.[26]

While Shayer found work and patrons in Southampton, Frederick Lee Bridell (1831–63) travelled extensively across Europe copying old masters before finally settling in Rome, where he married fellow artist Elizabeth Florence Fox. Exhibiting at the RA between 1851 and 1862, he enjoyed the support of a Southampton patron, James Woolf of Bevois Mount House.[27] Bridell was essentially a one-hit wonder, creating a masterpiece, *The Colosseum at Rome by Midnight* (Southampton City Art Gallery). Dying at the age of 32, of consumption, he never fulfilled his promise.

One local painter who did fulfil his potential was George Elgar Hicks (1824–1914), born in Lymington, the second son of a prosperous Hampshire magistrate, Edward Hicks, JP.[28] Today, few people would recognise Hicks's name or identify him with the famous images of Victorian life that he painted, but it was this very subject matter, which demanded an intimate knowledge of urban life, that secured for him a national reputation. A serious rival to William Powell Frith (1819–1909), Hicks painted the *General Post Office, One Minute to 6* (Private Collection), exhibited in 1860, *Billingsgate Fish Market* (1861, Worshipful Company of Fishmongers), and *Changing Homes*, shown in 1863 (Geffrye Museum, London). Such works, relegated since the Second World War to museum storerooms, have re-emerged as social documents, used to illustrate historical textbooks or, more generally, as a commentary on Victorian life. *Changing Homes*, an ideal wedding card, illustrates a typical upper middle-class home caught up in the marriage celebrations after the return from church:

> Mr Hicks is a disciple in the Frith School. He glides smoothly over the surface of society; he depicts character with a point seasoned often by satire; and for execution no man is more brilliant. *Changing Homes* is a subject quite to his taste [. . .] and affords in the bridal robes, the general gay attire, and the wedding presents, favourable opportunity for the artist to display his dextrous touch.[29]

Yet the painting was denounced by *The Times*, in a scathing review: 'Mr Hicks is, in short, Mr Frith gone to wreck on the shoals of prettiness and sentimentality'.[30] While the public pushed and shoved to see his paintings at exhibition, the critics condemned them as meretricious, vulgar and 'of precisely the kind to please unformed tastes', supreme examples of 'the vulgar naturalism, the common realism, which is applauded by the uneducated multitudes who throng our London exhibitions'.[31] Hicks, like Frith, did not use art in the cause of social reform; he did not highlight social injustice, as the social realists would only a decade later.

Hicks's climb to fame continued with *Women's Mission* (Tate Britain), also shown in 1863, and *An Infant Orphan Election at the London Tavern. Polling* (1865, Private Collection). He exhibited his last major modern-life work, *Before the Magistrates* (Private Collection), in 1866, for which he received 300 pounds. Some six years later, this work could only achieve 129 pounds at auction. Such were the rapidly changing tastes of the London art market. Ever resilient, from 1875, Hicks concentrated on portraiture, which was much more lucrative; in 1882, his earnings peaked at 4,352 pounds and 10 shillings.[32] Although, Hicks never reached the 30,000 pounds a year allegedly achieved by Millais, Hicks gained a sound income. He acquired successively larger houses in Bayswater and Notting Hill. At the pinnacle of his career, as a society portrait painter, Hicks moved in 1883 to the grandest of his London homes; 108, Westbourne Terrace, in fashionable 'Tyburia'. On his father's death in 1861, Hicks was left nine properties in Lymington, valued at 2,500 pounds. He invested his money in solid, low-yield stock, mostly railway shares. Careful to the last, his estate was valued at 11,500 pounds, in contrast to the 1,300 pounds left by Frith five years before.

Despite the popular success of his major modern-life subjects, Hicks was never elected Royal Academician. Frith achieved this in 1853, on the strength of his historical costume work, but, despite his prestigious commission to paint *The Marriage of the Princess of Wales, 10th March 1863* (shown 1865, Royal Collection), Frith was never knighted, his artistic reputation apparently tainted by his popular success. Finally elected to the Royal Society of British Artists in 1889, Hicks exhibited his last work at the RA: *The Traitor*, in 1903. Dying at Odiham, Hampshire, on 4 July 1914, he spent the last years of his life doing good works and tricycling round the Hampshire countryside. Hicks led the life of a solid Victorian gentleman, 'like many mid-nineteenth century artists he remained both eminently respectable and conventional'.[33]

Like Millais, Hicks was a 'gentleman of the brush', coming from a privileged background, while Shayer was but the son of a publican. Hicks benefited from a preparatory education in a private London art school before entering the RA schools. His art training began rather late, as his parents had urged him to study medicine. After three years 'arduous and disagreeable study' at University College, Hicks went to Sass' Academy (the Bloomsbury School of Art) and, in

1844, entered the RA schools.[34] This career progression was denied to many from the lower ranks of society. For the next generation, the schools of art provided new opportunities at a local level. They would prove to be facilitators, enabling even those from humble backgrounds to pursue a career in the arts.

5   Herkomer and the Southampton School of Art

The finest product of the Southampton School of Art in the Victorian era was Sir Hubert von Herkomer (1849–1914), regarded by many as the natural successor to Millais as a society portrait painter. Although on familiar terms with the royal family, Thomas Hardy and John Ruskin, eventually replacing Ruskin as Slade Professor of Art at Oxford, the Bavarian-born Herkomer never won total acceptance from the British. Rising from humble beginnings, Herkomer went on to be awarded an academic professorship and knighthood. Having emigrated from Bavaria to America in 1851, citing family and political reasons in the wake of the 1848 'year of revolution', Herkomer's father, Lorenz (1825–88), a master woodcarver, found there was little call for elaborately decorated furniture in Cleveland and believed a better future lay in England; Southampton was a major port for immigrants as well as those leaving the home country. Hubert, barely eight years old, arrived with his family in Southampton in 1857. The artist later recalled that his father, after a brief visit to London, opted to stay in Southampton as the town pleased him and it appeared prosperous.[35] But that affluence was not translated into a taste for the arts, and the Herkomers found themselves on the breadline. They certainly suffered from prejudice. Hubert recalled being called 'a Dutchman, Foreigner, Roman Catholic, Brigand, Vagabond, Half-Caste'.[36] Herkomer's German origins would dog him for the rest of his life; he maintained his failed bid for the presidency of the Royal Watercolour Society in 1897 was because he was perceived to be a 'forriner'.[37]

Young Herkomer inherited his father's love of craftsmanship and his mother's appreciation of music. His mother, Josephine Niggl (1826–79), an accomplished pianist, supplemented the family income by giving lessons and came to enjoy a certain celebrity.[38] Although Lorenz Herkomer was a skilled woodcarver, there was little demand for his craft in Southampton, and his mother's music lessons provided the main source of income. Through his mother, Herkomer became an accomplished musician, able to play piano, zither and to sing 'songs in character with dramatic action'.[39] Mrs Herkomer was convinced that music was Hubert's forte. Her sister and brother-in-law, Mr and Mrs Wurm (changed to Verne), who had also settled in Southampton, supported her. Four of the Verne sisters had musical careers; Adela (1877–1952) was considered 'one of the world's greatest pianists'.[40] But Herkomer Senior was determined to make his son a painter. This caused some family friction. Relatives 'instilled into his mother's mind the prevalent idea that the profession of an artist was of doubtful respectability and that starvation was bound to follow'.[41]

On his fourteenth birthday, in 1863, young Herkomer was enrolled at the Southampton School of Art rather than enslaved in an apprenticeship, although Edwards, Herkomer's biographer, rather misrepresents the artist's two years at the school as a 'disaster'.[42] Herkomer later indicated how he felt about the teaching methods at Southampton, which followed the 'absurd "South Kensington" routine'.[43] The head of the school, W. J. Baker, 'was one of the earliest artists to obtain an appointment at an Art school connected with the South Kensington System'.[44] Naturally, he followed the national course guidelines, which were weighed down with copying: 'outlines from flat copies, studies in coloured crayons from life studies [. . .] watercolour copies of landscape sketches by the master of the school and [Herkomer] was at the end of all this somewhat purposeless labour promoted to do chalk drawings from the cast'. [45] Few artists enjoyed this kind of exercise – most wanted to draw from the live model.[46] Although such exercises were uncongenial, they did provide a solid basis: Herkomer was awarded a bronze medal, by Solomon Hart, RA, for Michelangelo's *Moses* drawn from a cast.[47] Herkomer would institute new educational practices, especially drawing and painting from the live model, at his School of Art at Bushey, Hertfordshire, founded in 1883.[48] However, he never referred to his formative experiences as 'crippling', as Edwards suggests; rather, he recalled that his first attendance engendered 'a great deal of excitement [. . .] though not unmixed with disappointment, for I was set to copy those stupid outlines of casts'.[49]

In 1865, Lorenz Herkomer, after receiving an important commission in Germany, decided to continue his son's art education at the Munich Academy, 'the place best suited as he thought for the purpose'.[50] After six months, they returned, Herkomer, always forthright, declaring that, after Munich, Southampton 'seemed arid and stupid'.[51] It was time to head for London. In 1866 and 1867, Herkomer spent two summer terms at the National Art Training School. Again, he found the teaching intolerable: 'The studies that I made from the nude model at the South Kensington Schools were purposeless and aimless; and the teaching [. . .] was worthless to me'.[52] The system of teaching did not 'encourage the student to "dig" for his own identity'.[53] Yet the young artist returned to Southampton brimming with new ideas, demonstrating to his fellow students how to drawn and paint the nude. He later recalled,

> We soon developed a consciousness that we were pioneers in the town, and that it behoved us – nay, it was our duty- to show the townspeople that there was a nucleus of young artists amongst them of which they were unaware.[54]

Combining forces in 1868, Herkomer and his friends, 'men who were longing to be painters but were tied to some business', staged an art exhibition in Southampton at Samuel J. Wiseman's gallery, situated over his shop in the High Street.[55] The group gathered together some 65 works, including landscapes, portraits and recent studies from the nude. Herkomer reminisced that the works shown were 'tolerably good' – although only three works were sold.[56] Their expenses were covered by the sale of a sixpenny catalogue. Charles Frederick Williams (1810–94), a local artist who attended the exhibition, purchased a watercolour landscape of *Southampton Common* for 2 guineas, prophesying 'this young fellow has the right stuff in him and will make a name'.[57] Ironically, a large collection of pictures and studies by Williams, who had been trained by David Cox and praised by John Ruskin, was given to the city in 1895: 'it is much to be hoped that this noble gift may have the effect of quickening the Art faculties of students in this town and of the raising up of a band of artists who shall make themselves famous'.[58]

However, Herkomer believed that Southampton did not possess the wherewithal to support an ambitious artist: 'Southampton began to choke me, for I was handicapped on all sides, which my natural ambition resented'.[59] Unlike Shayer and Bridell, Herkomer bemoaned the lack of local support. While it could be argued that the Victorian art market was becoming increasingly centred on London in the 1860s, the dearth of local patrons might suggest that Southampton's art-buying clientele had deserted the city for more fashionable climes. The industry generated by the docks obviously made Southampton less attractive as a place of residence.

Herkomer returned to London aged 20, where he soon found critical acclaim and buyers, *Leisure Hours* (untraced) being 'hung on the line' at the Royal Academy in 1869. Herkomer attended the private view in a hired dress suit.[60] The *Hampshire Independent* congratulated him on his success, boasting that Southampton was not barren of artists and had now produced a successor to Millais in Herkomer.[61] Millais's successor shot to fame following the national and international success of *The Last Muster: Chelsea Pensioners in Church or Sunday at the Royal Hospital, Chelsea* (1875, Lady Lever Art Gallery), the poignant image of an old soldier who has died during the sermon. When

The Last Muster was sent to the Paris International Exhibition of 1878, the painter received, alongside Millais, the coveted *Medaille d'Honneur*.[62] Herkomer was elected Associate of the Royal Academy in 1879 and gained full membership in 1890, by which time he had exhibited over 65 works at the RA. In 1899, Bavaria awarded him the Order of Maximilien, which permitted him to add 'von' to his name, while in Berlin, Kaiser Wilhelm II bestowed upon the artist, whose citizenship was sometimes questioned, the Officer of the Legion of Honour, Foreign Knight of the Prussian Order of Merit.[63] Edward VII knighted him for services to British art in 1907, although sadly his art school at Bushey was denied a royal charter and forced to close in 1904 due to mounting debts.

5 Herkomer's legacy

Of Herkomer's fellow students only Edward Gregory (1850–1909), born in Southampton, achieved national fame. The son of an engineer, Gregory entered the drawing office of the P&O Company, but attending the Art School awakened his aspirations. When both Herkomer and Gregory were simultaneously invited to join the Royal Institute of Painters in Watercolours in 1871, Herkomer commented:

> Gregory and I were boys together in Southampton and it is a satisfaction to me to think of my words to his mother when the question of his art career was put to me for decision I said 'he has more real talent than any of us.[64]

Following in Herkomer's footsteps, Gregory moved to London in 1869, where he studied at the National Art Training School and later at the RA Schools. He exhibited his first work at the RA in 1875, being elected an associate in 1879. Like Herkomer, he worked for the *Graphic*, from 1871–5, where, no doubt, he acquired his taste for illustrating scenes of everyday life. William Thomas, the founder and manager, encouraged his artists to 'go out into life and humanity [. . .] to wander the London streets in search of subject matter'.[65] Frederick Wedmore noted in 1884 that Gregory's speciality was modern genre, although he also painted a series of Venetian scenes and lucrative portraits:

> The outward aspect, therefore, of the things and persons of the day – and not so much their inner significance – has come to be the material out of which Mr Gregory weaves his work [. . .] Gregory will be found but little devoted to that art which has monopolised the title of 'imaginative'. Not for him the world of the past.[66]

Wedmore concluded:

> If Mr Gregory had manifested a great dramatic faculty the sympathy of the large
> public might have been more absolutely his. But as it is, he is dependent practi-
> cally upon the suffrages of the cultivated; and of the cultivated, many are weak
> and a few are strong. When he is truest to himself he paints modern themes, but
> he is far too sincere an artist to treat them meretriciously. Thus – it has to be
> admitted – in a certain measure he escapes wide popularity[67]

However, Gregory was to achieve that illusive fame for *Boulter's Lock: Sunday
Afternoon*, now one of the stars of the Lady Lever Art Gallery, Port Sunlight.
Shown at the RA in 1897 but begun in about 1882, the *Art Journal* observed that
'it is the kind of picture which foreign critics recognise as national; it is in fact
the three volume novel in art, the guide book and encyclopaedia of the
manners and customs of the English people'.[68] The intellectual *Academy* was
more scathing:

> Mr Gregory's great lock picture is dull for all its cleverness. He has piled it with
> all the signs of vivacity, he has laid all his difficulties low and his painting is
> extraordinary; nevertheless it would be difficult for a less able man to paint a less
> desirable picture; the bridge itself is enough to make one look away.[69]

Despite such comments, the picture was widely regarded as Gregory's masterpiece – it was even admired by John Singer Sargent – and probably secured
Gregory's election to the RA in 1897–8.[70]

Herkomer maintained links with the city of his youth and the school that had
enabled his career. His friend and fellow art-school student George W. Sandell
(1851–c. 1943) encouraged the successful artist to present gifts, perhaps making up for the lack of local patronage in their own day. In 1912, Herkomer gave
the Art School his favourite palette, later transferred to the Tudor House
Museum and thence to the Southampton City Art Gallery in 1976. Sandell also
presented his own palette and brushes to the Tudor House Museum in 1942.
Sandell did not pursue a professional career as an artist; he became a shipping
broker in the family firm, Sandell Brothers Ltd, of 6 Canute Road,
Southampton. But he maintained his passion for the arts, becoming Honorary
Secretary of the School of Art and founding an art club that organised annual
exhibitions. He often invited artists trained at Herkomer's Bushey School of
Art to open these events, thus keeping Herkomer's name alive in the city.
Herkomer also requested that the portrait of his father, executed in 1882, be
given to the city. This wish was finally realised in 1930, when, at the suggestion
of Sandell, Lady Herkomer gave the portrait to the city. Herkomer also
returned to the city to visit friends and to lecture. During his 1910 visit,

Herkomer paid a nostalgic call to his old home in Windsor Terrace. He noted with pride that it was called 'Herkomer House', and he presented the occupants with an autographed edition of *The Herkomers*.

Conclusion

After such a promising start, what was the fate of the Southampton School of Art? Its evolution is certainly confused, as the *Southampton and District Pictorial* noted in 1912: 'No one in the course of its history has deemed it worthwhile to place the sequence of events on record [. . .] There is a distinct need for some precision, moreover, because some of the events in the early history of the School have been matters of controversy'.[71] In 1871, the school moved into special accommodation at the Hartley Institute. Unfortunately, Mr Baker, the Head of the School, fell out with Dr Bond, the chief of the Hartley staff, and resigned. Art classes continued at the Hartley under a Mr Pratt, but Mr Baker's supporters rallied to his side and re-established him as the head of a new school in the upper part of the Philharmonic Hall. '[It] was a break in the chain', but the school went on under his successors.

The School continued to have a chequered history, moving to the former Savings Bank building on Havelock Road in 1908. In May 1939, the Art Gallery and School moved into the newly completed Civic Centre, erected on the former West Marlands Park only yards away from the Herkomer's Windsor Terrace home. Alas, in November 1940 the building received a direct hit during a daylight bombing raid. Fifteen students and three staff were killed including the Deputy Principal. After temporary refuge in a local junior school, the School moved to Winchester. In 1945, the Art Gallery was re-established in the Civic Centre, but there was no accommodation available for the Art School. Rooms were allocated in the girl's wing of Deanery School, Marsh Lane, and the Art School remained here until moving to the new campus on East Park Terrace in 1974. The Art and Technology Colleges were merged in 1978 to form the Southampton College of Higher Education. The story ends with the merging of various institutions into Southampton Institute of Higher Education in 1984.

In the post-war era, the School of Art still provided a gateway for local artists. Graham Ovenden, born in Alresford in 1943, studied at the School of Art between 1960 and 1964, where his tutor and mentor was James Sellars (1927–2000), 'artist-writer-teacher'.[72] He then progressed to the Royal College of Art from 1965 to 1968, before collaborating with Sir Peter Blake. But he did not return to Hampshire. Like so many 20th-century British artists, he headed for Cornwall. In 1975, he was one of seven artists who joined together to form the 'Brotherhood of Ruralists', a reconfiguration of the famous Pre-Raphaelite Brotherhood (1848–53), whose seven members included Millais, Hunt and Rossetti. Composed of Ovenden and his wife Annie, Peter Blake and his then wife Jann Haworth, Ann and Graham Arnold and David Inshaw, the group held together until 1981. Although Blake and Inshaw left, the Ovendens and Arnolds still hold to the original sentiments of the Brotherhood and exhibit together.[73]

The Art School has certainly played its part in the furtherance of British art, even though a local school never emerged. Circumstances appear to have changed in Southampton; while Shayer could sustain his success without recourse to London, Herkomer and his generation could not. Clearly there were not enough Hartleys and Chipperfields, Buchans or Wisemans to invest in local artists. The success of Southampton as a port was not celebrated in its cultural institutions. Today, Gregory's *Boulter's Lock* and Herkomer's *The Last Muster* both hang in the Lady Lever Art Gallery. Liverpool's gain, is once more, Southampton's loss.

Acknowledgements

I would like to thank the staff of the Southampton City Art Gallery, especially Tim Craven and Esta Mion-Jones. New information on Herkomer comes from Mike Bucknole, 'Sir Hubert von Herkomer: His Southampton Life, Artistic Influences and Later Achievements', (unpublished BA dissertation, Southampton Institute, 2003).

Netley Hospital.

31·12·07

JWS 71

Figure 5 Netley Abbey, near Southampton, 1907, Copyright, the author.

Chapter 5: Hampshire Gothic

The ruin, regeneration and apocalypse of Netley Abbey

Philip Hoare

> We re-create the horizons we have abolished, the structures that have collapsed;
> and we do so in terms of the old patterns, adapting them to our new worlds.[1]

As a boy growing up on the eastern side of Southampton, its suburbs still scarred by bomb sites, I would make up for the apparent blandness of my provincial surroundings by fantasising about the past. My school, set on a hill overlooking Southampton Water, occupied an 18th-century house to which Jane Austen had been a visitor; below lay the site of Clausentum, the Roman outpost, while down in the town itself was the forbidden territory of the Docks, seen fitfully on school trips, its wharves piled with crates of bananas from the Caribbean, complete with hairy spiders, and its massive dry docks carved out of the reclaimed land like industrial amphitheatres. These mysterious, imported images coloured a black-and-white city for me; they gave it a romance, albeit one which its 1960s concrete carapace sought to obscure.

Thirty years later, Southampton's uncertain place in the national identity was the starting point for my book, *Spike Island: The Memory of a Military Hospital*.[2] I wanted to reclaim a role for the city in which I was born and in which I grew up; to give substance to the romance with which I had invested it as a boy. And, almost by default, the story of Netley's Royal Victoria Military Hospital fulfilled that role. Standing just outside the city's boundaries, yet inevitably affecting it, the gigantic building – constructed in the aftermath of the Crimean War and destroyed a century later – was a paradigm for this historical ambiguity; and, just as its own written record is distinctly lacking, so it seemed to echo an almost wilful obscurity with which Southampton had surrounded itself.

It is one of the paradoxes of the city that its site is responsible for both its positive and negative presence. This is not a destination, but a place of transition; a place seen or experienced on the way to other places. Yet the topography of

Southampton Water has also made it a microcosm of the waves of influence that formed modern Britain: from Roman invasion, Saxon raids and medieval piracy, to less sensational changes in its economy, trade and immigration, all assisted by its double tides, one of the port's geographical blessings. But just as it is physically, socially, culturally and economically determined by its proximity to water and its connections to the rest of the world, so Southampton is limited and threatened by that nexus. Lodged gynaecologically within the underbelly of England, it bears a graphic yet ambiguous relationship to the mother country, her colonies, dependencies and enemies.

As it entered modern history, Southampton still seemed to be suffering the predations of visible and invisible enemies. It lived in the lingering after-effects of the Interregnum's apocalypse, when the world had turned upside down; the plague of 1665 was claimed to have been brought to the town when a misguided humanitarian gave sanctuary to an infected child from London.[3] Depopulation combined with economic downturn to threaten the port with a kind of ghost-town existence, and, thus, when he embarked on his 1724 tour of England, Daniel Defoe announced,

> Southampton is a truly antient town, for it is in a manner dying with age; the decay of the trade is the real decay of the town; and all the business of the moment that is transacted there, is the trade between us and the islands of Jersey and Guernsey, with a little of the wine trade, and much smuggling.[4]

Yet within 20 years, Southampton had regenerated itself – as a spa resort. Fashionable 18th-century society demanded two particular nostrums: mineral waters and sea bathing; and Southampton could supply both. A spring was discovered to produce chalybeate waters – a homoeopathic solution charged with the power to cure all manner of ills, from leprosy to hydrophobia – and visitors to Southampton were advised by tourist guides that 'Bathing has generally been attained with the best effect'.[5]

Its water now had a magical new attraction. Tidal sea-water baths were built below the medieval walls; Long Rooms and a promenade known as the Beach were also constructed for public assembly. By the time Horace Walpole visited Southampton in the summer of 1755, it was already 'crowded; sea-bathers are established there too'.[6] A month or so later, his friend Thomas Gray was complaining,

> This place is still full of *Bathers*. I know not a Soul, nor have once been at the rooms. the walks all round it are delicious, & so is the weather. lodgings very dear & fish very cheap. here is no Coffeehouse, no Bookseller, no Pastry-Cook: but here is the Duke of Chandos.[7]

Part of Southampton's physical allure lay in its countryside, a source of diversion for an age alert to the sublime and restricted in its Grand Tours by Continental war. Lying on the then pristine eastern banks of the water, Netley Abbey was a Cistercian abbey founded in 1239 by monks from Beaulieu and built with stone from Quarr on the Isle of Wight. Centuries before the emergence of spa town Southampton, it had established the monastic reputation of hospitality and healing, a place of health-giving waters, with a leper hospital situated near what would become the site of the Victorian hospital. Water and health were ever entwined in Netley's fortunes, as they were in Southampton's.

With its dissolution in 1538, the abbey was acquired by William Paulet, Lord High Treasurer to Henry VIII. He converted it into a domestic residence; the impacted red brick of Paulet's tenure can still be seen, patched like lesions into the grey Quarr stone. But by the 18th century this crumbling corpus had collapsed into a picturesque ruin, and it was in this state that Horace Walpole, on his visit in 1755, saw Netley. That encounter fixed the abbey in the modern imagination as a Gothic site; for the future creator of Strawberry Hill, Netley seemed to fulfill his dreams:

> The ruins are vast, and retain fragments of beautiful fretted roofs pendant in the air, with all the variety of Gothic patterns of windows, wrapped round and round with ivy – many trees are sprouted up against the walls, and only want to be increased with cypresses! A hill rises above the Abbey, encircled with wood; the fort, in which We would build a tower for habitation, remains with two small platforms [. . .] on each side breaks in the view of the Southampton sea, deep blue, glistening with silver and vessels; on one side terminated by Southampton, on the other by Calshot Castle; and the Isle of Wight rising above the opposite hills. In fact they are not the ruins of Netley, but of Paradise.[8]

In the late 18th and early 19th century, Netley assumed a new prominence on the tourist map. It was hymned by poets, fictionalised in novellas, dramatised in operas and painted by innumerable artists, from Turner to Constable; in one recent discovery, the abbey's ruins even decorated a fine and extravagant porcelain vase, a rich souvenir for some 19th-century visitor.

In September 1807, the Austen family arrived by ferry from Southampton, walking through the woods with a sense of discovery and anticipation. As the party came upon the abbey, the prospect of its ruins entangled with ivy and sprouting mature trees proved too much for Jane Austen's impressionable 14-year-old niece. Like Catherine Morland in her aunt's Gothic satire,

Northanger Abbey – itself probably inspired by Netley – Fanny Austen attempted to capture her astonishment in a breathless letter to her governess:

> Never was there anything in the known world to be compared to that compound of everything that is striking, ancient and majestic: we were struck dumb with admiration, and I wish I could write anything that would come near to the sub-limity of it, but that is utterly impossible as nothing I could say would give you a distant idea of its extreme beauty.[9]

By the 1820s, attracted by such charms, the gentry had colonised the eastern side of Southampton Water with a series of large houses such as Peartree, Hamble Cliff and Sydney Lodge. In 1826, on one of his 'rural rides', William Cobbett visited William Chamberlayne at his marine villa, Weston Grove, whose grounds ran down to Netley. Cobbett's rhetoric reads like a 19th-century watercolour in words:

> To those who like water scenes (as nineteen-twentieths of people do) it is the prettiest spot, I believe, in all England [. . .] The views from this place are the most beautiful that can be imagined. You see up the water and down the water, to Redbridge one way and out to Spithead the other way. Through the trees, to the right, you see the spires of Southampton, and you have only to walk a mile, over a beautiful lawn and through a not less beautiful wood, to find, in a little dell, surrounded with lofty woods, the venerable ruins.[10]

The visitors kept coming. In June 1856, Nathaniel Hawthorne, the master of American Gothic, visited Netley, taking away with him a memory of its 'once polished marble pillars', now 'so rude in aspect'.[11] But by that time, Southampton's reputation as a place of gentility, patronised by Georgiana, Duchess of Devonshire and members of the royal family, had been sundered by the coming of the railway.

In the 1850s, Philip Brannon – artist, entrepreneur, aerialist and utopian – imagined Southampton as a future imperial city laid out in rational lines like Napoleonic Paris. He described its present-day facilities in almost Edenic terms for potential tourists:

> The Whale and Grampus have been captured in Southampton Water, and on such rare occasions there have been of course the usual arrangements for sight-seers. Small shoals of Porpoises often visit the estuary; and the visitor from inland counties may be pleasingly surprised, as he walks the Quays and Platform, to see at a short distance from the shore many of these singular fish rolling and springing on the surface of the water, then disappearing, and rising again at another point to renew their awkward gambols.[12]

But now, as the iron lines separated the town irrevocably from its pleasure beach and sporting cetaceans, fashion shifted down the water to Cowes and Osborne. In the process, the town changed again – for the worse, according to the yachting diarist for *Vanity Fair*:

> Southampton July 26 [1875] ... Here is this town, which is endurable enough, and which I have seen look more beautiful than Venice in that delicious moment when the sun has just set ... here it is bedecked with flags, hideous with blatant bands, peopled no longer with decent work-day people, respectable with evidence of labour, and smug citizens hurrying to effect a job, but with hideous attempts at fine feathers which would make the angels weep.[13]

Netley, too, had changed. By the time of Hawthorne's visit, the abbey had become a venue for picnics, and where poets once discerned romance they now found discarded sardine cans. But that year, 1856, it was announced that Netley was to become a new focus for national attention – in the attenuated shape of a military hospital, about to be built on what were monastic lands, now owned by the Chamberlayne family.

The hospital's beginnings lay in the trauma of the Crimean War, during which only one in ten casualties died of wounds rather than disease. But its genesis also emerged out of imperial myth, and a royal visit to Fort Pitt at Chatham, when Victoria witnessed the inadequate provisions made for her ailing troops and declared the urgent need for a dedicated military hospital. Such a high command suited the portentous qualities of Netley's new, secular foundation; but it is clear that the movement was already under way to construct a large military hospital, and that Victoria's dictum was employed – if not prompted – as part of the political impetus to get it built.

Herstmonceux, Portchester and Appuldurcombe were all considered as possible sites, until the Queen's Surgeon, Sir James Clark, spotted the open shoreside at Netley from the boat on his way to Osborne. Once more, royal intervention, albeit by one remove, was vital to the new hospital's inception. Clark informed the War Department Surveyor, Captain Laffan, of its 'numerous advantages': 'Sir James handed me a strip cut from the Ordnance Survey of Hampshire, upon which he had marked the place he wished [me] to examine'.[14]

Netley and its common had an historical military presence, used since the medieval period, as a mustering place, training ground and an encampment. From here, Henry V's army set out to fight at Agincourt, while Netley's coastal fort had been manned – albeit fitfully – since its construction, using stoned robbed out from the abbey, during Henry VIII's reign. During the Napoleonic Wars, troops were stationed on Netley Common. Now a new royal command would bring back the military, albeit for recuperative, rather than defensive reasons.

Laffan's survey revealed good 'brick earth', a resource that would enable the hospital to rise out of its own footings. But there were detailed objections to the miasma given off by the mud of low tide and effluent discharged from Southampton; the once pure waters, now bespoiled by the industrial era, compromised this locus of health and succour. The spectres of cholera (an invisible but constant 19th-century threat, with its own newspaper billing as a 'Dreaded Visitor' whose invasion no 'streak of silver sea' could prevent) and even malaria (as if imperial conquest had imported tropical malaise) were raised.[15] Other protests came from local gentry, 19th-century nimbys who objected to the building of a military hospital so close to their estates. (Yet more so when they learned that an asylum for 'military lunacies' was also planned.)

Nevertheless, five fields of 109 acres were purchased from William Chamberlayne's son Thomas for 15,000 pounds, and on 19 May 1856, Victoria and Albert arrived by royal yacht and barge from Osborne to lay the foundation stone. The proposed building would appear 'as though a Venetian palace had been erected on the scale of Versailles with traditional English materials', rivalling Chelsea Hospital 'in extent and beauty', reported the *Hampshire Independent*.[16]

However, when Florence Nightingale, the icon of national and martial care, was shown the plans as a matter of courtesy by the Secretary of State for War, Lord Panmure, her reaction was forceful and negative. The designs militated against all modern notions of medical architecture (as would be displayed in her patronage of St Thomas's hospital on another waterside setting, that of London's South Bank), which tended towards 'pavilions' of separate blocks and large wards – easier to air and keep clean. Not only were Netley's wards small (in order to impose military discipline), but they lay at the north-east rear of the building, cut off from its healthy sun and sea-facing aspect by impractical, quarter-mile-long corridors.

In his debunking, post-First World War biographical essay on Nightingale in *Eminent Victorians* (1918), Lytton Strachey has his heroine marching from her home at Embley Park to nearby Broadlands to lobby the Prime Minister, a family friend. Convinced, or harried, Lord Palmerston instructed Panmure,

> It seems to me that at Netley all consideration of what would best tend to the comfort and recovery of the patients has been sacrificed to the vanity of the architect, whose sole object has been to make a building which should cut a dash when looked at from the Southampton river [...] Pray therefore stop all progress in the work until the matter can be duly considered.[17]

Yet such was the relentless nature of Victorian bureaucracy that Netley seemed unstoppable. In her book, *Pugin's Builder*, Patricia Spencer-Silver notes that George Myers, her antecedent and the contractor responsible for Netley, 'would have to be paid 70,000 pounds to demolish the partly constructed building and start again'.[18] Myers was also responsible for building the army camp at Aldershot, the new lunatic asylum at Colney Hatch (later known as Friern Barnet, whose design signature also lay in its long corridors), and Broadmoor Prison for the criminally insane – a track record which underlines the perceived institutional grimness of Netley's Leviathan, rising at the same time as these other Victorian monuments to asylum, care and social control.

The hospital's troubled origins remain the subject of speculation. A later report in the *Lancet* suggests that Charles Barry had a hand in its conception: 'It possesses a bold façade as seen from the water, though the original design by Barry was marred by a piece of economy [. . .] which necessitated the curtailing of the central dome'.[19] Yet although its style bears comparison to Barry's, I have been unable to find any records to contradict the official line that Netley was purely the product of the War Office architect, E. O. Mennie. Similarly, another rumour surrounding this semi-mythic building – as if its very size and contrastingly royally approved, yet near-abortive beginnings encouraged such eddying apocrypha – was that it had been erroneously designed from plans made for a similar institution planned for India.

This persistent if useful story was applied to at least one other hospital of the same period built in Ireland. It could explain why the building's wards were cut off from its healthy sun and sea aspect by long corridors which, in a warmer climate, would have been protective and cooling but which here were suspected, by Nightingale and others, of providing a conduit for infection (just as Southampton Water and its miasmous shores posed the same threat). Whatever the truth, 'one of the first problems' that confronted Netley's commandant, Sir Thomas Longmore, according to his grandson, 'was having to glass in the open verandahs [. . .] which were open to the south west gales!'[20] Thus, these contemporary cloisters were closed in around their inhabitants, doomed to pace their eternal linoleum, just as Netley's small, unaired wards were calculated to foster military discipline rather than healing, in a reflection of the monks' cells of Netley's abbey as places of medieval 'little ease'.

Much delayed, the hospital was completed in 1863 at a cost of 350,000 pounds (approximately 24 million pounds today), against the original estimate of 150,000 pounds. Thirty million bricks (probably shipped from the nearby brickyards of Bursledon along a purpose-built causeway to the south-east of the site) and 3 million cubic feet of stone were used on a 200-acre estate.[21] The materials themselves – Hampshire clay, Welsh granite and Portland stone – were emblematic of the building's British provenance. The hospital also boasted its own 3-million-gallon reservoir, three artesian wells, a swimming pool pumped by windmill with sea water, hydraulic lifts, gasworks, stables, married quarters and a state-of-the-art screw-pile pier, built by Eugenius Birch, elsewhere responsible for Bournemouth and Brighton piers. Entire lives could be contained on this site: from a school for service children, to a royal chapel for 1,000 worshippers, prison cells for errant soldiers and a cemetery, tactfully placed at the end of the causeway, for those who would never leave Netley. This all-encompassing embrace employed the industrial architecture of the period, here applied to the victims of war, disease and imperial policing; an accommodation that echoed the neo-utopian constructions of northern industrialists such as Titus Salt, who built Saltaire in Shipley, Yorkshire, for his cotton-weaving employees.

The building was certainly a splendid sight from Southampton Water (which was practically the only place from which its entirety could be seen). Pevsner's guide to Hampshire would later describe its skyline as 'distinctly romantic, with the rhythm of towers, turrets, cupolas, and central dome, rising above the trees which hide the main bulk of the building'.[22] Yet the first-time visitor entering the hospital would be greeted, not by the sight of scurrying nurses and doctors, but by the skeleton of a mammoth, stuffed fish flying up the walls and vitrines containing spiralling snakes in formaldehyde and mummified human heads arranged by racial type as an index of imperial conquest. This display of natural history asserted scientific and cultural progress, the neural cortex of Empire – just as the body of the building was coursed by arterial corridors, running in either direction from its central chapel dome, as if to emphasise its muscular Christian, pan-global reach.

Even its name – the Royal Victoria Military Hospital – underlined its place in the imperial identity, as did Her Majesty's patronage of the hospital: the Queen-Empress would make at least 22 visits to the hospital during her reign. Indeed, it is a measure of her attachment to Netley that Victoria's visit to the hospital in May 1863, shortly after it opened, was her first public appearance after Albert's death in 1861. During its construction, he had often visited the site; now Netley became a vast memorial to the Prince Consort and his scientific ambitions, in the same way that the Albert Hall commemorated his passions for the cultural advancement of his age.

The Queen's visit was marked by a biblical engraving in the *Illustrated London News*, with its plangent caption, the words of a paralysed soldier over whose deathbed Victoria stands: 'Thank God he has allowed me to live long enough to see Your Majesty with my own eyes'.[23] It was as if, in the absence of Nightingale's patronage, the hospital had acquired another taffeta-clad, universal nurse. At one point, Victoria used her own funds to pay for a prosthetic limb for each amputee. She also knitted a pink and white woollen shawl to be worn by the most valiant inmate, although, as this often meant the most seriously wounded, it was not a popular gift. One trooper was reported to have said, 'Oh, not that ruddy Shawl for me, no thank you, it means I'm a gonna'.[24]

Such visual parables indicated Netley's greater impact, beyond the immediate area, with the eastern side of Southampton and its market gardens, soft-fruit holdings and its labour force now becoming a supply area to the hospital, serviced by the railway line built in 1866 for that purpose, rather than to connect Southampton with its historic rival, Portsmouth. Netley quickly established its presence in the national and local newspapers – there are weekly reports on its activities in the late 19th- and early 20th-century editions of the *Southampton Times* and the *Hampshire Advertiser* – as the hospital replaced the Gothic fantasy of the abbey, albeit with its own fictive identity. Arthur Conan Doyle's first Sherlock Holmes mystery, *A Study in Scarlet*, written while he was a practising GP in Southsea and published in *Strand* magazine in 1882, opens with Dr Watson training at Netley: 'In the year 1878 I took my degree of Doctor of Medicine of the University of London, and proceeded to Netley to go through the course prescribed for surgeons with the Army'.[25] Such was its renown that Doyle did not need to explain the significance of Netley to his readers.

With its image commodified in postcards, prints and chinaware, the hospital's ministry was worldwide, and, despite the equally unsatisfactory venture of the South African War, the new century saw the glow of Empire upon Netley, secure, even complacent, in its role. Important research work conducted by Almroth Wright – who experimented (on himself and his students) with an anti-typhoid vaccine – was rejected by the Army, which was reluctant to use it in South Africa; while the bureaucratic intransigence and lack of foresight which Nightingale had discerned at the hospital's inception came back to haunt it as casualties sent back from Bloemfontein and Simon's Town found themselves stacked in beds arrayed along the corridors in a kind of permanent holding pattern. This terminal inadequacy was soon to be proved in an even more vivid manner, with the advent of a truly mechanised war and its multiplying victims.

From 1914 until the end of the First World War, Netley became part of the military production line. A series of Red Cross hutted hospitals were built on the plateau behind the main hospital, doubling its capacity; this was Netley at its most numerous, a medicropolis of thousands. As the British Expeditionary Force was shipped down Southampton Water, ambulance ships brought back its casualties to Southampton Docks and, from there, by train, into the hospital itself on a dedicated railway line which had been built in 1900 to cope with the South African War. After heavy offensives at the Front, as many as three trains a day would arrive at Netley. (One visitor to a talk I gave on the hospital told an anecdote of his great-uncle, a young teenager during the war, being employed to wash the blood out of the carriages after use). An alarm bell would sound on site, and all available staff would stop work and go to help. Depending on their wounds and conditions (both physical and mental), the casualties were sorted into their sometimes final destinations: the main hospital, the hutted hospital or the military asylum, known as D Block.

Netley's population was now swollen with an international admixture of British and Germans, Russians and Japanese, French and Belgians; there was even a *ghat* built for the cremation of Hindu and Sikh soldiers, enabling their ashes to float down Southampton Water and eventually to mingle with the waters of the Ganges. Imprinted with the efficient routes of modern war and its ancilliary requirements (the quick turnaround of troops able to be returned to the Front), Netley was another node in the network. This bustling place of thoroughfares, radiating out from the main hospital through the hutted hospital and into the outbuildings beyond, was mediated anew in hundreds of different postcards which became, in effect, propaganda images for the Allies' global war. A recently discovered postcard album, assembled by a Red Cross worker from 1914 to 1918, is a remarkable record of the sheer extent of the hutted hospital, portraying its strange conflation of semi-civilian, semi-military life.[26]

Women with babies on their shoulders stand by the railway line as detachments of orderlies march past with empty stretchers, having deposited their burdens at the hutted hospital. Moustached officers in jodphurs gather for a group photograph outside their hut, the very image of doomed gallantry. Pale-skinned consumptives lie in open-sided huts. And outside the Goodman Reading Room, one patient – presumably an officer – has been carried out on his iron bedstead and set in the sun with a cotton sunshade tied over his bed-head, his legs covered by a protective cage. The linen glows luminously through the sepia photograph; an eccentric, poignant vision, resonant with a certain power. It is redolent of the schizophrenic site itself: the massive Victorian building, the ever-expanding, temporary township behind it and the madness which impels it all. It is as if this little bit of Hampshire was itself demented, shell shocked by the reverberations across the Channel.

It is remarkable that almost none of the surviving photographs from the First World War were taken within the main hospital itself; this was still army territory – as opposed to the semi-civilian site of the Red Cross hospital – and, as such, subject to stringent regulation. That sense of a policed, protected zone – an extended asylum – was underlined by the fact that German prisoners of war were kept in the main building, for security reasons, prompting a brief strike at Woolston's Vosper Thorneycroft in 1917, where workers objected to the idea of their fellow countrymen being kept and treated in huts and tents while the enemy were treated in supposedly better conditions. (Other accounts maintain that German prisoners of war wore red discs on the front and back as targets to aim for should they attempt escape. At least two did try to get away, climbing onto the buffers of a train at Southampton like modern-day asylum-seekers and making it to Waterloo before being caught.) In fact, the modern equipment in the Red Cross huts – which included electrical treatment and whirlpool baths – was superior to that in the older and already decrepit 19th-century building.

Yet to modern eyes, photographs of these rows of grey-painted huts at the end of the railway line evoke nothing so much an English Auschwitz (ironically, their predecessors had been donated by the German Red Cross during the South African war, when the British had become notorious for their use of concentration camps). Equally sombre was D Block, Netley's dedicated military asylum and the first of its kind, completed in 1870 under the aegis of the surreally named Commissioners in Lunacy.

Set back from the main hospital in the woods, its high walls, barred windows and padded cells encouraged morbid speculation; the reality was probably worse. One report from 1875 tells of an inmate who had been found in the bathroom, having cut open his stomach with a razor (left by a careless workman) and incised a 4-foot section of his intestine. 'I told him he was dying', said Surgeon Major Buckley, who found the man with his excised gut lying beside him, 'and asked him if he wished to see his clergyman? He said no, he was not going to die, and he should be alright in the morning'.[27]

Shortly before the First World War, D Block was given a vaguely neo-Georgian extension of wards and cells, and from 1914 to 1918, it treated more than 14,000 shell-shock casualties – at least half of the total number to be brought back from the Western Front.[28] Among them was Wilfred Owen, who was brought to Netley in June 1917 and who spent a week there ('I cannot believe myself back in England in this unknown region', he wrote to his mother) before being sent to Craiglockhart Hospital outside Edinburgh, where he would meet Siegfried Sassoon, another poet victim of shell shock.[29] At D Block, the army employed physical cures for mental conditions; in the absence of drug therapy, hypnosis, manipulation and 'abreaction' were used. One doctor proposed a patient's tendons be cut to release frozen limbs. The proposed subject of this treatment was Private Meek, whose fate was featured in the 1918 British Pathé film, *War Neuroses*.[30] Meek was haunted by the ghost of a German whom he had shot on the Somme; every night this Teutonic wraith appeared at Meek's bedside to confront him with his crime. In the film, Private Meek – even his name seems pathetically emblematic, a supine figure from a First World War *Pilgrim's Progress* – is seen sitting in a wheelchair, held by a nurse while his paralysed legs are manipulated, with no little degree of vigour, by a booted, Sam Browned officer-doctor. The pathos and pain of this sequence is heightened by the fact that Meek laughs throughout it.

With the end of the war, Netley settled into its own, uneasy post-traumatic period. The hutted hospital was dismantled (many huts were sold off, including one which was re-erected at St Patrick's Catholic Primary School in Woolston – itself founded by the Victorian Catholic chaplain to the hospital – and where, 40 years later, it became my first classroom). In the 1920s and 1930s, the main hospital continued to be used for long-term care; one wing was given over to tubercular patients. The now dilapidated interior, with its peeling paint, cracked windows and long, gas-lit corridors – complete with screeching feral cats – was already resembling a Gothic ruin, taking up the role Netley's abbey had fulfilled a century earlier. Now silent where it had once resounded to war, the hospital's empty corridors conjured stories of the Grey Lady, a Victorian nurse who had mistakenly given a fatal overdose to her soldier lover and who subsequently committed suicide by jumping from the top of the building. Her ghost – attested to by many hospital employees (including its chaplain) was claimed as an augury of death – although in the cavernous building echoing with the coughs of mortally ill men, death was a daily occurrence even without such spectral omens.

As the hospital languished in Netley's backwater, as if stranded on a permanent low tide, Southampton swelled and prospered, enjoying its inter-war boom as a transatlantic passenger and trading port. Its architectural cynosure – the modern counterpoint to the hospital's crumbling Victorian brick, was the Portland stone-clad, neo-Georgian Civic Centre, begun in 1929. The same waterway that had witnessed the passing of *Titanic* and that, during the war had turned black with troopships, now saw the passage of glamorous ocean liners, their upper decks filled with film stars and aristocrats, the lower decks with émigrés and refugees. For them, the verdigris dome of Netley's hospital chapel was the last man-made structure they saw before the verdigris torch of the Statue of Liberty loomed in New York harbour. Yet many were sent back from Ellis Island (whose waterside architecture bears more than a passing resemblance to Netley's) to Southampton's Atlantic Park Hostel, a camp set up in First World War airport hangars (themselves built by German prisoners of war) on the site of what is now the city airport and where, from 1922 to 1931, transmigrants – often Jewish – languished for up to seven years.[31]

More 'welcome' passengers arrived at or left from the South Western Hotel. This building, its Victorian swagger almost contemporaneous with Netley's hospital (it opened in 1872), now had its own, art-deco extension and seemed to restore Southampton's spa-town sheen. Where Netley's hospital pavements were a parade ground for quivering victims of shell shock like grotesque silent comedians, this brief stretch of (reclaimed) territory, from the deluxe hotel to the transatlantic ship, was a photographed, filmed, flash-lit zone of celebrity, a media arena for the likes of Charlie Chaplin, Noël Coward or the Prince of Wales. It was a notion of imported sensation emphasised when the cowboy star, Will Rogers, rode his horse through the lobby and re-echoed in another act of Hollywood appropriation half a century later when James Cameron recreated Southampton's docks via computer-generated imagery for his 1995 blockbuster *Titanic* – only instead of the terraces of Woolston in the background, the eagle-eyed viewer would discern the golden beaches of Mexico where the film was actually shot.

During the Second World War, Netley hospital received wounded from the evacuation of Dunkirk in June 1940, but its antiquated facilities had to be updated by a modern one-storey complex built behind it – a concrete version of the Red Cross huts – in order to cope with the new casualties. In 1944, as Churchill and Eisenhower met at the South Western Hotel to plan D-Day, the keys of Netley hospital were handed over to the US Army and Navy. Horrified American nurses looked aghast at the drainage which conducted effluent in open channels across the floor, while GIs, having little patience with quarter-mile-long corridors, drove their jeeps along them. (Since the writing of *Spike Island*, I have heard three eyewitness accounts of what I had thought to be another of Netley's suburban myths. Indeed, one nurse told me that the wounded were brought into the ground floor of the hospital by ambulances which drove up the stairs of its main entrance and into the building).

During 1944–5, 68,000 casualties – 10,000 of them German prisoners of war – were treated by the American medics and nurses. In the meantime, the British retreated to D Block (which would remain as a functioning psychiatric unit for the services until 1978), and where, in 1951, R. D. Laing was sent on his National Service. The future proponent of 'anti-psychiatry' was shocked by Netley's proactive use of insulin coma therapy, during which the subjects were kept comatose for up to three days in darkened wards – the process made their skin acutely photosensitive. In the low light, doctors administering tubes used to feed patients could puncture lungs. Other treatments such as malaria therapy and electro-convulsive therapy, the use of Sodium Pentothal (the so-called American 'truth drug' to loosen war-paralysed tongues and thoughts) led others to wonder if such applications were ethical, while Lang's witness of institutional abuse – especially in situations in which conscripted soldiers were suspected of cowardice and of feigning illness – led him to call D Block a 'place of torture, and anguish, and despair'.[32] It was, perhaps, Netley's nadir, although soon after, a more enlightened regime, capitalising on new drug therapies (soon dubbed 'chemical straitjackets') took its place, and the new commandant declared his intention to tear down the high walls of the asylum, metaphorically, if not physically.

By now, the main hospital was retreating from its useful history, its antiquated turrets and spires a sharp contrast to the gleaming silos and gantries of Fawley's oil refinery now rising on the far side of the water; a post-war challenge to Netley's Victorian skyline. Netley, an imperial project outmoded by the changed global geography of conflict, was costing the Army 50,000 pounds a year in upkeep. In 1963, a fire started by children living on the site sealed its fate.

But, at the last, the hospital had a brief, final starring role when Dr Jonathan Miller used it as a location for his reimagining of *Alice in Wonderland* (his own father had served at Netley during the Second World War). The film – in which key roles were played by Ralph Richardson, John Gielgud and Peter Cook in Victorian dress – was a trippy, 1960s take on Lewis Carroll's book, and Netley's Victorian Gothic air was well suited to Miller's psychopathological aesthetic; the Mad Hatter's Tea Party, in particular, looked as though the director had cast it with the Commissioners in Lunacy in mind.[33]

That year, 1966, the order was given to demolish Netley, thereby accomplishing what the Luftwaffe's bombs had failed to do. (One reason advanced for the hospital's wartime preservation – apart from the fact that it was treating German as well as Allied wounded – was that it proved a useful landmark for bombers raiding Southampton Docks, a story which has its correlation in the similar preservation of the Civic Centre, supposedly identified as a regional headquarters for invading Nazis.) And if the hospital's origins were wreathed in bureaucratic obfuscation and error, then so was its end. A week before the heavy plant machinery moved in, the decorators commissioned by the Army had just finished work on one wing of the building (which had recently been reroofed). And even this final indictment of the unwieldy institution had its coda when Perry's, the contractors, employed the hospital's own staff to pull the place apart.

Within a year, Netley was reduced to 250,000 cubic yards of rubble and metal – all to be recycled, as Perry's proudly stated in a press release: 'Thus next year's new car may contain traces of Netley Hospital. And next year's new road may have some of Netley Hospital in its foundation'.[34] My elder brother, then a pupil at St Mary's College, remembers watching from his classroom window as the rubble was ferried in trucks down Lance's Hill and, from there, to Totton, where it did indeed become the basis for a dual carriageway. It was a deconstruction with its own echoes of the transatlantic connection, one which began with the *Mayflower*'s first departure from Southampton, to land, not at Plymouth, but at Provincetown on Cape Cod and which, in another act of export shortly after the Second World War, saw rubble shipped as ballast (there being little else for post-war Britain to export) from blitzed Southampton to New York, where it was used as the foundation for Manhattan's East River Drive.

As the dinosaurean diggers and cranes moved towards the sacred heart of the hospital complex, they came to a halt in front of the foundation laid by Queen Victoria 110 years earlier. On 7 December 1966, the granite block was raised, and a metal casket retrieved. This time capsule was found to contain coins of Her Majesty's Realm, a contemporary edition of *The Times*, plans of the hospital and an early Victoria Cross. These Victorian fossils marked the defoundation of the hospital, and it seems emblematic of the inconstant sense of its history that the casket and foundation stone should be preserved, not at Netley's modest 'heritage centre', but at the Royal Army Medical Corps museum in Aldershot. At the last, it seemed, there was a determination, con-scious or not, to withdraw from this place any semblance of its importance.

The park was opened up to public recreation by Hampshire County Council in 1980. But the stain of memory still lies on this landscape. The quality of Netley's destruction has a lingering, residual, centrifugal impact. Bits of china, clay pipe, brick, glassware – even medals – push up out of the turf and under-growth, as if the Victorian behemoth had imploded, leaving an absence which is in itself a memorial – a cenotaph, in its original meaning as an empty tomb; a site invested with 'the usual touch of melancholy that a past-marked prospect lends'.[35] Like the yawning void of Southampton's dry docks, its emptiness serves to commemorate a greater loss.

Shortly before his tragic early death in 2001, the German émigré, W. G. Sebald wrote of a similarly gargantuan Gothic institution, the Palais de Justice in Brussels:

> At the most we gaze at it in wonder, a kind of wonder which in itself is a form of dawning horror, for somehow we know by instinct that outsize buildings cast the shadow of their own destruction before them, and are designed from the first with an eye to their later existence as ruins.[36]

So it seems that Netley, too, lives on in the memory of its ruins, its own past-marked absence.

Figure 6 The Gordon Memorial, Queen's Park, Southampton, unveiled October 1885, by permission of Southampton City Council.

Chapter 6: Gordon of Khartoum

Reluctant son of Southampton

Miles Taylor

General Charles Gordon (1833–85) ranks alongside David Livingstone as the most famous icon of Christian martyrdom in the late 19th-century British Empire. News of his death on 26 January 1885 at the hands of the Mahdists at Khartoum in the Sudan produced an unprecedented wave of public grief across Britain. For the next few months, there was a flood of poems and songs, sermons, portraits, jugs, tracts and popular biographies celebrating the life and mourning the loss of this deeply religious soldier who, almost single-handedly, had attempted to suppress the slave trade of the Sudan and put down the anti-Egyptian 'jihad' led by the Mahdi. The Bishop of Newcastle led a memorial service at St Paul's on 14 March; Queen Victoria broke with protocol to inform publicly the Prime Minister, W. E. Gladstone, of her displeasure at the manner in which Gordon's forces had been left stranded in Khartoum; and Parliament stepped in immediately to vote 20,000 pounds for the support of Gordon's extended family of siblings, nieces and nephews. In time, grief and remorse gave way to memorialisation. The Lord Mayor of London opened a public subscription for a more permanent national memorial to Gordon, which eventually took the form of the Gordon Boys' Home (now Gordon's School at Woking). To Boehm's monument to Gordon in St Paul's were added statues in Trafalgar Square, in Chatham, Gravesend, Melbourne and in Khartoum itself (Gordon depicted astride a camel). Medallions such as the 'Khartoum Star' were struck bearing his bust, a stained glass window was dedicated to Gordon in Manchester Cathedral, and in 1912 a cathedral at Khartoum was consecrated in his name.[1] The death of Gordon, immortalised in George Joy's famous painting of the hapless general about to be speared to death by 'dervishes' on the steps of the Khartoum garrison, was a turning point in the British imperial conscience. Later commentators such as Lytton Strachey might ridicule Gordon's credentials as a saint, and, in retrospect, his soldiering seems maverick and undisciplined. But in the later Victorian period, no other episode revealed so tellingly the consequences of absent-minded imperialism. Gordon's determination to stamp out slavery revived evangelical enthusiasm for overseas mission, whilst his doomed last stand became a rallying call for the 'national efficiency' campaign, inspiring its demand for strong imperial leadership.[2]

In October 1885, the town of Southampton added its own tribute to General Gordon: an 'architecturally unimpressive', granite-columned memorial, some 60 feet high, erected in Queen's Park, near the docks. Surmounted by a cross, the memorial bears the inscription, 'Soldier, Administrator and Philanthropist', records Gordon's principal military exploits in the Crimea, China and Sudan, and also, with pathos, the last entry in his famous Khartoum diary.[3] Southampton too had joined in the wave of national bereavement that followed news of Gordon's death reaching Britain in the first week of February. However, the town felt especially bereft: 'the sad intelligence comes to very many in Southampton with all the poignancy of personal loss'.[4] For Gordon had been a sometime resident of Southampton since the mid-1860s. Gordon's father, a lieutenant general in the Royal Artillery, had retired to Southampton in 1857 and, on his death in 1865, the family home in 5, Rockstone Place passed to Augusta, Charles Gordon's elder sister. Whenever Gordon was back in Britain during a break from the series of colonial missions he undertook over nearly 30 years, he divided his time between London and staying with Augusta in Southampton. It was during one such stopover in Rockstone Place in January 1884 that Gordon was pitched back into the problems in Sudan. W. T. Stead, editor of the *Pall Mall Gazette*, sought out Gordon at home in Southampton, and the subsequent interview scoop proved decisive in winning over Gladstone's cabinet to supporting a Gordon mission to Darfur. On the eve of his departure on that final fateful expedition in January 1884, Gordon took communion in his sister's church, St Luke's.[5] In these ways, the town felt it had played a special part at the outset of Gordon's venture to the Sudan. Just as Southampton had received Livingstone's mortal remains a decade earlier, now the town bore direct witness to Gordon's last act of altruism.

The story of Southampton's memorial to Gordon has never been told. As in the case of the reception of Livingstone's corpse, it is partly a tale of municipal self-importance and civic patriotism, as local councillors sought to associate the town with the national sense of loss in 1885. It is also a case study of the highly contingent and contested ways in which public memorials often emerge, as what the Town Council thought worth commemorating was at odds with the Gordon family's wishes. Most important of all, the Gordon memorial is a reminder of how ambiguous a part the town and port of Southampton played in the imperial imaginary of the late 19th century. In his lifetime, Charles Gordon valued Southampton for the quiet sanctuary and sleepy refuge it offered, away from both onerous duties overseas and metropolitan society at home. Yet in his death, the town sought – unsuccessfully as it turned out – to claim his reputation as an imperial hero.

The following chapter is in three main parts. First, it looks at the national campaign for a Gordon memorial, and the debate it provoked over what was the most appropriate form of commemoration to the slain general. Second, the chapter describes the local efforts that led to the Queen's Park memorial and the tension that caused between the councillors and Gordon's sister, Augusta. And, finally, an account is provided of a second less-noticed Southampton memorial to Gordon – the Gordon Boys' Brigade headquarters, opened in Ogle Road in the town centre in 1889.

I

Within days of the announcement of Gordon's death there were calls for statues and monuments to be built in his memory. Vacant pedestals in Trafalgar Square and on Blackfriars Bridge were suggested as suitable sites.[6] Towards the end of February, George Nottage, the Lord Mayor of London, established the 'Mansion House Fund' and invited subscriptions towards a memorial managed by a committee whose members included the Prince of Wales, the Duke of Edinburgh, the Lord Chancellor and Cardinal Manning. As the subscriptions mounted over the coming months – totalling 18,000 pounds by mid-summer – various schemes were put forward as fitting tributes to Gordon. They included the navigation of the Nile (suggested by the Anti-Slavery Society) and a new national church erected with the monies from a penny subscription.[7] But the scheme favoured by the Mansion House committee was the construction of a hospital on a site at Port Said in Egypt, offered by the Suez Canal Company. It was considered that this historic meeting point of East and West, Christian and non-Christian, would be the most appropriate way of recognising Gordon's good works, as well as a much-needed addition (supported by Florence Nightingale) to modern medicine in the area.[8] Not everyone went along with this memorial which, however laudable, would be out of sight to the British public, and pressure grew for something closer to home.[9] Pressure grew not least because of the behind-the-scenes support which Gordon's sister, Augusta, and brother, Sir Henry Gordon, a Crimean veteran, gave to alternative schemes.

Augusta and Henry Gordon had long been custodians of their younger brother's reputation. Charles Gordon had joined the ranks of military notables in the aftermath of his role in the suppression of the Taiping rebellion in China in the early 1860s, when he had not only put down the revolt but also refused the rewards offered by the Chinese Emperor, whom he distrusted. But his family were always keen that he be known not just as 'Chinese' Gordon, the formidable soldier, but as a Christian philanthropist at home and abroad. Sir Henry Gordon oversaw the publication of Gordon's Sudan letters in 1881, which brought out the evangelical motivation behind his governor generalship.[10] Even so, Augusta later noted that despite all the books written about her brother, Charles, too little was known about his religious life.[11] On his return from China, for example, he spent six years at Gravesend in Kent, in charge of the erection of forts at the mouth of the Thames. At Fort House he devoted himself to philanthropy, in the local workhouse hospital, and by providing shelter and sustenance to 'ragged' boys off the street. This was a side to Gordon that his family were anxious to promote. In 1885, Augusta wrote a preface to an account of Gordon's work at Gravesend, as well as sanctioning the publication in Southampton of Gordon's own reflections on Holy Communion.[12] Symbolically, after his death, she passed on to Queen Victoria the bible owned by her younger brother.[13] In cultivating this image of Gordon as active Christian philanthropist, Augusta was joined by Gordon's friend, the cleric Reginald Henry Barnes, whose biography of Gordon was one of the few amongst the many published in 1885 that could speak of actual intimate acquaintance with its subject.[14]

As the Mansion House committee amassed subscriptions and commissioned preparatory work at Port Said, Augusta and Sir Henry Gordon made known their objections to many of the suggestions for a Gordon memorial. Augusta wrote that her younger brother would have found statues and monuments 'distasteful' and hoped that instead the subscription might support the establishment of a boys' home. Sir Henry went along with this, hoping that the fund might benefit poor children generally – 'the poorer the better and if the children have lost one eye or are cripples it should not exclude them' – and specifically not be used for buildings or establishments, and certainly not for one in a 'foreign' country.[15] Both of them lent their support to a proposal for a boys' home at Gravesend.[16] Round the coast at Dover, the local orphanage, founded several years earlier by Thomas Blackman, was renamed the Gordon Boys' Orphanage. And so the campaign for a more philanthropic national memorial gathered momentum. In April 1885, the Ragged School Union and the Council of the Reformatory and Refuge Union joined forces to raise subscriptions for the establishment of seaside or country holiday homes for poor children as a memorial to the general. To this new 'Gordon Boys' Camp Fund', Augusta contributed 2,000 pounds.[17] The Port Said project was losing support. In April, Nottage, the Lord Mayor, died suddenly, and his successor (who had also been his predecessor) was Robert Fowler, the Conservative MP for the City of London. Fowler had been a prominent supporter of the Gordon family in Parliament, helping to secure the 20,000-pound provision. Fowler was instrumental in redirecting the Mansion House Fund away from the Port Said hospital, towards the boys' home scheme. At a meeting of the committee in June it was reported that an engineer's survey had found the Port Said site to be unsuitable for a major construction, and the decision was taken to amalgamate the Mansion House Fund with the 'Gordon Boys Camp Fund'. The combined subscriptions, totalling 21,000 pounds, were invested in a boys' home and school, initially at Fort Wallington at Fareham in Hampshire, which opened in October 1885 with its first nine boys.[18] So, by default and by design, the Gordon family got their way. Statues and monuments of Gordon the soldier may have gone up here and there, but the outcome of the public subscription was a permanent testimony to his philanthropy.[19]

II

Similar divisions emerged in Southampton as to what form a Gordon memorial should take. In mid-March 1885, the Town Council responded to the establishment of the Mansion House Fund with a proposal of their own, put forward by the Mayor, James Bishop, for a local memorial to Gordon. Porters' Meadow Common Field, a dock-side site already under redevelopment, was earmarked as a suitable place for a monument, designers were commissioned and a subscription fund opened.[20] Within a week, however, the Gordon family's objections to statues and monuments and their preference for a philanthropic project were being faithfully reported by the local Conservative newspaper, the *Southampton Observer*, and, for the next two months, this paper led the attack on the Council's scheme.[21] By the end of March, Conservative councillors were demanding that townspeople be consulted on the form of the memorial and, at the very least, that the wishes of Gordon's sisters be ascertained. Instead of a statue, one councillor said, 'a friend of the sisters said they had intimated a preference for a memorial [. . .] of a benevolent character [. . .] for example, a ward at the infirmary, or something in connection with the Orphan Asylum'.[22] Inevitably, the memorial was becoming politicised. It was reported that the slogan, 'Who killed Gordon? G. O. M.' (i.e., Gladstone) was scrawled on the palings outside the Gordon home in Rockstone Place, and in the weeks that followed news of Gordon's death, local Conservative associations and Primrose League habitations proved especially diligent in publicising their expressions of condolence to Augusta.[23]

Plans for the Southampton memorial also became enveloped in local evangelical enthusiasm. At the beginning of April, the *Southampton Observer*, with Augusta's public endorsement, published an edition of Gordon's thoughts on Holy Communion. The paper noted that although the pamphlet was written in a 'somewhat mystical manner, following a line of thought peculiar to himself', Gordon was a modern-day Puritan.[24] At the same time, a local Quaker published an account of Gordon, describing in detail his final prayers in Southampton before departure the previous year.[25] A month later, Wesleyan Methodists organised a musical celebration of Gordon's life at the town's Philharmonic Hall. A choir of 80, drawn from local Wesleyan chapels across the region, sang; there were biographical readings; and Salim, a missionary student and former slave from Khartoum, told of Gordon's role in quelling the slave trade and administering the affairs of Sudan.[26]

Proceeds from this event went towards the memorial fund, but by the spring it was becoming clear that the councillors' scheme was proving unpopular. At the end of April, the local subscription fund amounted to only 129 pounds, and it was reported that several local dignitaries, such as Canon Basil Wilberforce (Rector of St Mary's and son of the former Bishop of Winchester), Sir O'Brien Hoare and Revd G. C. White would only subscribe to the memorial if it took a different form to a statue or monument. A prominent voice in all this was that of the Eyre Crabbe family, one of whom, Captain Eyre Crabbe, was currently serving in Egypt. His sister pointedly sent a subscription to the Mansion House Fund, but withheld any local donation.[27] Despite Conservative objections, however, the Liberal majority on the Council prevailed: an amendment for further consideration of the memorial project was lost at its mid-May meeting, and in June it was announced that the design for the memorial, by James Bennett, had been approved and would go as originally planned in the newly laid-out Queen's Park. Most significantly, the Mayor reported that Gordon's family approved of the memorial 'subject to certain small matters of detail being observed'. A few weeks later, a photograph of the final design for an obelisk was shown to Augusta Gordon, and she wrote back to the Mayor that she thought it 'most suitable'.[28] The family's approval secured, the subscriptions revived, and plans were made for the unveiling of the memorial in October.

What had happened to win over Augusta Gordon, whose opinion on the form taken by the Southampton memorial to General Gordon clearly mattered?

Unfortunately, there are no remaining records of the designs submitted to the Town Council for the Queen's Park memorial, but it is reasonable to assume that some modification was made to the original plan for a monument – the crucifix atop the obelisk may have been one of the 'small matters of detail' that required adjustment in order to satisfy the family. It was also the case that by the time the decision was taken in June to go with Bennett's obelisk, the national Mansion House Fund had been diverted into the Boys' Home scheme, similar 'benevolent' memorials were underway in Kent, and the Gordon family may have felt sufficiently placated as to be comfortable with the Southampton monument. Moreover, a local boys' camp providing for 60 boys was formed at West Marlands in the town in June, and conspicuous as the reader of its first attendance roll was James Bishop, the Mayor.[29]

So everyone was reasonably pleased by the time the Gordon memorial was unveiled in the middle of October. The robed members of the Council made up a procession from the town centre to the park, and the 'light and elegant struc-ture' of granite and marble, with its cross, inscription and faintly exotic embell-ishments of Chinese characters and an Egyptian landscape was revealed to the small crowd who attended the ceremony. In his speech for the occasion, the Mayor made a point of stating that Augusta Gordon had requested to him to say 'how happy' the family were with the memorial.[30] And there, for the moment, the town's preoccupation with its famous sometime resident remained. Whether out of mischief or as a gesture of conciliation it is not clear, but two weeks later Augusta presented to the Council a giant parade spear that Gordon had been given by M'Tesa, the King of Uganda, as well as two smaller spears.[31] By the time of the general-election campaign in November 1885, much of the local partisan-ship over Gordon seems to have died down. It is striking that although local Conservative candidates were fiercely critical of Gladstone's desertion of Gordon in the Sudan, there was very little overt reference on the hustings to the General as a local man, or any attempt made to attach the Gordon family name to the Conservative cause, as had occurred earlier in the year.[32] The town had its Gordon memorial, although the memorial might just as well been dedicated to anyone, for only up close does its subject become clear. And the Gordon sisters (Sir Henry died in 1887), who had come to Southampton for a quiet life near the sea, could go back to their pious, retiring ways.

III

However, the evangelical response to Gordon's death lingered on in the town after 1885 and went on to provide the initiative behind a local version of the 'benevolent' memorial that his family had so ardently desired. In March 1888, two local men – Stone and Isted – wrote to local newspapers calling attention to the need to find employment for unemployed youths in the town. Both men had already been involved in city mission work and were now joined in their philanthropic endeavours by H. L. Sanders, who convened a meeting at the Deanery in Winchester, in order to consider possible schemes. Sanders had investigated the work of Dr Barnardo in London and concluded that creating a boys' brigade to provide messenger, household and gardening services would be suitable for Southampton. The meeting was attended by, amongst others, Sir Charles Wilson (Director-General of the Ordnance Survey, based at Southampton), Canon Wilberforce, Augusta Gordon and the Mayor (Henry Coles). The Gordon Boys' Brigade was established, its first headquarters were in the High Street, and, within 18 months, some 80,000 commissions had been completed, with 70-80 boys employed fetching and carrying across the town, keeping ¾ of what they earned for themselves. Inevitably, the Brigade had the overtones of social control typical of much charity and philanthropy of the period. A register of boys was held, their background and circumstances investigated, a savings bank provided, and, where possible, permanent employment or even emigration sought. The boys were adorned in a blue serge uniform and subjected to drill every morning. The Brigade quickly outgrew its home in the High Street, and the following year its patrons supported a move to a new and larger premises in Ogle Road. Here, the proposed narrow Gothic three-storey building would not only house a registry and changing facilities for the messengers, as previously, but also a library, reading room and gymnasium – resources which would be used to offer evening classes. In the mid-summer of 1889, extravagant plans for the laying of the foundation stone of the new home were agreed, involving a royal visit.[33]

On the second Saturday of August 1889, Princess Beatrice, fifth daughter and constant companion of the widowed queen, together with her husband, Prince Henry of Battenberg (later to lose his life in the Ashante war of 1896), visited Southampton from the Isle of Wight, to attend the ceremony in Ogle Road and also visit the Ordnance Survey Office at the bottom of the Avenue. It was the first official royal visit to the town for some time and confirmed the special relationship between the royal family and Gordon's memory. The town turned out to welcome the couple, with firms and shops vying with one another for the best showing of flags, banners and floral displays. Adams and Scanlan, the photographers, arranged a window devoted to Gordon. The ceremony at Ogle Road fused the memory of Gordon as philanthropist with Gordon as imperial adventurer, together with a sprinkling of Highland kitsch.

Attended by boys from the Brigade and a regiment of Hampshire Volunteers, Prince Beatrice arrived, carrying a bouquet of orchids and stephanotis, over which were draped the colours of the Royal Engineers and Gordon tartan. She laid the foundation stone, using a trowel the handle of which was made from coco de mer wood, brought home from the Seychelles by the late Gordon – Augusta kept a box of the wood amongst her treasures at Rockstone Place, occasionally making gifts of it to establishments such as Kew Gardens. From Ogle Road, the royal party moved onto the Ordnance Survey, before concluding the visit with tea with Augusta at Rockstone Place.[34]

The Gordon Boys' Brigade in Ogle Road was not the official civic memorial to Gordon, but it was the more authentic. The prominent involvement of Augusta Gordon and local establishment figures such as Charles Wilson and Canon Wilberforce, the large turnout by weekend crowds, the touch of royalty – all attested to a way of remembering Gordon that was uncontroversial and more compatible with his reputation as a Christian soldier-philanthropist than the Queen's Park obelisk. The building was finally completed a few years later, and until 1938 the Boys' Brigade operated from there.

IV

In subsequent years, General Gordon became inscribed into the town's memory and topography in other ways. Southampton celebrated the British reconquest of the Sudan, when General Kitchener led forces that defeated Khalifa's army at Omdurman in 1896, and two years later reoccupied Khartoum. In the 1880s and 1890s the suburban estates which were built to the east of the Avenue and towards Highfield celebrated the famous resident – with the Gordon estate of small villas, opened in 1886, and later roads named Nile, Omdurman and Khartoum.[35] Although Gordon's remains were never recovered, the family tomb in the Old Cemetery was a partial mausoleum to the general. Augusta passed away in 1893, but Helen, the last of Gordon's sisters, remained alive long enough to experience the last twist in the saga of the town's curious relationship with its most famous adopted son. In 1910, Edward Wise, retired Portswood grocer and property developer, and town councillor (he had been mayor in 1903), offered to fund a new stained-glass window in St Luke's church, of which he was a member and office-bearer. The window, promised Wise, would depict Gordon taking communion alongside some of the apostles. The vicar thought it would be the best window in the church.[36] But Wise failed to mention that he intended to include a study of himself in the commission, together with the martyr and saints. Helen Clarke Moffitt (Gordon's remaining sister) objected vehemently in a letter to the *Echo*; the national press picked up the story as an example of provincial liberal bumptiousness, and Wise was forced to change his design and scrub his image from the work. It was a reminder, as if it were needed, of the political opportunism that often went with the privilege of having Gordon as a local hero.

The story of Southampton's memorials to Gordon is not only a tale of the Town Council's attempt to appropriate as much of the national grief over Gordon for local consumption in the face of political opposition and contrary to the wishes of the Gordon family. It is also an indication of the fundamental ambiguity that surrounded Southampton's status as a gateway to the British Empire. The obelisk, with its overt military and imperial symbolism, was a contested memorial, its location away from the town centre on the dock-front, marginal to the civic life of Sotonians, whereas the Gordon Boys' Brigade Home was at the heart of the bustle of town life, its charitable mission closer to the wishes of the town's elite, and its boys actually providing a service to businesses and residents. When it came to imperial heroes in the late 19th century, Southampton opted for business as usual.

Acknowledgement

I am grateful to Roy Newman of the Old Gordonian Association for furnishing me with information about General Gordon, and for his hospitality during my visit to Gordon's School.

Figure 7 The Winchester Pageant of 1908.
Source: Illustrated London News, 27 June 1908.

Chapter 7: Commemorating the past in Edwardian Hampshire

King Alfred, Pageantry and Empire

Paul Readman

Introduction

Recent years have seen a great upsurge in historical interest in the impact of Empire on the British domestic scene. Building on the pioneering work of John Mackenzie, scholars have examined the variety of ways in which empire has affected British culture, society and politics.[1] In doing so, they have paid particular attention to the late 19th and early 20th centuries, the period in which imperialist sentiment is usually thought to have reached its height. At this time, so it is claimed, Empire and its ideologies exerted a powerful hold over the experiences of contemporary Britons, surfacing in contexts as disparate as Joseph Chamberlain's tariff-reform crusade, advertisements for food, cigarettes and other items, music-hall songs and children's literature.[2] This cataloguing of the multifaceted impact of Empire has led to a further suggestion, also common in recent scholarship, that modern British national identity was, to an important extent, imperial in character. It is now widely agreed that Victorian and Edwardian Britons saw themselves as belonging to an imperial nation (or nations).

However, it is possible that historians have exaggerated the importance of Empire to conceptions of national identity. It certainly seems to be the case that the empire was less important to ideas of *English* – as opposed to *British* – identity. Few contemporaries spoke of an 'English Empire'. This paper affirms the persistence of a powerful sense of cultural Englishness in the Edwardian period. At a time when imperialist sentiment was at its height, English people retained cherished ties of belonging to an older, island past. And quite possibly, these historic ties exerted a stronger pull than the ties of Empire. The following discussion fleshes out this claim by examining the cultural significance of the English past in the early years of the 20th century. There are three parts to its argument. First, and in contrast to much recent scholarship, it stresses the continued prominence of national history in contemporary cultural life. Second, it suggests that the English past provided an important focus for patriotic sentiment, at least as important as that provided by the Empire. Finally, it advances the view that nationalistic interest in English history reflected the high value contemporaries placed upon the preservation of continuity at a time of change. Despite the undeniably powerful impact of Empire, English men and women sought to maintain imaginative links to a more discretely defined nation, one that pre-dated the acquisition of vast swathes of overseas territory.

This argument is developed by means of a local case study of commemorative activity in Edwardian Hampshire. Such activity took a variety of forms, ranging from the commemoration of contemporary events of national significance, such as the sinking of the *Titanic*, to centenaries of key moments in the longer narrative of British history, such as Nelson's great victory (and death) at Trafalgar in 1805. But three events stand out as particularly suitable for the analysis of attitudes to the English past in a Hampshire context. First, the commemoration in 1901 of the 1,000th anniversary of the death of Alfred the Great, whose capital was on the site of modern-day Winchester; second, the Romsey Historical Pageant of 1907, conceived as part of Romsey Abbey's millenary celebrations; and third, another larger-scale pageant, this one styled a 'national pageant', which was held at Winchester in 1908.

I   Alfred the Great and Edwardian Hampshire

We now know that Alfred the Great died in 899. At the end of the 19th century, the year of his death was widely thought to be 901. The King Alfred Millenary, as the 1000th anniversary came to be called, was organised under royal patronage by a national committee, formed in 1898 on the prompting of the positivist thinker Frederic Harrison. The commemoration took place in Winchester, where King Alfred had been buried.[3] Held between 18 and 20 September, its organisation was largely the work of Alfred Bowker, Mayor of Winchester and Honorary Secretary of the Commemorative Committee. Bowker and his colleagues put on an impressive programme. Scholars, clerics, politicians, local luminaries and other dignitaries were invited to participate in visits to historic sites, speeches and lectures and celebratory luncheons. Events open to the general public included a special service at Winchester Cathedral, a dramatic reading by Sir Henry Irving, a firework display and the roasting of 'King

Alfred's ox'. For three days, Winchester was en fête; businesses closed early, and souvenir-hunting crowds milled around the medieval streets, whose shops and buildings were festooned with flags, bunting, fairy lights, balloons, flowers and other decorations. But the real highlight of the festivities came on 20 September, with a ceremonial procession through the city centre, culminating in the unveiling, by Lord Rosebery, of the 16-foot-high bronze statue of Alfred that stands on Winchester Broadway.

The anniversary in general and the celebrations at Winchester in particular attracted considerable attention. This was reflected in the newspaper coverage, which was both extensive and enthusiastic. Lengthy editorials and blow-by-blow reportage filled many columns in the Winchester and Southampton papers, as well as in the national press.[4] But people were not content merely to read about the millenary. Many came from near and far to experience the celebrations first-hand. Hundreds drove into Winchester from Hampshire villages, while thousands travelled from Southampton and London, large numbers of them by cheap trains specially laid on for the occasion.[5] The procession and unveiling ceremony was especially popular, with the streets being filled with enthusiastic crowds throughout the day. One observer felt that 'the crowds that lined both sides of the streets as the procession approached were almost overwhelming, and it was with difficulty the police could ensure quiet'.[6] Some spectators were literally overwhelmed, fainting in the crush, while others had money and personal items filched by professional pickpockets – a number of whom had also taken advantage of the cheap trains from London.[7] In the excited throngs, vendors of Alfredian merchandise had a field day. Large numbers of books and programmes were sold, as well as cheap illustrated leaflets that presented factoid accounts of 'what Alfred did' in a format suitable for mass consumption.[8] Other souvenirs were also sold. As the *Daily Mail* reported, these included decorative teapots and plates, china loving cups, plaques depicting the head of Alfred, and – perhaps unsurprisingly – 'King Alfred' cakes.[9]

So, despite the waning of the idea of a 'Norman Yoke',[10] the public response to the millenary suggests that the Anglo-Saxon past still had considerable cultural purchase. To be sure, the celebration at Winchester was organised by the social elite, but it elicited a popular response – as borne out by the cheering crowds, the demand for commemorative Alfrediana, and the spontaneity of much of the popular enthusiasm generally. Significantly, the cornucopia of street decorations was the doing of local residents and shopkeepers, not the city authorities.[11] Had he lived to see it, the historian Mandell Creighton – a member of Bowker's Committee – would not have been surprised at the public response. At a Royal Institution lecture given in 1897, Creighton had told his audience that

> there can be no doubt that in late years there has been a very decided increase of general interest in history amongst us [. . .] In small towns and villages, historical subjects are amongst the most popular for lectures; and historical allusions are acceptable to all audiences. It was not so fifteen years ago.

At that time, Creighton continued, exhortations directed at working-class audiences 'to act worthily of their mighty past [. . .] fell upon dull ears [. . .] working men cared neither for the good nor the evil of the past; their minds were set upon the present, and that was enough for them'. Creighton's conviction that such 'indifference' to the past 'would not be shown nowadays' was one shared by other contemporaries.[12] Speaking at Winchester Guildhall on the day of the statue's unveiling, Rosebery paid tribute to public interest in Alfred with an anecdote about two girls overheard excitedly discussing the millenary at a free library. The girls' conversation showed what Rosebery called 'a great sign of the times'. 'A quarter of a century ago', he continued, 'there was not the same passion for raising memorials of our great historic heroes'.[13]

Rosebery's remarks can be set in the context of the contemporary cult of heroism. At a time of growing social and political tension at home and new challenges to Britain's international position (not least that posed by Boer farmers), there emerged a growing preoccupation with 'great men' who had displayed leadership, courage and other exemplary virtues during periods of national crisis or in the face of overwhelming odds. This cult of the hero was exemplified by the enthusiastic commemoration of the centenary of Nelson's death in 1905 and the continued prominence of General Gordon and the Duke of Wellington as inspirational embodiments of 'character' in contemporary discourse. It was with such figures that Alfred was compared, and, like them, he was held up as providing a salutary example of right action. Speeches connected with the millenary, such as that given by Frederick York-Powell at Winchester in June 1898, hammered home this message. Doubtless judging that Gordon and Wellington had a special meaning for Hampshire audiences, the Oxford Regius Professor of History asserted that 'this English king a thousand years ago faced his foes with all the patience and perseverance of the Iron Duke himself [. . .] and [with] the simple and trusting faith of Gordon'. Expressing the widely held fear of looming international threats, York-Powell 'did not think they could do wrong to look back at such men as Alfred to see how in their day – a very dark day it was for England – they managed by courage and perseverance, by never knowing when they were beaten, and by sticking to what they knew to be right to pull the country through'.[14]

II   Historical pageantry in Edwardian Hampshire

The Alfred Millenary reflected the passion for memorialising exemplary historic heroes and, in this way, illustrated the prominent part played by the past in early 20th-century culture. But the past could be commemorated in other, less personalised ways, and the historical pageants held at Winchester and Romsey bear this out. The Edwardian pageant craze has received little attention from scholars,[15] but it was a major cultural development. It is important to stress that this was a new departure: pageant performances had of course taken place before the 1900s. But earlier forms of pageantry (of which the annual Lord Mayor's Show was a vestigial example) had focused on the here and now, not on the past.[16] While early 20th-century pageants had aesthetic affinities with their predecessors (the element of spectacular, sumptuously costumed display was retained), the emphasis on the past was entirely new. Held out of doors before huge audiences and involving thousands of volunteer actors, costume-makers and other helpers – nearly all of whom were locals – the typical Edwardian pageant presented history as community drama. Arranged in short chronological episodes, it told the story of town and national life over the course of about three hours. This distinctively historical conception of pageantry was the brainchild of Louis Parker, a well-known playwright, who had organised the first major performance at Sherborne, Dorset, in 1905. Its success stimulated what contemporaries called 'pageant fever', with many other towns across England following Sherborne's example. While Southampton remained immune to the contagion, its Hampshire hinterland did not.

Romsey was first off the mark, holding a pageant in 1907 in connection with the 1,000th anniversary of the founding of the town's abbey. Four performances were staged between 25 and 27 June in the grounds of Broadlands Park. Though not as large-scale as some other pageants, it was still a major event: 1,200 performers were involved, and covered seating was provided for 3,000 spectators.[17] The pageant traced the history of Romsey – and, by extension, of England – from the tenth to the 17th centuries. Benefiting from royal patronage (Princess Louise officiated at the opening ceremony) and the expert theatrical assistance of the distinguished Shakespearian impresario Frank Benson, who acted as Pageant-Master, the performances were very popular.[18] Almost 7,000 people, many from Southampton, travelled to Romsey by train to see the pageant, and tickets (especially for the cheap seats) sold out quickly.[19] Indeed, such was the demand for tickets that an extra evening performance was put on, which attracted an audience of 4,000.[20]

The Winchester Pageant of 1908 was perhaps still more of a success. Spread over eight days and involving a total expenditure of more than 7,600 pounds,[21] it was a much larger undertaking than its Romsey counterpart. Organised over the course of nearly two years by a committee of Hampshire notables presided over by the Marquess of Winchester, it was staged in the grounds of Wolvesey Castle, where over 2,200 performers entertained sell-out grandstands of about 5,000 spectators.[22] The pageant featured nine episodes, beginning – inevitably – with Alfred the Great and closing with the visit of Charles II to Winchester in 1683. Benson (an Old Wykehamist) was again put in charge, and his production was again hugely popular. As was the case at Romsey, tickets sold very quickly, with the cheaper tickets selling fastest of all, and supplementary evening performances had to be arranged to meet the demand.[23] These extra shows were deliberately designed to accommodate working-class people, many of whom were unable due to work commitments to attend in the afternoons.[24] The scene outside the pageant-ground before the final performance, which drew an audience of 8,000, was little short of mayhem. As the *Hampshire Independent* reported,

> Several thousands were awaiting admission at six o'clock, before the afternoon performance had concluded. Special trains brought in hundreds of visitors, who crowded the precincts of the pageant ground. The crush at the gates leading to the ticket office was terrible; women screamed and fainted, and frantically tore their way out of the dense, swaying, pushing, surging mass of humanity behind. When the gates opened the constables were almost overcome, and again around the ticket office the crowd screamed and fought for the little piece of paper which entitled them to admission. At length the crowd were appeased, but hundreds were unable to get into the ground. The grand stand was crowded to excess; every inch of standing room on the ground was occupied, and even the performers' stand had to be utilised for the accommodation of the crowd.[25]

At the close of the proceedings, Benson was borne away on a shield in triumph by ecstatic cast members (as had also been done at the close of the Romsey pageant), and the National Anthem was sung.[26]

There is no doubt, then, that historical pageants appealed greatly to all sections of society, including the many working-class people who snapped up the cheap seats and attended the special evening performances, as well as the dress rehearsals – for which cheap tickets were also offered. But pageants did not simply draw popular audiences; they also involved high levels of popular participation. Like the Alfred Millenary, the Hampshire pageants were organised by committees of local luminaries. But while these events were elitist in this sense, they had an important socially inclusive dimension. In line with Parker's insistence that pageants should be 'absolutely democratic' celebrations of history,[27] the volunteer performers, costume-makers and other helpers who took part were recruited from all sections of the local community. It was a cause of considerable satisfaction to the organisers of the Romsey pageant that 'all classes' – 'rich and poor, gentle and simple' – were involved in the event.[28] Mechanics at the Berthon Collapsible Boat Works in Romsey Town, for example, voluntarily built the Danish ships used in Episode III (which, immediately after the last performance, were also used in an unscheduled race between two of the boat crews – an event suggestive of popular pride in proletarian craftsmanship).[29] Other workers, apparently acting on their own initiative, fashioned crosses, picture frames, walking sticks and other items from the 600-year-old oak which had been removed from the roof of Romsey Abbey in the course of its restoration. These were sold in the pageant ground, the proceeds being donated to the Abbey Restoration Fund.[30]

It is true that some of this activity was organised and supervised by middle-class committee members actuated by a desire to 'improve' the lower orders. In the early stages of planning the Winchester Pageant, a memorandum to the Costume Committee suggestively referred to how 'at Romsey many of the "properties" such as brass helmets, shields etc have been made by men who were in some cases practically "loafers" who have been organised by a clergy-man & taught their craft by a County Council teacher'.[31] Nevertheless, working people readily volunteered their time and services, for which they received no financial inducement. Moreover, there is evidence that levels of enthusiasm were high, as illustrated by the case of Romsey's Danish boats. At Winchester, members of the group of working-class volunteers who made spears, shields and other props at local-authority workshops for the Winchester Pageant often took their work home with them.[32]

What, though, about the pageant performers? In common with other his-torical pageants, the vast majority of cast members had no prior acting experi-ence: those who did were usually upper- and middle-class people, or clerics, and these individuals – who also had the most spare time to devote to rehearsals – tended to get the most prominent parts. But pageants were conceived as community events, and a real attempt was made to offer parts to people from all social groups. This appears to have been successful at Romsey, where at least one-quarter of the town's total population took acting roles.[33]

But the evidence relating to Winchester is still more compelling. From the out-set, the organisers resolved to appeal to the 'General Public' for volunteers, and advertisements calling for prospective performers to come forward were widely circulated.[34] In addition, as a means of encouraging the less well-off to participate, reimbursement was offered to cover the cost of costumes.[35] Such expedients reflected a determined effort to involve as wide a range of people as possible, and this effort was remarkably successful. Cross-referencing names and addresses in the pageant cast books with the 1901 Census returns gives an indication of the social composition of the pageant performers.[36] From this, it is clear that cast members were drawn from all social groups, and all parts of the town. Working-class inhabitants of Hyde Abbey Road, Union Street and Eastgate Street, among others, provided performers, as did the domestic ser-vants living on St James' Terrace and Southgate Street. Many of the grocers' and drapers' assistants, clerks and dressmakers employed in the shops and businesses of Winchester High Street also took part. While it is true that the most important parts did go to local notables, working-class cast members were often given status-transcending roles: the wife of a railway worker was a Saxon noblewoman; a boot and shoe operative was a Benedictine monk.

III   Hampshire and the English national past

Whether or not the interest excited by commemorative occasions like histori-cal pageants or the King Alfred Millenary provides an accurate gauge of the importance of the past in English culture is debatable. It could be suggested that participants in pageants might simply have warmed to the thrill of dressing up in costumes; that the crowds on the Winchester streets during the millenary might have been mainly attracted by the prospect of an exciting spectacle. Contemporary evidence does exist for such views. Writing in the *Southampton Times*, Wyndham Hill advised readers that the best way to 'get full enjoyment' out of the Winchester Pageant was

> to leave the 'inspiration and aspiration' part of the business to work uncon-sciously and at its own convenient season; to go to Wolvesey Castle unfettered by any feeling that one ought to learn something, and when there, just sit and feast one's eyes on the long succession of pretty spectacles and listen to the music without bothering in the least to understand what it is all about.[37]

However, while some spectators, perhaps particularly those from Southampton, might have approached the Hampshire pageants with such a mindset, comments like those of Hill's were the exception and not the rule.

Generally speaking, press coverage of the Winchester and Romsey pageants – in Southampton as elsewhere – was heavy with historical detail, précis of episodes and testaments to prevailing high levels of public engagement with the past. This was even true of the *Southampton Times*, which no doubt judged such material would be of interest to its readers.[38] (Significantly, the *Southampton Times* also carried extensive regular coverage of the antiquarian doings of the Hampshire Field Club, as well as a weekly 'Historical Calendar' detailing notable anniversaries.)[39]

On balance, it seems reasonable to conclude that the level of public interest in commemorative activity in Edwardian Hampshire reflected popular attitudes towards the past. This activity, after all, was inescapably *historical* in character. Such did not escape Arthur Quiller-Couch, whose novel *Brother Copas* was set in a fictional cathedral city (Mercester; a dead ringer for Winchester) at the time of a pageant. Towards the end, Quiller-Couch has his protagonist observe:

> So the Pageant went on unfolding its scenes. Some of them were merely silly [. . .] Indeed, much of the Pageant was extremely silly. Yet, as it progressed, Brother Copas was not alone in finding his heart lift with the total effect of it. Here, after all, thousands of people were met in common pride of England and her history. Distort it as the performers might, and vain, inadequate, as might be the words they declaimed, an idea lay behind it all. These thousands of people were met for a purpose in itself ennobling because unselfish [. . .] the rite took possession of them, seizing on them, surprising them with a sudden glow about the heart, sudden tears in the eyes. This *was* history of a sort.[40]

Quiller-Couch's account was a fictionalised one, to be sure, but one informed by his first-hand experience of the Winchester Pageant, for which he had written two of the episodes. As it suggests, a person's experience of an historical pageant or the Alfred Millenary was not just about the fun of the fair, or the excitement of spectacle, or the pleasure of participation – though these and other factors might have played some role. After all, thousands of people bought verbose pageant programmes (often heavy with historical disquisitions on the town in question), books of words and other literary-historical merchandise before and after witnessing a performance.[41] Apropos of the Romsey Pageant, the *Southampton Times* reported that '"The Pageant Book" was completely sold out on the second day, and the booksellers' shops were besieged on Thursday by eager applicants for copies, which were not obtainable'.[42] The Winchester pageant prompted a slew of historical writing, not least a novel by former Mayor Alfred Bowker, set in medieval times.[43] As for the

Alfred Millenary, the quantity of pamphlets, speeches and books on the great king's life and times published to coincide with the event was positively diluvial.[44] Written for the mass market in a style more accessible than scholarly, thousands of copies were sold. Indeed, the flood of publications, and their popular success, was sufficient to prompt an ex-cathedra denunciation by the eminent Anglo-Saxon historian Charles Plummer. In his opening Ford lecture of 1901, Plummer observed somewhat crossly that there had been 'a "boom" in things Alfredian lately; and the literary speculator has rushed in to make his profit'.[45]

Plummer's perception that unscholarly popularisers were able to cash in on Alfred's memory in this way is symptomatic of the prominence of a historical-minded dimension to Edwardian cultural life – a prominence also illustrated by the public reception accorded the Millenary Commemoration itself and the pageants at Romsey and Winchester. Such a conclusion is of historiographical significance, as it calls into question the generalisations many scholars have made about the increasingly 'modern' and, as such, increasingly ahistorical character of English culture at this time. According to Raymond Chapman, Jose Harris, Peter Mandler and other writers, the rapid pace of social, political and technological change after 1870 resulted in a significant dehistoricisation of cultural life.[46] Harris has written of what she calls 'the unique dominance of the present time' in these years.[47] Chapman has asserted the existence of a 'growing sense that the past [was] simply irrelevant' to modern concerns.[48] More recently, Peter Mandler has offered the judgement that 'English culture became less interested in history'. Indeed, Mandler has gone so far as to say that 'history in general was marginalised' by modernising late-century trends. These included the increasing speed of travel, the prevalence of photographic images, even imperial expansion (which directed attention away from the English past and towards here-and-now happenings on the frontiers of Empire).[49] In the light of the evidence presented here, such claims seem in need of revision. The commemorative activities that took place in Edwardian Hampshire indicate the still-important place occupied by the past in English cultural life. But what do these activities say about the *use* of the past at this time?

IV   The past and patriotism

First and foremost, the past was used as a vehicle of English patriotism. Commemorative activity was invested with a strong patriotic charge by its organisers, participants and outside commentators. The Alfred Millenary occasioned much flag-waving, with Alfred being presented as a patriotic hero, the founder of England, the personification of national virtue. In an 1898 address at Winchester Guildhall promoting the idea of the millenary as a 'national memorial', Bowker claimed that 'there would have been no England had it not been for Alfred, and [. . .] the country would have been Dane-land'. The following year, at the same venue, the Liberal politician G. J. Shaw-Lefevre told the burghers of Winchester that Alfred 'combined with the highest attributes of mankind all those qualities which England most admired, which we claimed to be the especial attributes of the highest and best of Englishmen'.[50]

As for pageantry, press opinion was unanimous in regarding it as patriotic celebration with a patriotic function. In a leader article on the Winchester Pageant, the *Hampshire Independent* claimed that historical pageants were

> above all [. . .] the most powerful incentives to patriotism which have been invented in the memory of man. As our thousands of men, women, and children watch the history of their home unfolding before their eyes, in moving pictures, with striking song, with mirth and tragedy, they are unconsciously learning to love England, to fear God, and to honour the King.[51]

Such opinions were not surprising, given the avowedly patriotic agenda of pageant organisers. As Parker himself explained, historical pageantry was 'the great incentive to the right kind of patriotism: love of hearth; love of town; love of country; love of England'.[52] For Parker and other pageant organisers, this patriotism was a feeling of communitarian belonging that extended 'from the county to the country'.[53] In a sermon given on the occasion of the Romsey Pageant, the Revd A. J. Grieve voiced similar sentiments. 'In modern England', Grieve told his Congregationalist flock, 'our patriotism is a threefold cord, combining love of land, of county, and of town or village'.[54]

Such a perspective testified to the currency of the idea that English national loyalty was bound up with love of locality. Historical pageantry was consonant with this mainstream conception of Englishness. Pageants gloried in the history and traditions of particular towns or cities, and the performances at Romsey and Winchester were no exception. Care was taken so that the story told was one of local relevance. At Winchester, the Staging and Music Committee of the pageant resolved 'that the Episodes [. . .] be in no case unconnected with Hampshire', and blocked Benson's attempt to bring in a 'scene relating to Birinus, the words and incidents of which properly belonged to the north of England'.[55] At Romsey, the opening lines of the preface to the official programme proudly and proprietorially proclaimed 'our Pageant' to be 'an endeavour on the part of the people of Romsey to represent some of those historical scenes which have taken place in the town since the founding of the Abbey in the year 907'.[56]

Yet despite this local emphasis, the community dramas at Romsey and Winchester were not narrowly parochial. In both pageants, local experience was deliberately merged with a grander national story. Winchester was explicitly conceived as a 'national pageant' – its promoters being desirous of commemorating the past of 'this beautiful old city [. . .] the cradle of English history, the ancient capital of the English nation, Alfred's city [. . .] where the foundation of our national greatness was laid'.[57] Their conception was realised in the content of the pageant episodes, which told the story of England through the idiom of local experience. National events and national figures loomed large. The Roman invasion, King Canute and the waves, the 'anarchy and misrule' of Stephen's reign and the 16th-century Anglo-Spanish rivalry were among the subjects traversed. In the opinion of the *Southern Daily Echo*, 'the central idea of the pageant, "the making of England" runs like a golden thread through the fabric'.[58]

Telling the story of 'the making of England' was easier at Winchester, which – as a former capital city – had a more glorious, more eventful and more 'national' past to draw upon than the small town of Romsey. But if Romsey's pageant was necessarily more locally oriented, it too was suffused with national meaning and connected to a national narrative. As at Winchester, many of the scenes took the form of local illustrations of larger developments in English history, with the audience being alerted to the national dimension by the words of the performers and the gloss provided in the pageant programme. Episode VIII, for example, featured King James I at Broadlands in 1607, a visit that had seen him grant a charter of incorporation to the town of Romsey. This event, the book of words made clear, was of more than parochial relevance: it was intended to illustrate 'the growth of municipal life which was taking place all over England' at that time.[59] In this way, the organisers of the Romsey Pageant sought to demonstrate how 'it is but a step from the story of each English town, to the wider scenes and the grander Drama of our National History'.[60]

Relating the local to the national was both an assertion of civic pride and an assertion of the significance of Romsey and Winchester in the broader tapestry of English history. As such, the Hampshire pageants reflected the nature of early 20th-century English identity. This identity involved deep attachment to the locality, and – as K. D. M. Snell has recently shown – could even encompass strong feelings of hostility towards neighbouring localities.[61] Yet, in contrast to continental countries like Italy, for example, where the pull of local loyalties sometimes ran counter to the prerequisites of a wider sense of nationhood, there was in England little tension between local and national ties of belonging. The two fed into and supported one another. 'High levels of local patriotism', as Snell has written, 'could often coincide with and buttress national patriotism'.[62]

V   Hampshire, Empire and national identity

As mentioned earlier, many scholars now point to the Empire as a focus of national identity in the late 19th and early 20th centuries. Empire certainly excited interest, and from time to time even passion – as at the general election of 1900.[63] But its impact should not be overestimated. The commemorative activity of Edwardian Hampshire also provides evidence that qualifies the impact of Empire and, specifically, its impact on English identity.

The Alfred Millenary was organised in the late 1890s, at a time when impe-rial issues were at their most prominent. Held during the Boer War, the celebration at Winchester was seen as an appropriate context for the recogni-tion of valour on the frontiers of Empire. Among the servicemen who took part in the ceremonial procession before the unveiling ceremony were Volunteers and Imperial Yeomanry who had fought in South Africa; and the presentation of medals to these men was incorporated into the day's proceedings.[64] Moreover, the Millenary Commemoration was attended by claims that the foundations of Empire were laid in the Alfredian past. As a prominent 'Liberal Imperialist', Rosebery gave passing expression to this view in the course of his speech at Winchester Guildhall.[65] But such a perspec-tive was not representative of contemporary comment on the millenary in general. Local press coverage did not put an imperialist gloss on Alfred's reign and achievements. In fact, in the run-up to the millenary and during the commemoration itself, imperialist readings of the Anglo-Saxon past were very largely absent, being given en passant, if at all. Speeches by supporters and organisers of the events at Winchester – not least Rosebery's own – tended to emphasise Alfred's exemplary character and domestic 'success as a states-men and a ruler' of England above all else.[66] As originator of the idea of the millenary and a prominent member of the organising committee, Frederic Harrison emphasised from the start how the example of Alfred showed that 'true human greatness needs no vast territories as its stage, nor do multi-tudes add to its power'.[67]

This is not to say that Alfred's military achievements went uncelebrated. Much was made of his supposed formation of a navy, and, indeed, a state-of-the-art cruiser (the *King Alfred*) was launched in connection with the millenary on 28 October.[68] Unsurprisingly, given the proximity of Southampton port, Hampshire opinion was especially susceptible to this association of Alfred and the nation's sea power. Articles in the local press repeatedly emphasised his role as a pioneer of maritime warfare. And, significantly, as the Southampton newspapers were particularly keen to report, it was the naval brigade (not the khaki-clad soldiers from South Africa) who received the loudest cheers of all the participants in the procession through Winchester.[69]

But Alfred's military activities, including his supposed establishment of a navy, were generally presented as actions in defence of an English homeland, not precursors to imperial expansion. As a newspaper broadly supportive of the South African war, the *Hampshire Independent* presented Alfred not as a martial hero who might serve as inspiration for contemporary imperialists, but as a 'true reformer', a godly and selfless lawmaker who had done much to improve the education and social condition of his people. While his small fleet had formed 'the embryo of the naval glory of old England', his overall 'policy was one of peace and development of his kingdom. Warrior though he was, he left the thirst of conquest to others'.[70] Others agreed. In the opinion of the Mayor of Winchester, 'pride in his country rather than love of conquest was the form [King Alfred's] patriotism took. He never attacked except to defend'.[71]

Historical pageantry had a similarly prominent inward-looking dimension. The Empire was not ignored in pageant performances. But it was peripheral to most, including those that dealt with 18th and 19th-century history.[72] It is true that the national stories told at Winchester and Romsey closed in the 17th century, thereby limiting the scope for imperial excursuses. But the lack of teleological commentary on the Empire at such festivals of patriotic commemoration is significant. At Romsey, the Empire was entirely absent, receiving no mention in the words or programme notes of the pageant. In acclaiming the pageant as a great patriotic celebration, the Hampshire press made no reference to the Empire.

At Winchester, things were slightly different. Some newspaper coverage did mention how the foundations of the 'mighty empire' were laid in the city, but there were very few such references, and those that did appear were brief and allusive. As regards the pageant itself, Empire and imperialism cast their shadow on none of the episodes. As in the millenary, King Alfred was portrayed as a wise, virtuous ruler, who took up arms in defence of his people against aggression; his naval achievements were again presented in defensive rather than expansionist (or proto-expansionist) terms. To the cheers of the audience, Alfred declaimed in Episode IV that ''Twas by our fleet we broke the Danish power. I'll leave my England this for legacy. There's your defence – the sea – Look to your ships!'[73] Even Walter Ralegh was not shown in an imperialist light at the pageant. Sir Walter – who appeared in Episode VIII – was simply depicted as a great naval commander, who had defeated the aggressive Spanish. Despite a programme note describing him as 'the first apostle of the true imperialism', Ralegh's speech made no mention of his 'imperialist' doings on the high seas, and he was not presented as a hero of Empire in other commentaries.[74]

As the Alfred Millenary and the Hampshire pageants reveal, then, patriotic commemoration of the national past did not necessarily involve the Empire, or even reference to the Empire. Given the centrality of history and memory to conceptions of national identity, this raises questions about the importance of Empire to English nationhood – an importance that many scholars might well have exaggerated. While the imperial spirit did not run directly counter to mainstream ideas of Englishness, it did not have much influence over these ideas either, which were grounded on the long continuities of English history, reaching far back into the pre-imperial past. Even in the age of 'high imperialism', the historic ties of English national belonging stood independent of Britain's far-flung empire.

Conclusion: national identity and the continuities of the national past

In Edwardian England, interest in the national past was widespread. Historians who say these years saw a dehistoricisation of English culture are mistaken. Ironically, though these scholars rightly reject Martin Wiener's famous caricature of a culturally retrogressive England, their views – like his – seem predicated on the idea that deep-set concern for the national past was incompatible with the spirit of modernity.[75] But we should not suggest that the processes of change necessarily implied a sharp diminution in the cultural significance of the past. In England, as this essay concludes by suggesting, the transition to the 20th-century world went hand in hand with regard for the continuities of national history.

In a number of ways, the Alfred Millenary reflected strong concern for these continuities. Much of what was regarded as good in the English national character could be traced back to Alfred. These attributes included the refusal to be beaten, the manly, upright, faith in God, the selfless devotion to duty and the commitment to truthfulness (which – according to Rosebery – was something that 'Englishmen love').[76] The national virtues identified in Wellington, Livingstone, Gordon and other latter-day heroes found their first personification in Alfred. But Alfred's legacy was traced through to the present by other means, too. His achievements as ruler laid the groundwork for future progress. As Rosebery said at the unveiling ceremony, Alfred was

> [T]he pioneer of England's greatness. With his name we associate our metropolis, our fleet, our literature, our laws, our first foreign relations, our first efforts at education [. . .] His rude councillors were the ancestor of our Parliament; his flotilla of galleys was the foundation of our fleet [. . .] He breathed the earliest inspiration of education into England [. . .] And he [. . .] gave us the London which we know.[77]

Aside from his successes as ruler, Alfred's status as ruler was also tied into the long continuities of English history. In the eyes of contemporaries, Alfred was not only King of Wessex but also King of England – a leader inspired by love of England and prophetic dreams of national unity. Indeed, much was made of the idea that Alfred was first in a long line of English monarchs – a line that ran unbroken to the present day. This was a matter of national pride and was itself seen as emblematic of the still-continued continuities of English identity. In a volume of commemorative essays edited by Alfred Bowker, Frederic Harrison spelled this out: 'In the history of modern Europe', he wrote,

> there is nothing which can compare in duration and in organic continuity with the unbroken evolution of our English nation. And [. . .] there is no dynasty in Europe which can be named in the same breath with that which has seen a succession of forty-nine sovereigns since Alfred; nor has any King of Caesar a record of ancestry which can compare with that of the royal lady who through thirty-two generations traces her lineal descent to the Hero-King of Wessex.[78]

Victoria's death just before the Winchester commemoration did not dampen the enthusiasm for tracing such royal lineages. Family trees printed in newspapers even endeavoured to show that Alfred's blood still flowed in the veins of Edward VII (who would have been present at the unveiling had his mother not died when she did).

The pageants at Winchester and Romsey provide an even better illustration of the importance of the continuities of the national past. Following Parker's example, the presentation of 'the grander Drama of our National History' in the form of a continuous narrative, related to the local context, was the declared aim of the pageant-makers' game.[79] With their episodic, chronological structure, the Hampshire pageants traced the course of history from the pre-Christian era to the 17th century, a time defined by Romsey's book of words as marking the beginning of 'the modern period of English History'.[80] Such emphasis on continuity was borne out by the elision or watering down of discontinuity. At Winchester, there was no episode dealing with the Civil War, and Charles II received very favourable treatment.[81] At Romsey, although the Civil War was not avoided, a distinctly royalist spin was in evidence. In the final episode, showing Charles I in captivity after his defeat, stress was laid on the maintenance of monarchical traditions in spite of the Roundhead victory. In the closing words of the episode, a schoolmaster urges remembrance of 'him who goes to his death for England's Church and for his people'.[82] Other historical caesurae were also smoothed over – that of 1066, for example. While much 19th-century opinion would have seen the Norman invasion as marking a diversion from the English national *telos*, this perspective was absent from the content of and commentary on the Hampshire pageants. Episode III of the Winchester Pageant featured the execution of the Saxon rebel Earl Waltheof in 1076. But though the Earl was presented in a positive light, the lesson imparted was that his death symbolised 'the broadening of the national life by the influence of Norman vigour and Norman largeness of statesmanship'.[83] The Conquest did not represent the imposition of any 'Norman Yoke', but a step forward. Saxon and Norman attributes were combined to create the modern English race. This point was also made at Romsey, where the moral of the early episodes, which featured conflict between Saxons, Danes and Normans, was that through war these groups 'were slowly welding together the England that was to be'.[84] Episode IV, which featured the wooing of Princess Eadgyth by the future King Henry, marked the completion of this process: 'In a few months more the joy-bells of Westminster ring out at the wedding of the Norman Prince and the English maiden, and the two warring nations are blended in one English people'.[85]

In Hampshire pageant narratives, stress on continuity was coupled with stress on progress. At Romsey, the declared aim was

> to mark how disorder and barbarism have given place to order and civilisation, how clank of mail and stroke of sword have hammered out national unity and social law, and how, though it were through the jar and fret of contending factions, our land has swept into clearer knowledge and not less strenuous life.[86]

Commemorating the past did not take the form of threnodic regret at the passage or time, nor did it seek to turn back the clock to the 'good old days'. Indeed, as an active vice-president of the Romsey Pageant Committee, the Bishop of Winchester drove this point home in a special service of thanksgiving on the Sunday before the first performance. The 'so-called "good old days" of England', he declared, 'were times of [. . .] deep-seated ignorance, profound superstition, wide-spread poverty, constant civil strife, violence, lawlessness, coarseness, and oppression [. . .] as they looked back, they knew their land was better'.[87]

But the function of the past was not simply to act as a benchmark against which the better present could be judged. In both the Alfred Millenary and the Hampshire pageants, the past was used as a vehicle of moral instruction and, as such, was firmly directed at the future. Pageants were designed to show how the achievements and progress made by people in the past, often in the face of great hardships and difficulties, provided a lesson to modern-day Englishmen and women. By attending to the message of the pageant, they might, as the Bishop of Winchester put it, 'learn from the pages of history [. . .] how best to consecrate and ennoble their inheritance' and so foster progress underpinned by a sense of continuity.[88] This was a view shared by the organisers of the Alfred Millenary. They also welcomed change while emphasising salutary continuities. The attitude was that the nation would be much the poorer if the ideals and achievements of the great king were forgotten. In a speech publicising the millenary, Frederic Harrison spoke of how 'in this age of Progress and of never-ending pursuit of new things, new men, new ideas, we feel ever more and more in the bottom of our minds, the need to base these on just traditions of the Past'.[89]

How far patriotic commemoration of the English past resonated with ordinary people, and their conceptions of national identity, is, of course, debatable. But widespread engagement with the English past cannot be denied. Pageant fever was too extensive for it to be otherwise, the contagion affecting even the forward-looking inhabitants of the port city of Southampton. The commemorative activity surveyed in this essay can be seen as a response to industrial, urban modernity. But it did not imply cultural rejection of the modern world. Neither, for that matter, did it imply rejection of the imperialist tendencies, attitudes and outlooks which had a cultural purchase that was undoubtedly significant – even if scholars might have exaggerated this significance. Rather, engagement with the English past was an imaginative counterpart to daily life in town and city, at the heart of the British Empire. For Englishmen and women, the maintenance of connections with an imagined national past provided a sense of rootedness and belonging at a time of change and uncertainty. Affording reassurance that continuity existed between the nation's past, present and future, it aided and abetted the process of modernisation – in Hampshire as elsewhere in England.

Acknowledgement

This essay is an offshoot of work done for a larger project, published as 'The Place of the Past in English Culture, c. 1890–1914', *Past and Present*, 186 (2005). For permission to include it here, I am grateful to the editors of *Past and Present* and Oxford University Press. For advice and comments, I should like to thank Jon Parry, Kristina Spohr Readman and Barbara Yorke.

Figure 8 The *Titanic* Memorial, Southampton, unveiled April 1914, by permission of Southampton City Council.

Chapter 8: The *Titanic* and the port of Southampton

Stephanie Barczewski

S outhampton's docks are located near the end of the 8-mile inlet known as Southampton Water, which extends in a north-westerly direction from Calshot Spit in the Solent, the stretch of water that separates the Isle of Wight from the Hampshire coast. The Solent is shaped like a chevron, with the entrance to Southampton Water at its point. Larger ships usually enter it along the eastern channel, while smaller or less heavily laden vessels enter from the west. At their peak, Southampton docks handled almost half of the ocean passenger traffic of the UK, with as many as 17 passenger liners arriving or departing each day. In the mid-1930s, 10 of the 12 largest ships in the world regularly called at Southampton.[1]

In contrast to Liverpool, whose development was closely connected to the industrial growth of the midlands and the expansion of the canal system, Southampton grew as a port primarily because of its ideal geographical location. Situated halfway along the south coast on the routes leading to the English Channel and the North Sea, Southampton was a convenient port of call for journeys to and from the Continent. Moreover, the short distance between Southampton and London enhanced the port's attractiveness to passenger traffic. Above all, however, Southampton owed its success to its position adjacent to the Isle of Wight, which protected it from the open sea and created a commodious and sheltered deep-water harbour with wide approach channels. 'A seaport without the sea's terrors, an ocean approach within the threshold of the land', proclaimed one 19th-century commentator.[2] Southampton's location also resulted in a unique double tide caused by the port's position at the midway point of the Channel, combined with the Atlantic Pulse and the relative positions of the sun and moon. As the tide ebbs down the Channel towards the Atlantic, enough water is diverted by the projecting spur of the Ryde peninsula to reflood the entire estuary. This phenomenon produces a greatly extended period of high tide, giving large ships a much longer window in which to dock, and making lock entrances unnecessary as must be done at London, Liverpool and Bristol.[3]

Southampton's history as a port is long and rich. As Philip Hoare has written:

> Centuries have passed through this inseminal conduit. From Roman barges to ocean liners; from plague ships to Pilgrim Fathers; from French marauders to Hollywood film stars; from Francis Drake's *Golden Hind*, laden with Spanish gold for the Virgin Queen, to Goering's bombers, heavy with a deadlier cargo. Enemies or tourists, missionaries or immigrants, they all entered or left the land here, and in some other age their phantoms are still processing along Southampton Water.[4]

In 1415, Henry V's army embarked from Southampton on its way to France and the Battle of Agincourt. In 1620, the Pilgrims departed from Southampton on their famous journey to New England in the North American colonies, though they put in briefly at Plymouth when the *Speedwell* started leaking so badly that it had to be abandoned and continued their journey in the *Mayflower*. But the most famous historical association of the Southampton docks is one that occurred much more recently: on 10 April 1912, the *Titanic* set sail from there on its ill-fated maiden voyage, a voyage that ended abruptly five days later in the middle of the North Atlantic.

For Southampton, the sinking of *Titanic* was devastating. The vast majority of *Titanic*'s 900 crew members lived in the city, and almost 700 of them died. The impact was immense, as hundreds of families were left bereft of their primary breadwinners, hundreds of wives were left widows, and hundreds of children were left fatherless. Nothing of this magnitude had happened to Southampton since the French sacked the town in the early stages of the Hundred Years War in 1338, and nothing was to have such a major impact again until the German bombing raids of 1940. At a single school, Northam Council School, 125 children suffered the loss of a parent or other close relative.[5] The nature of *Titanic*'s relationship with Southampton means that there the story is not the romanticised tale featured in Hollywood films or even the heroic myth that prevailed in Britain immediately following the sinking.[6] In Southampton, 'women and children first' had a less noble ring to the local citizenry, because that order condemned their husbands, fathers, sons and brothers to an icy death. There, perhaps more than anywhere else in the world, the sinking of *Titanic* was a very real and immediate tragedy. In Southampton, there was no myth of *Titanic*, only cold reality, and this continues to shape the city's relationship with the disaster to this day.

I

On 9 June 1815, the steam yacht *Thames* travelled up the Solent into Portsmouth, a harbinger of a revolution that was to change the face of the Solent ports, and Southampton in particular. Previously, the city's development as a port had been limited by the long haul for sailing vessels up the English Channel and Southampton Water, but steam power transformed Southampton into the most important commercial port in the British Empire. In 1827, 2,000 passengers entered or left Southampton by steamship every week during the summer months; by 1830 that total had increased to an annual total of over 100,000.[7]

Southampton's future as a port, however, was precarious without a better land connection to London, which did not exist until 1839 when the first rail service began. This in turn encouraged further expansion of the docks, funded by a new group of investors from London who called themselves the Southampton Docks Company. They opened their first dock in 1840; three years later, Southampton's future as a commercial port was secured when the British Government chose it to replace Falmouth as its principal packet station. The departure of emigrants from Southampton to North America began the following year, when the port was selected as the emigrant station for Canada. Soon, ships were carrying emigrants to South Africa and Australia as well.

The dramatic increase in size of steamships over the course of the 19th century necessitated the continual expansion of commercial dock facilities. By the century's end, Southampton's docks were in danger of obsolescence, and there were rumours that several of the bigger lines, including P&O and Union Castle, might pull out of the port. In 1890, the London and South-Western Railway agreed to provide a loan of 250,000 pounds to finance the construction of the huge new Empress Dock. Two years later, the railway purchased the Southampton Docks Company outright for 1.36 million pounds, an event that led to the city's meteoric rise as Britain's main passenger centre. The railway's infusion of capital permitted expansion projects that would have crippled the previous owners. By 1895, the London and South-Western Railway had spent more than 2.2 million pounds, and passenger traffic through the port had increased by 71 per cent. In 1905, a huge tidal dock and dry dock was opened that could accommodate the very largest passenger vessels.

Over the next decade, one North Atlantic line after another moved its operations to Southampton.[8] In 1907, the White Star Line transferred its North Atlantic Express Service from Liverpool, opening offices in Canute Road.[9]

Within five years, Southampton had overtaken Liverpool as Britain's busiest passenger port.

II

The *Titanic* arrived in Southampton after its overnight journey from Belfast at midday on 4 April 1912. After some initial confusion following the replacement of the *Titanic*'s original chief officer, William Murdoch, by Henry Wilde at the request of Captain Smith, the officers settled into their usual routine.[10] When not on watch, they were accustomed to being permitted to go ashore, but there was so much to do on board the *Titanic* that trips into town were infrequent. The *Titanic* had arrived not quite ready for its maiden voyage: staterooms and public rooms still lacked carpets, paint and furniture, mattresses and bedding had to be distributed and mirrors and draperies put into place.

The situation was further complicated by a massive national coal strike that had been going on since January. Although the strike was finally settled on 6 April, it was not possible to get newly mined coal to Southampton in time for the *Titanic*'s departure. The *Titanic*'s coal, therefore, had to be cannibalised from the other White Star liners in the port. This made the coaler's job much dirtier and more difficult than it ordinarily was, for every spare pound of coal had to be removed from the holds of the other ships and transferred to the *Titanic*. But with little else going in and out of the port due to the lingering effects of the strike, the coaling firm of R. & J. H. Rea was happy to have the work.

Equally pleased were the numerous Southampton firms involved in provisioning the *Titanic*. Miller's Naval Tailors were in charge of providing uniforms for the crew. Due to the unusually large number, they had to perform the job in a hurry, and one exhausted tailor told a crewman when he came to pick up his uniform, 'I hope I shall never see this again'.[11] Sadly, many of the bills for these uniforms were not issued until long after their purchasers had ceased to require them. The *Titanic* exhibition in the Southampton Maritime Museum displays a bill for 4 pounds and 4 shillings from Miller's dated June 1912 for the uniform of Steward Sidney Sedunary, who did not survive.

The *Titanic*'s 57,000 pieces of crockery and 29,000 pieces of glassware were supplied by Stonier and Company, who were based in Liverpool but had a store at Southampton docks. The ship's 15,000 bottles of beer came from Charles George Hibbert and Company, who issued special posters declaring that they provided 'bottled beer for the White Star liner *Titanic*, the largest vessel in the world'. Decorative plants, some 300–400 of them, were supplied by F. G. Bealing and Son; 11-year-old Eileen Lenox Conyngham later remembered the *Titanic* as a 'ship full of flowers'. Paper goods came from W. H. Smith and tablecloths from Edwin Jones (now Debenham's). Most of the food was provided by Grey and Company: the *Titanic* required 75,000 pounds of meat, 40,000 eggs, 40 tons of potatoes, 7,000 heads of lettuce, 10,000 pounds of sugar, 36,000 oranges, 1,500 gallons of milk and 6,000 pounds of butter.[12]

Alongside the provisioning of the *Titanic* came the recruitment of the ship's crew. Only the senior officers had accompanied the ship from Belfast; the remainder of the crew was recruited locally. In 1912, passenger liners did not have permanent crews. Instead, they were hired for one voyage at a time and paid off when it was complete. They therefore could not depend on steady employment, though they might remain with the same ship year after year if they performed good work and the signing-on officer knew them. Waiters and stewards in particular could become favourites of passengers, who would alter their bookings in order to be on their ships. Most of the time, though, crew members served on a variety of ships and with a number of different lines.

Despite the steady growth of the passenger shipping trade in Southampton, there always seemed to be more men seeking places on the big liners than there were jobs. The city's population had expanded rapidly, from 25,000 in 1836 to 120,000 in 1912, as a steady flow of people arrived looking for employment, which they did not always find. The situation in the winter of 1903–4 was particularly grim, as the *Southampton Times* reported:

> In almost every street numbers of working men were aimlessly about idle. Men went out in the early morning to look for work, pulling their belts tighter to make up for their lack of breakfast, while their children went to school cold and with their hunger only partly satisfied and their weary eyed wives perhaps pawned something more in order to find some sort of an apology for dinner in the family. Large numbers of men wandered about near the docks and haunted Canute Road like ghosts, those nearest the dock gates hoping to be among the fortunate ones when workers were called for; all with a hungry look in their eyes that turned to one of hopeless misery if the work was supplied without them, and they were condemned to go home as they came out, with empty pockets as well as stomachs.[13]

The situation had improved somewhat by 1912, thanks in part to the formation of a number of trade unions, including the National Sailors' and Firemen's Union of Great Britain and Ireland, the National Union of Ships' Stewards, Cooks, Butchers and Bakers, the British Seafarers' Union, the National Union of Stewards and the Dock, Wharf, Riverside and General Labourers Union.

The previous year, a labour dispute had arisen when porters had received orders to begin coaling the *Olympic* at 6 a.m., but then had to wait until 11 a.m. before they could begin. They were refused 'standing by' money and went on strike. The *Olympic*'s firemen, seamen and stewards also struck, citing the 'special difficulties' of working on such a large vessel. Shipping in the port was at a standstill for several days until Southampton Corporation was able to arrange a settlement with the shipping companies. In June 1911, White Star and the other lines grudgingly agreed to recognise the unions.

In April 1912, however, Southampton's dockworkers and seamen were in no position to demand further concessions. The coal strike left many ships idle, and idle ships meant idle men. More than 17,000 men were out of work, forcing many families to rely on municipal and private charity. The logbooks of Northam Girls' School reveal the extent of the problem. On 14 March, the headmistress Annie Hopkins recorded, 'twenty-two free meals given today. The distress is daily becoming more acute owing to stagnation caused by the coal strike'. Eight days later, she added, 'Distress is great amongst [the] children'. Northam was one of several suburbs that sprang up in the late 19th century to accommodate Southampton's growing population of people who worked on the large liners. In a city where the neighbourhood in which one lived reflected one's shipboard status, Northam ranked near the bottom: its inhabitants were lowly firemen, greasers and trimmers. In the spring of 1912, Northam was emerging from a difficult winter, in which unusually cold weather and flooding in early March had forced many families to rely upon the charity of the parish. The coal strike added to the distress, both by putting breadwinners out of work down at the docks and by causing a shortage of fuel for home heating.[14]

The *Titanic*'s arrival in Southampton therefore came as a welcome relief, at least for those men – and a few women – who would find employment either on its maiden voyage or in helping to prepare the ship for it.[15] White Star had promised the ship would sail despite the strike, although its speed would be limited to 20 knots in order to conserve coal. This meant that, from the beginning, Southampton's relationship to the *Titanic* was thoroughly pragmatic rather than romantic: the ship was a source of jobs, not of celebration. When *Titanic* docked on 4 April, there was relatively little fanfare; the *Hampshire Independent* reported that 'quietly and unostentatiously without any blare of trumpets, the *Titanic*, the world's latest and biggest ship steamed up the silent waters of the Solent and docked at Southampton'. And as *Titanic* lay moored in its berth for a week, the local populace was fairly blasé. John Wright, who saw the ship from Southampton Common, recalled that 'the *Titanic* was just another ship to us at the time [. . .] We thought not an awful lot about her until the terrible happening'.[16]

But if there were no cheering and flag-waving crowds as there had been when the ship had sailed from Belfast, there were thousands of local citizens eager to apply for positions as crew members in the tight labour market of April 1912. In signing on for the *Titanic*, 699 of the 898 crew members gave Southampton as their current address, though some listed temporary lodgings in hotels and boarding houses.[17] Of these, the majority were not originally from Southampton and its environs; only about 40 per cent of the crew can be identified as Hampshire-born. The rest were from all over Britain and Ireland, with a substantial number from Lancashire who had followed White Star from Liverpool to Southampton in 1907.[18]

Only after they were among the lucky ones who were selected could the *Titanic*'s crew members appreciate the finer qualities of the ship. 'Like the *Olympic*, yes, but so much more elaborate', said baker Reginald Burgess:

> Take the dining saloon – *Olympic* didn't even have a carpet, but the *Titanic* – ah, you sank up to your knees. Then there's the furniture. So heavy you could hardly lift it. And that panelling [. . .] They can make them bigger and faster but it was the care and effort that went into her. She was a beautiful wonderful ship.[19]

The families of the crew members, meanwhile, felt themselves fortunate that their husbands, brothers, sons and, in a few cases, daughters had been chosen. The *Daily Graphic*, which sent a reporter from London to cover the *Titanic*'s departure, reported that 'all these Southampton women were proud that their men had entered into service on the greatest vessel ever built by man. They prattled of the *Titanic* with a sort of suggestion of proprietorship'.[20]

III

That pride, of course, rapidly changed to despair and grief when the news that the *Titanic* had sunk reached Southampton. The shock was made even more cruel by the fact that the first press accounts reported that all passengers and crew had been saved and that the ship was being towed to Halifax. Soon, however, more accurate reports confirmed that there had been a grievous loss of life. Stephen Townsend, a young boy at the time, recalled the pandemonium that prevailed in the city:

> There was no radio or television or anything like that, naturally. People were running round the street 'the *Titanic* sunk' panic, panic stations everywhere. Women

running out and going down to the Shipping Office, you know, down near the dock gates there and the *Titanic*, they can't sink the *Titanic* because everybody talked about the *Titanic*, it was the unsinkable ship [. . .] And even as young as I was it impressed me because there wasn't a family in the whole of the area that never had anybody associated with that ship. Fathers and sons on board, grandsons and all this sort of thing, to be on the great *Titanic*, you see. And well they were all shipping community, shipping and dock working community and, as I say, everybody down there, all of us. It was real panic, I can see it now, I can visualise them. The women running out, you know, in their aprons they were busy doing their household chores and forgot everything and all run down to the Shipping Office.[21]

Soon, the initial shock turned to despair. The *Southern Daily Echo* reported that 'the pathetic scenes in Southampton [. . .] after the dread news of the *Titanic*'s foundering had been confirmed would have moved the hardest heart to compassion'.[22] Virtually every major London paper sent a reporter to the port, and their stories were almost identical. The *Daily Chronicle* described the city as being in 'the depth of gloom' on 17 April and the next day asserted that 'the same cloud of grief covers all alike'.[23] Its reporter compared the scene in Southampton to 'the semi-darkness of the pit's mouth while the kindred of ghastly, distorted remains were seeking to recognise, yet fearing to know'.[24] The *Daily Mirror* stated that 'hopeless misery has cast its wing over the town' and that 'nothing approaching this appalling blow has ever fallen upon the port'.[25] Flags flew at half-mast all over the city, and numerous public functions were cancelled.

Specific information about who had survived and who had perished was frustratingly slow to trickle in. After the first notice of the disaster was posted outside of the White Star offices on Monday, hundreds of people gathered frantically seeking further details about the fate of their loved ones. The Salvation Army sent in special 'slum officers' to watch the children so that mothers could go down to White Star and try to get information regarding their husbands, fathers and brothers. The correspondent from the *War Cry*, the organisation's newspaper, wrote:

None but a heart of stone would be unmoved in the presence of such anguish. Night and day that crowd of pale, anxious faces had been waiting patiently for the news which did not come. Nearly every one in the crowd had lost a relative. Some of the poor little women in black, who were bearing their overwhelming sorrow with wonderful courage, notwithstanding their tears, stood with little children in their arms and toddlers at their skirts.[26]

Tuesday passed with no additional news other than the fact that five of the *Titanic*'s officers had survived. Captain Smith's wife, Eleanor, a Southampton resident, posted a message to her 'poor fellow sufferers' offering her sympathy: 'My heart overflows with grief for you all, and is laden with sorrow that you are weighed down with this terrible burden that has been thrust upon us'.[27] On Wednesday afternoon, a workman appeared and nailed a large blackboard to the railings outside the offices, in obvious preparation for posting the names of the survivors. The board, however, remained stubbornly blank, and every time a White Star clerk came outside, the crowd would plead for information. 'We haven't any', they were told. 'As soon as we hear anything it will be posted up'.[28] Other messages of sympathy appeared, including ones from King George and Queen Mary and from the Queen Mother, but they had little effect. The people of Southampton were not interested in public expressions of grief and grandiose commemorations; what they wanted was the news that their loved ones were safe.

By Thursday, tensions were nearing the breaking point. 'Is there any hope? They must know something inside', a woman in the crowd pleaded with one of the policemen guarding the door. 'They know nothing yet', he told her. 'The moment they do the names will be posted'. An itinerant preacher attempted to offer religious consolation, but his efforts only further strained already frayed nerves, and the crowd's discontentment convinced him to desist. Finally, early on Friday morning, the first lists of survivors' names were received. A clerk came out of the office holding a long strip of paper, which he pinned to the blackboard. The crowd pressed forward, trying desperately to read the names. A few people burst forth with exclamations of gratitude when they saw their loved one's name, but for most the search was in vain. Of *Titanic*'s 898 crew members, only 212 survived.

IV

Many parts of the city were utterly devastated. In the summer of 2001, I drove through Southampton with Brian Ticehurst, the President of the British *Titanic* Society, as he rattled off the list of victims from each street that we passed. Few were omitted, and on some streets as many as one in four houses suffered the loss of a family member. In the *Daily Mirror* on 18 April, the wife of a crew member on the *Olympic* described the situation in her neighbourhood:

Mrs May across the way lost her husband and oldest son [...] The son was married a year ago and his wife had a baby six weeks ago. Mrs Allen around the corner lost her husband, George [...] And the young girl there in black [...] is Mrs Barnes. She lost her brother [...] The woman going into the shop is Mrs Gosling. She lost a son [...] And Mrs Preston of Princes Street, a widow, she lost her son too.[29]

The press featured a plethora of heartrending stories, including those of a family of seven children left fatherless and a house where five lodgers were among the missing.

Nowhere, however, was more devastated than the district of Northam, which provides a microcosm of the impact of the sinking of *Titanic* on Southampton. 'Old Northam, where I lived, was plunged into mourning', recalled one local resident. 'Nearly every house in Northam had lost a son or husband [. . .] every blind was drawn'.[30] On 16 April, Annie Hopkins wrote in the logbook of Northam Girls' School, 'A great many girls are absent this afternoon owing to the sad news regarding the *Titanic*. Fathers and brothers are on the vessel and some of the little ones in the school have been in tears all afternoon'. Two days later, when many families' worst fears had been realised, she continued, 'I feel I must record the sad aspect in school today owing to the *Titanic* disaster. So many of the crew belonged to Northam. It is pathetic to witness the children's grief and in some cases faith and hope of better news'. The school did the best it could to help the pupils cope with the trauma. On 7 May, clothes were distributed to the victims' children, and on 23 May the Mayoress visited 'the orphans of the *Titanic*'.[31]

Many of the bereaved had more to contend with than their grief, for the loss of income meant serious economic deprivation for families that had already been suffering for months from the effects of the coal strike. 'The distress in the stricken quarters of Southampton is incredible', reported the *Daily Mail*:

> During the coal strike many breadwinners were out of work, furniture was sold or pawned, and numerous families received notice to quit. Then came the *Titanic*, and firemen, greasers and trimmers, who had known no work for many weeks, eagerly joined the big ship to save their homes. To-day hundreds of women are clamouring for food for themselves and milk for their babies.[32]

Mayor George Bowyer declared that the corporation was caring for 600 families, with an average size of five members each. 'I wonder if your readers quite appreciate the position here', he told the *Daily Chronicle*.

> For than a month most of these families [. . .] had been kept alive by the mayor's fund raised in connection with the coal strike, and many of them have sold or pawned everything that could raise money. Now, even where husbands are safe, they have lost all their clothes and not infrequently the money they possessed.[33]

Bowyer immediately travelled to London to discuss the possibility of funds being diverted from the national relief effort to Southampton. Several trade unions and the Seaman's Friendly Society also set up relief depots in order to distribute food and other necessities. Some people wanted more than material aid; one woman threw the tickets entitling her to relief back in the face of the union representative who gave them to her: 'I want news of my son, I don't want tickets!'[34] Most people, however, were glad to get whatever they could. In St Mary's parish, there were 61 'cases' that arose from the disaster, the majority of which involved the loss of young men who had been wholly or partially supporting their parents. Tom James recalled that his father, the new vicar of St Luke's Church, had as one of his first tasks 'to visit the bereaved families, and in some cases to carry the news for the first time'.[35]

V

The tragedy that struck Southampton when the *Titanic* sank was, thus, of a very different type from that which the rest of the world experienced. Elsewhere, on both sides of the Atlantic, a '*Titanic* myth' very quickly took shape that sought to extract meaning from the disaster by emphasising the heroic conduct of the first-class male passengers. Account after account depicted these elite men as chivalrously stepping aside so that women and children, including those travelling third class, could board the lifeboats first. The evidence to support this view was flimsy at best, but that was of little consequence, for it supported contemporary British conceptions of patriotism and of class and gender hierarchies.

To the bereaved families of Southampton, however, this mythic interpretation of the disaster offered little solace. What comfort could they derive from the notion that first-class men had saved third-class women and children, even if it had been true? This view not only ignored their loved ones but displaced and diminished them, for missing from it was any effort to commemorate the heroism of the crew. There was no way, therefore, for Southampton to participate in the kind of myth-making that quickly subsumed the real story of what had happened. In Southampton, the tragedy was, quite simply, a tragedy; there is no 'myth of the *Titanic*' there, but only the story of a very real, very painful and, for many residents, very personal disaster.

This helps to explain why Southampton is not eager to exploit the *Titanic*'s potential to attract tourism. On visiting the city, one might expect to find numerous attempts to capitalise on the tourist interest created by the discovery of the wreck in 1984 and the success of the 1997 James Cameron film. There is, however, very little. A flip through the relevant section of the Southampton phone directory reveals that there is not a single business – no pub, no restaurant, no souvenir shop – named after the *Titanic*.

This is despite the fact that Southampton offers few other obvious entice-ments to tourists. Physically, it is an odd and incongruous mix of new and old, often side by side. Portions of the old city wall snake through modern tower-block developments; sagging, half-timbered Tudor buildings stand next to brand-new shopping malls. On most residential streets, Victorian houses are interspersed with modern dwellings in haphazard fashion. There is a simple explanation for Southampton's chaotic appearance. During the Second World War, the Luftwaffe did its best to level the city, and it is still easy to pick out where the bombs fell by identifying the buildings constructed since 1945. Couple this with some poor decisions by city planners in the 1960s and 1970s to pull down many of the older neighbourhoods and replace them with modern blocks of flats, and the result is a place lacking obvious historic charm.

The *Titanic* seems a surefire magnet to lure visitors who might not otherwise be interested in Southampton, but the city seems unwilling to take advantage of the association. To be sure, there is a display in the Maritime Museum, though it pales in comparison to the *Titanic* exhibitions found in other cities, Belfast and Liverpool in particular, with close connections to the disaster. Southampton City Council's web site features a '*Titanic* Trail' for visitors to walk and see various sites associated with the ship, including some of the numerous public memorials which are scattered around the city. But there is little else. In a world in which everything having to do with the *Titanic* is ruth-lessly exploited for every penny of profit that can be squeezed out of it, this is surprising, perhaps even astonishing.

Certainly, there are some practical problems. The site that would be most attractive to *Titanic* tourists is Berth 4, the spot from which the ship departed on its maiden voyage. Berth 4, however, is still an important part of the working docks and is all but inaccessible to the public, with entry to see the small memo-rial plaque strictly controlled by Associated British Ports. There are, however, plenty of other sites. Why not promote them? The obvious explanation is that the story of the *Titanic* in Southampton was not the romantic, heroic tale told in the British press and elsewhere but a story of death and destitution that directly affected hundreds of local families. Given the intense devastation, both emo-tional and financial, that the sinking of the *Titanic* inflicted on Southampton, it is scarcely surprising that the city is not eager to turn the disaster into a theme park. Southampton's memories of the disaster are clearly not suitable material for a Disney-style animatronic ride.

It would be inaccurate to assume, however, that Southampton's reluctance to exploit its link to the *Titanic* stems entirely from the lingering impact of the disaster. As time has passed, demographic change has removed most of the immediate connection. Only a single *Titanic* survivor, Millvina Dean, still resides in the city. When the James Cameron film premiered in Southampton in early 1998, the British press predicted that it would meet with an 'icy welcome' because the story would be 'a little too close to home'. Instead, the film received the same enthusiastic reception as in other British cities and broke attendance records at several local cinemas. This was primarily because the young people who made up the film's primary audience felt little personal connection to the tragedy. A nine-year-old girl told an interviewer than she went to see it 'because Leonardo DiCaprio is in it and it's a really good film', an answer not substantially different from what one of her peers in New York or London might have given. If Southampton audiences acknowledged the link between the tragedy and the city at all, they merely remarked that it was 'cool' to be in the place from which the *Titanic* had departed.[36]

There is, however, another, more compelling reason why Southampton is uninterested in reminding itself of its role in the most famous maritime disaster in history. Commercial shipping has been the city's economic lifeblood for centuries. Why, of all the great ships that have come and gone from Southampton docks, should the city choose to remember the one with the least successful career? It might be appropriate for other places to wax romantic about what happened on the night of 14–15 April 1912, but Southampton prefers to get on with its business. In Sotonian eyes, the *Titanic* is hardly a good advertisement for the industry upon which it still depends. Why not focus on the *Olympic* instead, a ship that was equally as beautiful as its sister and far more successful as a passenger liner?

In a more general sense, Southampton's commercial focus means that it has not traditionally been inclined to focus on the past. This helps to explain why not only does the city downplay the *Titanic*, but also its role as Henry V's staging area for his army bound for France and as the true point of departure for the *Mayflower*. All these things seem ripe for the attraction of tourists, yet none of them are exploited. Lindsay Ford, Assistant Curator of the Southampton Maritime Museum, speculates that this attitude may be the product of the transience of the local population, who for centuries have tended to pass through without putting down roots, in keeping with the city's status as Britain's most important passenger port.[37] Moreover, unlike Portsmouth or Plymouth, Southampton has always viewed its orientation as a port city as private and mercantile rather than naval, which breeds a pragmatic attitude towards the sea rather than a romantic one. In Southampton, the sea is for making money, not history. T. P. Henry, a member of the Totton and Eling Historical Society, sees Southampton as a 'working city', a place that's more about 'ships and football' than about heritage. Southampton, Henry says, 'doesn't sell itself' on the basis of its history or culture, but rather on its status as a 'frontline port'.[38]

For some, this attitude can be frustrating. Nigel Wood, the curator of the city's West End Local History Museum, complains of a 'complacency' about Southampton's history, which he says is 'taken for granted'. The *Titanic*, in particular, is 'underexploited' by the local government, which has missed excellent opportunities to purchase prime sites for a museum devoted to the tragedy and to the golden age of passenger liners. The Ocean Terminal, where passengers waited to board the *Queen Elizabeth, Queen Mary* and other famous liners, was torn down in 1982; the White Star building on Canute Road was turned into offices; and the South Western Hotel, where J. Bruce Ismay and some of the *Titanic*'s wealthiest passengers stayed the night before the ship departed, has recently been converted into luxury flats. As proof of what *Titanic* could do for the city, Wood points to its impact even on his small museum, which generated considerable publicity from its dedication of a memorial to Captain Arthur Rostron of the *Carpathia* in 1999. 'We've got a lot of mileage on the back of *Titanic*', he says. 'You've got to exploit what you've got'.[39] Others, however, argue that Southampton's failure to take advantage of its connection to the *Titanic* is the product not of a lack of will but of wherewithal. Kevin White, Conservation Manager for Southampton City Council, told me that the Council is exploring the possibility of building a *Titanic* museum but that a lack of funding has, to date, kept plans from proceeding beyond the drawing board. 'We'd love to do more', he declares, 'but it's a question of funding and priorities'.[40]

For various reasons, then, the use of the *Titanic* for commercial tourism purposes is a problematic endeavour in Southampton, and the city's relationship with the *Titanic* is likely to remain an understated one. Even Southampton's public commemorations of the sinking are, in keeping with the nature of the tragedy that struck the city, intensely personal, emphasising individuals rather than groups, unlike *Titanic* commemorations elsewhere in Britain. While the exhibitions in the Ulster Folk and Transport Museum and the Liverpool Maritime Museum focus on the ship and refer only to a few of the most prominent passengers and highest-ranking ship's officers, the Southampton Maritime Museum devotes much of its display to Sidney Sedunary, a third-class steward. Similarly, the West End Museum and Heritage Centre focuses its *Titanic* display on James Jukes, a greaser whose body was never found. In addition, numerous local churches feature plaques and memorials to crew members from that parish, and the gravestones of *Titanic* victims and survivors have, through the years, been carefully tended by the British *Titanic* Society and other groups.

Even in those cases in which a local memorial is not devoted to a single person, there is still an effort to remember individual victims in Southampton. Dedicated in April 1913, the musicians' memorial on the public library lists the names of all eight members of the *Titanic*'s band above the inscription 'They Died at Their Posts Like Men'.[41] Unveiled the following year before a crowd of 10,000, the huge bronze and granite engineers' memorial in East Park includes 18 names; its inscription, from John 15:13, reads 'Greater love hath no man than this, than a man lay down his life for a friend'. These memorials serve as precursors to the kinds of public memorials that would become all too common in Britain during and immediately after the First World War, when the listing of the names of the dead functioned as a way to recognise ordinary people who had performed their duty in extraordinary circumstances. Rather than heroic deeds, these types of memorials commemorated those who 'stayed at their post' in the face of grave danger, much as many members of the *Titanic*'s crew had done. They do not celebrate 'service beyond the call of duty, but rather [. . .] faithful performance of an allotted role'. These memorials are inherently democratic, for they do not commemorate those who achieved special distinction and thereby stood out from the masses. Instead, naming the dead served as a recognition that they had 'all been equally valuable members of [the] community, because they had performed their allotted tasks to the extremity of death'. This style of commemoration began on war memorials in the mid-19th century, but it was not until the First World War that the ranks of those listed were eliminated and the names were listed in alphabetical order. This concept of the 'equality of sacrifice' was crucial to post-war commemorative efforts. It reached its peak of influence in 1920, when the Imperial War Graves Commission decreed that all British war graves in military cemeteries abroad would be marked by a single, unadorned cross. The idea, according to the Commission, was to assert that all were equally worthy of honour, 'great and lowly, peer and peasant, rich and poor, learned and ignorant, raised to one supreme level in death by common sacrifice for a common cause'.[42]

Southampton's memorial to the *Titanic*'s engineers thus represents an early manifestation of the type of memorial that would appear in many places in Britain during and after the First World War. This suggests the extent of the impact of the tragedy upon Southampton, an impact not unlike that of a major war, at least among certain social and occupational groups. To gauge this impact further, contrast Southampton's memorial to the engineers to its counterpart in Liverpool, on which none of the dead are named. This testifies to Liverpool's very different relationship to the disaster, for it was merely White Star's corporate home, and only a handful of people from the city died. Or contrast Southampton's engineers' memorial to Belfast's, which includes the names of the dead but lists them in order of rank rather than alphabetically. This greater concern with hierarchy stems from the smaller number of victims from the city. Belfast lost 22 citizens to Southampton's 700.

There is, however, one memorial in Southampton that does not list any names. On 27 July 1915, a Portland-stone fountain commemorating all of the *Titanic*'s crew members was unveiled on Southampton Common. Paid for by public subscription, the fountain remained on the Common until 1972, when vandalism caused it to be moved to the ruins of Holyrood Church, which had been destroyed by German bombs in the Second World War. In its current state and location, it functions as the most insular of all the city's *Titanic* memorials. The fountain offers little in the way of obvious aesthetic appeal. Exposed to the elements for almost 60 years, the bas-relief of the *Titanic* has almost entirely worn away, and the badly eroded inscription can barely be discerned:

> This memorial was erected in memory of the crew,
> stewards, sailors and firemen, who lost their lives in the
> SS *Titanic* disaster April 15th 1912.
> It was subscribed for by the widows, mothers and friends
> of the crew.

To the casual observer, this is merely a decrepit memorial in a ruined church. Knowledge of Southampton's history, however, allows the viewer to 'read' the memorial as a poignant statement about two devastating civic events: the sinking of the *Titanic* and the bombing by the Luftwaffe. Tourists familiar only with the romantic myth of *Titanic* or the James Cameron film would doubtless be unimpressed, but there could be no more appropriate commemoration of the city's two worst 20th-century tragedies.

It will be interesting to see if Southampton's reluctance to turn tragedy into tourism persists. With computerisation and the rise of container shipping, the docks employ far fewer people than they once did, creating a need for greater economic diversification. Belfast, which has a very different but equally intimate relationship with the *Titanic*, has begun to set aside its traditional reluctance to exploit the tragedy and make a big pitch for *Titanic* tourism. Will Southampton do the same? For now, the answer is no. Southampton is focusing on technology as the key to its future prosperity. In other words, as it has done for the past century, the city is getting on with its business. Looking forward, not back – that's the Southampton way.

Figure 9 Troop embarkation, Southampton docks, c. 1900s, by permission of Southampton City Council.

Chapter 9: Going to war

Southampton and military embarkation

Ian Beckett

Some years ago, Donald Headrick identified 'tools of empire' resulting from technological advances in areas such as medicine, modern weapons and communications, which had made European expansion possible in the mid- to late 19th century. In terms of communications, he had in mind railways, steam navigation, the electric telegraph and the submarine telegraph cable, all of which enabled imperial governments and colonial administrations alike to react more quickly to events.[1] Apart from opening up river routes into the interior of Africa and Asia, steam navigation shrank the time taken to reach distant colonies so that India could be reached from Britain in something between 30 and 45 days by 1852 using the overland route across Egypt, the time dropping by about a third after the opening of the Suez Canal in 1869. For the British, in particular, this was highly significant given the sheer extent of the Empire, the periodic need to relieve regiments in far-flung imperial posts and the likely occurrence of colonial wars necessitating hasty reinforcement.

Transport, or logistics in modern military parlance, is one of those unglamorous subjects rarely mentioned in historical accounts. Yet, it is vital to the success or failure of operations and of grand strategy. As Winston Churchill wrote in his contemporary account of the reconquest of the Sudan in 1898, *The River War*, 'Victory is the beautiful, bright-coloured flower. Transport is the stem without which it could never have blossomed'.[2] One particularly neglected aspect of British military logistics is sea transport, and it seems appropriate, therefore, to reconsider its significance in the context of the role of Southampton as a military port in peace and war during the Victorian and Edwardian period. First, this chapter will deal with Southampton's part in routine peacetime 'trooping'; second, with wartime expeditions; and, last, with the two greatest periods of the port's contribution to wartime mobilisation, namely the South African war of 1899–1902 and the First World War of 1914–18.

I

The practice of regular trooping in peacetime was as old as the Empire itself, certainly dating back to the acquisition of Tangier in 1661, while expeditionary forces had long been sent overseas, not least in the wars of the 18th century and early 19th century, by which the 'first empire' had been won and lost and a second established: the first large-scale transportation of an expeditionary force was that sent to Cartagena in 1740 during the War of Jenkins's Ear. Merchant ships, including 'East Indiamen', converted warships and ships of the line, were used as required for both trooping and expeditions. Though Portsmouth was usually the principal port, others were used on occasions, the 28th Regiment of foot, for example, embarking at Southampton in June 1794 for Ostend and the campaign in the Low Countries.[3] After 1815, Portsmouth was again the principal port for routine trooping, the Royal Navy operating its own five-strong transport fleet for the Indian Troop Service based in Portsmouth from 1860 until 1894. The trooping season extended from September to March, with two of the ships running between Portsmouth and Suez, and three operating between Suez and Bombay. Each was capable of accommodating 41 officers, 12 wives, 18 children and six servants in first class, 12 non-commissioned officers and 27 wives and children in second class; and 910 other ranks, 100 wives and 120 children in third class.[4] To give an indication of the scale of the routine logistics of Empire, the pre-season estimate for 1868–9 was that the service would carry approximately 10,798 officers and men to India and 11,983 back from India between September 1868 and March 1869. Inevitably, Kipling captured the essence of the service in 'Troopin':

> They'll turn us out at Portsmouth wharf in cold an' wet an' rain,
> All wearin' Injian cotton kit, but we will not complain.
> They'll kill us of pneumonia – for that's their little way –
> But damn the chills and fever, men, we're goin' 'ome to-day![5]

Commercial firms, however, were also involved in Indian trooping before 1860 and continued to be involved in trooping elsewhere after 1860. Trooping continued to Canada until 1871 and to the West Indies and southern Africa throughout the Victorian period. Notably involved from the commercial sector were the Bibby Line of Liverpool, the British India Line of Calcutta, Peninsular & Oriental (P&O), originally formed in Dublin in 1823) and the Union Line, which began as the Southampton Steam Shipping Company in 1853. In addition to Bibby, British India and P&O, and the Union Line, Donald Currie's Castle Line also started carrying troops in 1872. It competed with the Union Line on the Cape route until the two lines merged as the

Union-Castle Line in March 1900, the raising of the new line's flag on the *Dunnottar Castle* being cheered by troops leaving Southampton for South Africa on the Union Line's former ship, *Gaika*.[6] Moreover, commercial vessels still took military personnel to the East even after the Navy acquired its own, and such hired transports were frequently berthed at Southampton rather than Portsmouth.[7] Thus, the future Field Marshal Lord Roberts, for example, first sailed to India from Southampton in February 1852 on the P&O steamer *Ripon*, en route to Alexandria, crossing Egypt by the land route and continuing on the *Oriental* from Suez. Similarly, the future General Sir Richard Harrison saw off his brother's regiment to Jamaica from Southampton in June 1861, and the future General Sir Archibald Hunter also sailed from Southampton in 1875 to join his new regiment at Gibraltar.[8]

Moreover, when the Navy's own transports began to reach the end of their useful service life in the 1890s, it was decided not to replace them but to hire from the shipping companies and to relieve the pressure on Portsmouth by switching the operation of the Indian Troop Service to Southampton. Accordingly, in February 1894, No. 25 Berth in the Empress Dock was hired from the London and South-West Railway Company annually from September to March at a cost of 100 pounds per berthing vessel. This particular berth drew 25 feet of water and was chosen due to its proximity to a large shed, its railway line and its accessibility at all stages of the tide. The storage space cost an additional 50 pounds per annum for 2,000 square feet. Additional advantages over Portsmouth were that ships would not need to be moved from the berth to coal, and it was closer to the hospital at Netley for the transfer of invalids.

The first ship to use the new berth was the last of the ageing naval transports, the *Jumna*, in January 1895, followed immediately by P&O's *Britannia*, which was contracted, together with the same company's *Victoria*, for six months to cover the trooping season of 1894–5. Indeed, as both ended up in port together, the *Britannia* had to be berthed temporarily at an additional cost of 50 pounds, a practice that became fairly frequent with either a berth at South West Quay or the No. 3 Extension to Empress Dock being used. A reberthing scheme in 1905 saw the Indian Troop Service moved to No. 34 berth at Ocean Quay. On a few occasions, a ship was moved to meet the convenience of the dock company, as in January 1895, September 1896, March 1898, March 1901 and October 1907. The attempt by the Company to charge the Admiralty twice when the same ship was moved a second time in February 1906 resulted in a long-running dispute.[9]

Some indication of the usual routine for peacetime trooping from Southampton can be gauged from examples drawn from the 1898–9 season.

The British India Line's *Dunera*, for example, arrived from Bombay and Queenstown on 1 December 1898, disembarking returning troops at the second berth and commencing coaling. Fresh provisions were taken on board on 5 December and the ship cleaned. It moved to the trooping berth on 7 December; embarked horses, women and children on 9 December; embarked troops on 10 December; and sailed for Queenstown on 11 December, before going on to Bombay. The Admiralty's Transport Department had made innumerable adjustments to the passenger list through November and December, with more troops getting on at Queenstown and Malta and others leaving the ship in Egypt. In addition, it carried 1,000 of the new 'Burma' pattern water bottles in cases of 200, supplied by John Pound & Co. of London on the order of Colonel Eaton Travers of the 2nd Gurkhas.[10] P&O's *Simla* had sailed a few days before, bound for Bombay via Port Said and Aden, its outward voyage having been delayed by a late arrival in Southampton due to bad weather. It carried 23 officers, five wives, one child and one female servant in first class; two warrant officers – one a schoolmaster – and four children in second class; and 38 non-commissioned officers, 1,160 other ranks, 41 wives and eight children in third class, the officers and men drawn from 13 different regiments and corps. As Southampton was its last port in home waters before sailing, whereas the *Dunera* called in at Queenstown, the *Simla* was given its inspection at Southampton as required by the regulations, specifying the attendance of one or two naval officers, an army officer of field rank, a second army officer, an army doctor and, if appropriate, an army vet.[11]

II

If Southampton only emerged as the main peacetime trooping port in 1894, however, it had played a significant role in the despatch of troops in wartime much earlier. In the Crimean War, for example, Portsmouth and Southampton together saw the despatch of 20,000 men for the East by November 1854, the future Lieutenant General Sir Gerald Graham VC sailing from Southampton with his Royal Engineers company on P&O's *Himalaya* in February 1854. The first ship sailed from Southampton on 22 February 1854. P&O sold the *Himalaya* to the Government and another 11 of their ships were taken up, while the Bibby Line provided two and the Cunard Company also provided 11 ships. The Crimea was also the first occasion on which the new Union Line carried troops, all five of its ships being taken up. Indeed, the first shipment of new prefabricated wooden huts to accommodate troops through the Crimean winter went out through Southampton in the Line's ship, *Norman*. Similarly, some 33,166 officers and men were sent to India as reinforcements during the Mutiny of 1857–8, 21,406 of them between receipt of the news in England in June 1857 and November 1857. One memorial to the movement of troops for the Mutiny remains in the two fine paintings, 'Eastward Ho!' and 'Home Again' by Henry Nelson O'Neil, the first depicting women seeing off a regiment on board a troopship bound for the East in August 1857, and the second the return. It seems, however, that most troops left from Portsmouth.[12]

During the Zulu War, Southampton was used for the despatch of cavalry reinforcements to the Cape following the disaster at Isandlwana. Alexander Tulloch, who was responsible for the embarkation arrangements as a staff officer in Southern District, recalled later that this was especially difficult since cavalry officers 'as a rule disappeared below deck as soon as their regiment arrived, doubtless to look after the berthing of their men'. This compelled him to requisition naval personnel to help. Using brows and lifts, Tulloch devised a method of embarking 300 horses in just four hours.[13] In all, eight of the 21 vessels used to send reinforcements to South Africa sailed from Southampton between February and May 1879, carrying 3,443 officers and men and 955 horses, principally from the 1st Dragoon Guards, 17th Lancers, Royal Artillery, and 90th, 91st and 94th Regiments of foot. It represented 37 per cent of the total number of troops despatched and 51 per cent of the horses. Indeed, the very first ship to sail was the Union Line's *Pretoria*, leaving Southampton with the 91st on 19 February, having been taken up immediately on its return from its maiden voyage and reaching the Cape on 13 March in record time.[14] All four of the major-generals sent out to assist Lieutenant General Lord Chelmsford left from Southampton, as did Napoleon III's son and heir, the Prince Imperial, on the Union Line's *Danube*, being enthusiastically cheered on his arrival at the rail terminus and seen off by his mother, Empress Eugenie. Subsequently, his body was brought back through Woolwich, but the Empress left from Southampton when going out to visit the death site in March 1880.[15]

For the Egyptian campaign of 1882, Southampton despatched 11 ships between 7 and 10 August carrying 3,451 officers and men and 2,001 horses, principally from the 4th and 7th Dragoon Guards, 19th Hussars, Royal Artillery, Royal Engineers and 1st Royal Irish Fusiliers, representing 21 per cent of the troops and 36 per cent of the horses sent from British or Irish ports.[16] Unfortunately, while the overall figures of troops and ships are available for the two Suakin expeditions of 1884 and 1885 and the Gordon Relief Expedition of 1884–5, there is no detailed breakdown of the ports of embarkation. It would seem that over 100 vessels were used for the second Suakin expedition in 1885, of which 18 carried troops. Few, however, went from Southampton, though the Union Line's *Arab* did sail for Suakin from the port in February 1885, carrying command, artillery and medical staffs together with carts, wagons and ambulances.[17] Similarly, and sadly, it is difficult to discover if any ships sailed from Southampton in the attempt to rescue its most famous military son, Charles Gordon. The family home, to which he frequently returned, was at 5 Rockstone Place: it now contains luxury apartments with only a small plaque to commemorate its previous famous resident.[18] It would seem that most went from Portsmouth, Liverpool, Glasgow and Woolwich.

III

Undoubtedly, Southampton's finest hours as an imperial port in wartime came in the South African War and the First World War. It is customarily believed that the British Army performed badly in the opening months of the South African War, but the actual process of mobilisation, once the Government had finally and belatedly agreed to it, was an outstanding success. To put 10,000 fighting men and all their support services into Egypt within 40 days of the expedition being authorised in 1882 was remarkable enough, but the mobilisation and despatch of 112,000 regulars to South Africa between 7 October 1899 and 30 January 1900 has been characterised as 'an unprecedented achievement for Britain'. Moreover, Britain sustained a war 6,000 miles from the home base at a time when the French had to rent shipping from Britain to invade Madagascar in 1895, the Germans were unable to contribute even a battalion to an international peacekeeping operation on Crete in 1897, and the USA experienced extreme difficulties in invading Cuba but 90 miles from its coast in 1898. Some confusion ensued as a result of the decision to break up the army corps and send some to Natal rather than concentrate all at the Cape, necessitating re-embarkation at Cape Town. Similarly, the loading of freight had been done too hastily in some cases, but it was still a remarkable achievement.[19]

Military and naval, if not political, preparation had begun in April 1899, with meetings between the Admiralty's Transport Department headed by Rear Admiral Sir Bouverie Clark and the Transport Division of the Quartermaster General's Department of the War Office headed by Major John Cowans, later Quartermaster General during the First World War, as Deputy Assistant Quartermaster General. The first meeting of the War Office Confidential Mobilisation Committee was held on 17 June, being reconstituted as the Army Board for Mobilisation on 8 September. New fittings for horse stalls were deemed necessary and ordered in July, but the Government only authorised expenditure on such equipment on 23 September. Some 35 leading shipowners were then contacted confidentially on 28 September, though the Admiralty had already requisitioned two cargo vessels. The principal firms used were the Union-Castle, White Star, Cunard, Allan, Leyland, Anchor and North Atlantic Lines, including such well-known large ships to contemporaries as the White Star's *Majestic*, the Allan Line's *Bavarian* and the Union–Castle Line's *Kildonan Castle*, though, generally, it was better to use medium-sized vessels of around 5,000 tons. It should be noted, of course, that those vessels taken up required fitting out for troops and/or animals, which was carried out either by government contractors or the companies themselves. In most cases, provision was also made for more coal to enable the ships to make faster passages.

Mobilisation was finally ordered on 5 October, with the Royal Proclamation signed on 7 October and the War Office sending the first official requisition to the Admiralty on 9 October, requesting transport for 46,000 men and 8,600 horses, representing an army corps and a cavalry division, specifying numbers to be sent to each port. The Admiralty then allocated vessels and indicated their size and the date they would become available, the allocation being made on the basis of every man having a space of 18 inches at a mess table; later, 24 inches was allocated to the Imperial Yeomanry. Tonnage was calculated as 4 tons for a man, 11½ tons for a horse and 3 tons for a mule. In passing, it can be noted that tonnage as a basis of the calculation of troop numbers per vessel had been used as far back as the Cartagena expedition in 1740. Units were then specified and orders issued to units and railway companies accordingly so that units could be embarked in the morning and the ship sail in the afternoon. Subsequently, there was an attempt in 1900 to persuade officers to arrive at the docks earlier so that ships could leave promptly, pilots being concerned about navigating the Needles in winter mists and darkness.

The embarkation of supporting units from the Army Service Corps and Army Ordnance Corps began on 7 October, two days before the War Office sent the formal requisition to the Admiralty. The main embarkation began on 20 October with 25 trains running into Southampton. Some 5,000 men left that day, followed by another 5,615 on 21 October, 4,864 on 22 October and 6,335 on 23 October. Approximately 20,000 men were despatched in the first week, transports leaving at the rate of five a day. Lord Wolseley, the Commander-in-Chief at the War Office, saw off the 2nd Brigade of 1st Division from Southampton on 20 October, writing to the Queen, 'I never saw five finer Battns., not one man under the influence of drink. When the five ships carrying those 5,000 men had pushed off from the quays, the men crowding every possible part of the upper decks, sang "God Save the Queen"'. The first ship to leave Southampton on that day was the Union–Castle Line's *Roslin Castle*, which reached the Cape on 9 November 1899.

Primarily, Southampton was used for infantry since, despite the experience of the Zulu War, it was felt the rise and fall of the tide was not best suited to the embarkation of horses. Consequently, cavalry went mostly from Liverpool and Birkenhead, though some units also went from the Tilbury and Royal Albert Docks in London. By 17 November, when mobilisation was completed, 47,081 officers and men had been despatched, comprising four infantry divisions and a cavalry division. Another four infantry divisions and a cavalry brigade, however, were embarked between 24 November 1899 and 17 February 1900, together with auxiliaries such as the City Imperial Volunteers, the Imperial Yeomanry, volunteers service companies joining regular battalions, militia and reinforcing drafts. The 6th Division, for example, was embarked between 16 December and 1 January in five ships, of which three sailed from Southampton, namely the *Gascon*, the *Tintagel Castle* and the *Gaika*. By June 1900, some 12,000 men had gone out through Southampton, with over 150 vessels employed in their transport – without disrupting the port's ordinary dock work – under the able direction of the Admiralty's Divisional Transport Officer, Captain Graham White, assisted by five naval officers, and the Dock Superintendent, John Dixon. White specially commended the American-owned Richardson, Spence & Co for putting its plant and coal stocks at the Admiralty's disposal. Temporary stands were also erected for the handling of officers' baggage by a number of baggage agents including Thomas Cook & Son, the Army and Navy Co-operative Society and two Southampton firms, A. W. White & Co. and Hickie, Barman & Co.[20]

Among the troops were the commanders, General Sir Redvers Buller embarking at Southampton on the Union–Castle Line's *Dunnottar Castle* on 14 October amid much rejoicing, the scene recorded by the movie cameras of the Biograph Company. Buller, in mufti, declined the civic reception offered him by the Mayor but made a short speech of thanks at the head of the gangplank. As the ship sailed to the sound of 'Rule Britannia', 'For He's a Jolly Good Fellow' and 'God Save the Queen', he stood on the navigation bridge, waving his hat as the ship disappeared into a mist. Still widely popular despite his early defeats, Buller returned to Southampton to an equally enthusiastic reception on 9 November 1900, receiving the freedom of the borough from the Corporation. When sent out to supersede Buller, Field Marshal Lord Roberts also sailed from Southampton on the *Dunnottar Castle* on 23 December 1899, ultimately returning to Southampton on 3 January 1901 by way of the hospital ship, *Canada*, the Isle of Wight and a visit to the Queen at Osborne. The defender of Ladysmith, Lieutenant General Sir George White returned to Southampton on the *Dunvegan Castle* on 14 April 1900, the town clerk reading a welcome address on behalf of the Mayor and aldermen. Lord Kitchener, who succeeded Roberts in the South African command, returned to Southampton on the *Orotova* on 12 July 1902 to a rapturous reception, being driven through decorated streets to the Hartley Institute, where he received the freedom of the Southampton before catching a special train to London.[21]

There were also the remounts and stores required to sustain the campaign, a total of 459,663 animals and 1.3 million tons of stores being sent to South Africa. Most of the ships used for the carriage of remounts were chartered through Messrs. Houlder Brothers, and it is clear that, despite the previous concerns over the tide, Southampton was used for this purpose, along with Queenstown and the London docks, over 27,000 horses passing through the port during the war. At the end of the war, of course, the troops had to be brought home, many by freighters in the course of their normal work. By 1902, indeed, a total of 528,000 officers and men had passed through Southampton, either going to or returning from South Africa. Not a single life was lost in terms of wartime sea transport, and loss of animals was restricted to 4 per cent of horses and 1.9 per cent of mules.[22]

In some respects, of course, the sea transport of the army to South Africa was purely a logistical exercise in that the Boers possessed no warships to challenge the Royal Navy's control of the sea lanes, and there was no need to seize hostile shores. Thus, as suggested by Leo Amery, it was 'of the same character as troopship work in peace, but carried out on a gigantic scale'.[23] Of a different nature entirely, therefore, was the despatch of the British Expeditionary Force to France in August 1914 and the subsequent wartime use of Southampton as the officially designated Port Number One.

France and Russia had been seen as the principal threats to British and imperial interests in the 19th century. Increasingly through the early years of the 20th century, however, Germany was being identified as the most likely enemy for the future and the left flank of the French Army on the Franco-Belgium frontier as the most likely theatre of operations for the British Army. Notwithstanding the staff conversations between British and French General Staffs initiated in 1906, it was only between 1910 and 1914 that the mobilisation plan for a concentration of the British Expeditionary Force around Mauberge began to be formalised under the direction of Major General Henry Wilson as Director of Military Operations at the War Office. The choice of Mauberge led to the choice of the projected lines of communication running back to Le Havre as a main base, with Rouen as subsidiary base and Boulogne as a reserve base. In turn, the choice of Le Havre dictated that Southampton would become the main embarkation port for troops and ammunition, though mechanical vehicles were routed through Avonmouth and stores through Newhaven. Dover, Liverpool, Glasgow, Queenstown, Belfast and Dublin were all also used to a lesser extent, while Folkestone became the port handling leave arrangements. Detailed work was carried out to assess the French ports in November 1913 and final details only settled as late as May 1914 as a result of the work of the Admiralty's Slade Committee. In 1899, it had taken some four to five weeks to embark just over 47,000 men, but the projected need now was to ship 165,894 men and 60,368 horses in 12 days. It was intended that logistics support units embark between the first and third days, infantry between the fourth and sixth days, cavalry between the seventh and 11th days and artillery from the sixth day.[24]

Certain considerations had to be taken into account. At most, it was felt that 70 trains could be run into Southampton in 24 hours and that would require the urgent completion of double tracking at the port entrance. In the event, an additional line was laid alongside the existing double line into the port in just four days in August 1914, for only eight ships could be loaded simultaneously without it. The outflow from the French ports was limited to 60 trains a day and that could only be achieved from the seventh day of mobilisation. Moreover, Le Havre could handle only 30 ships a day, Rouen only 20 and Boulogne a bare 11. The small staffs in the Mobilisation Directorate and the Movements and Railway Transports Sub-division (QMG2) in the Quartermaster-General's Department also had to work in secrecy, liasing with the Admiralty and the London and South-Western Railway Company, which was responsible for coordinating timetables with the other rail companies.

As in 1899, calculations were made to sort units into train loads and the day upon which they would arrive at the port and, indeed, at which berth they were to be delivered by the rail companies. Then ships were allotted by sorting train-loads into shiploads – no unit was to be divided between ships – and requesting from the Admiralty the number of ships required for each day and the berths at which they would be needed. Some berths were not equipped to deal with some trainloads, and the capacity of ships also varied. Moreover, while trains arrived at a rate of five per hour, no train could be sent to a berth within an hour and half of the arrival of an earlier train at the same berth. Consequently, a special diagram board had been devised during an exercise at Southampton in June 1913 to keep track of these complications, divided into intervals of 12 minutes and by berthing slots, and on which various coloured cards could be fitted. There had also been earlier exercises in Southampton in 1912, practising putting troops on and off a ship in a single night. Until berths were ready, ships were anchored off the Brambles and Cowes. In all, 20 berths were utilised while the Embarkation Commandant would have a staff of 162 men.[25]

The scheme was so flexible that it coped easily with a number of changes. First, the Government had allowed the Territorial Force to go into summer camp in late July 1914, necessitating a two-day delay from 7 to 9 August for the start of embarkation as they had to be brought back to their depots. Second, there was the late decision by the Government to delay sending two of the six infantry divisions of the British Expeditionary Force to France, the 4th Division not leaving until 23 August, and the 6th not until 8 September. Third, there was three days of fog in the Channel, necessitating one 24-hour delay. Last, a change of base to the Loire became necessary as a result of the retreat from Mons, Boulogne being closed on 26 August and the Le Havre and Rouen bases entirely transferred to St Nazaire and Nantes, before all was transferred back to the original bases in mid-October 1914. Some difficulty was also experienced with poor-quality coal, supplies of first-grade coal having been made available only to warships. Nevertheless, within the first 24 hours, a train ran into Southampton every ten minutes, only one being late and that by only five minutes. Planning to put 350 trains into the port in the first 60 hours, the London and South-Western Railway Company achieved the target in but 45 hours. For 19 consecutive days, the port handled not 70 but 90 trains a day. Since the Royal Navy covered each end of the Channel, transports sailed singly or in pairs without escort, with an average of 13 ships sailing per day. On 13 August alone, 18 ships left the port with 20,513 officers and men, 1,262 horses, 383 vehicles, 20 motor cars and 219 bicycles. Thus, by 26 August, 65,814 officers and men had been safely transported to France.[26]

For individual units, the process was invariably smooth. The 2nd Royal Welsh Fusiliers, for example, entrained at Bovington in Dorset at 6.30 a.m. on 10 August, arriving at Southampton at 10.00 a.m. to embark not on the 'sumptuous Cunarder, with unlimited champagne at the Government's expense', as keenly anticipated, but on the *Glengariff*, described as a 'wretched pig boat'. During the process of embarkation, the Welsh were kept in the embarkation shed with boy scouts doing 'good deeds' such as 'running for fags'. The 2nd King's Royal Rifle Corps stationed at Blackdown near Aldershot entrained at Frimley in the early hours of 12 August, arriving at Southampton at 9.15 a.m. that same morning, embarking on the Union-Castle Line's *Gaika* from 9.20 a.m., and sailing at 5.20 p.m. to arrive at Le Havre at 4 a.m. on 13 August. The 115th Battery, Royal Field Artillery, part of 25th Brigade RFA in 1st Division entrained at Deepcut near Camberley on the morning of 17 August, embarking that same day on the Leyland Line's *Victorian* to cross to Le Havre. Similarly, the 1st King's (Liverpool) Regiment left Farnborough Station at 8 a.m. on 12 August, reaching Southampton at 9.30 a.m. and embarking at once on the Henderson and Company Line's *Irrawaddy*, sailing at 1.15 p.m. and reaching Le Havre at 5 a.m. on 13 August.[27]

Staff of General Headquarters, which had first been located at the Hotel Metropole in London's Northumberland Avenue, were ordered to report to the Polygon Hotel at Southampton by midnight on 12 August, embarking the following day for Le Havre, though Sir John French went to Boulogne in HMS *Sentinel*. There is apparently a plaque still in the dining room of the Polygon commemorating General Headquarters' brief stay. The two corps headquarters of Lieutenant Generals Sir James Grierson and Sir Douglas Haig arrived at the Dolphin Hotel on 13 August. In the case of Haig, his sister and brother-in-law arrived the following morning with a 'sumptuous champagne lunch', and they, with Haig's chief of staff, John Gough, and his two aides-de-camp dined in the landlady's sitting room. They embarked that evening on the *Comrie Castle* for Le Havre.[28] There is still a 'Haig Room' in the Dolphin.

The despatch of the British Expeditionary Force to France did not end Southampton's role, the port being commanded initially by Colonel A. B. Hamilton and subsequently by Brigadier General Sir Alfred Balfour, with town and port as a whole coming under command of Major General G. G. Blackader. Captain H. Strausberg, assisted by the manager of the docks, T. M. Williams, and the dock master, Captain E. W. Harvey, supervised the naval arrangements. In September 1914, the 42nd (East Lancashire) Division of the Territorial Force was shipped out through Southampton to Egypt, followed by the 43rd (Wessex) Division to India in October and the 44th (Home Counties) Division, also to India, in December, while individual territorial units were also despatched to Gibraltar, Cyprus and Aden. Moreover, into Southampton came regular garrisons pulled out of India and the colonies for onward transportation to the Western Front. By November 1914, indeed, Southampton had despatched 47,083 Territorials and had received 16,294 regulars. In all, by the end of November, Southampton had embarked 359,417 officers and men, 93,019 horses, 704 guns, 11,606 vehicles, 3,528 bicycles, 776 motor cars, 40 ambulances, 24,609 tons of stores. Disembarked in the same period were 16,294 officers and men, 1,621 horses, eight guns, 183 vehicles, 8,625 Belgian wounded, 1,852 Indian wounded, 1,340 German wounded and 4,746 German prisoners of war.[29]

Troop movements were constant. To take a few examples, in December 1917, orders were sent to the Director of Transports at Southampton to arrange passage to France for 620 officers and men on 24 December, 773 on 26 December, 1,797 on 29 December and 1,427 on 31 December. Between 16 and 18 December 1917, the port had also shipped back from France for repatriation 1,900 men of the South African Native Labour Corps. A year earlier, on 24 November 1916, Southampton saw its 10,000th troop train, while the expertise of the port staff was such that on 4 March 1917 it detrained and embarked one group in just 29 minutes. In 1917, the American Expeditionary Force was despatched to Europe, some 2.086 million men crossing the Atlantic of whom 1.025 million (49.1 per cent) went through eight British ports. Liverpool and London handled most, but 57,000 Americans came through Southampton. Then, in 1918, French and Italian troops were also routed through the port bound for Murmansk during the allied intervention in the Russian Civil War. After the armistice, Southampton became the principal disembarkation port, the largest number of men ever handled in a single day being 11,183 on 9 March 1919. Casualties and losses within the port from beginning to end of the war amounted to just four men, eight horses, eight wagons and one gun. In all, there were possibly as many as 7 million individual movements through the port during the war.[30]

Horses and all manner of stores were also shipped through Southampton. Again, the movement was constant. To take some examples, between 21 March and 19 April 1915, 24 vessels arrived in the port carrying, as well as personnel, 18 horses, 1,100 blankets, 188 bags of dhal, two steam wagons and four aeroplanes. In the week ending 29 May 1915, the port also handled 740 tons of forage, 462 tons of stores, 66 guns and limbers, 289 four-wheeled vehicles, 307 bicycles, 50 motor cars, 22,567 mailbags and 620 parcels. In all, perhaps 3.7 million tons of stores passed through Southampton. The port shipped 3,800 horses and mules in the week ending 22 December 1917, 1,600 in the week ending 29 December and 3,125 in the week ending 5 January 1918. The largest shipment of horses and mules in a single week was 10,500 in 1917. It is perhaps appropriate, therefore, that among war memorials in Southampton, there is one at the Municipal Golf Course to the horse, Warrior, which served in France throughout the war and was later presented to the police, dying only in 1935.[31]

IV

The Second World War lies beyond the scope of this paper, but matters were rather different due to the threat from the air and the fact that the coast of France was in hostile hands after June 1940. Part of the British Expeditionary

Force certainly went to France from Southampton in 1939–40, such as the 48th (South Midland) Division of the Territorial Army in January 1940, and some troops returned to the port from Dunkirk. Thereafter, however, most troop convoys used Liverpool or, in the case of American forces, Gourock on the Clyde. Southampton did play its part in D-Day and, with Allied armies safely ashore in France once more after June 1944, the port was occasionally used for troop convoys, part of the US 11th Armoured Division arriving in Southampton in October 1944, followed by the US 66th and 76th Infantry Divisions in December 1944. Dangers still existed, however: the *Leopoldville*, carrying part of the US 66th Infantry Division to France as reinforcements during the German Ardennes offensive, was torpedoed on 24 December 1944 with the loss of 802 lives. After the war, the *Queen Mary* brought 11,383 returning troops into Southampton on 16 October 1945, almost certainly the largest number of military passengers ever brought into the port by a single vessel.[32]

With peace restored once more, trooping resumed from Southampton until the advent of large-scale air transport in the 1950s, the last troopship to enter Southampton on its last voyage from the Far East being the Bibby Line's *Oxfordshire* on 18 November 1962.[33] It seemed unlikely that the port would ever again be used for military embarkation of any kind. Yet, 20 years later, in April 1982, the unexpected occurred, and once more a British expeditionary force sailed, this time for the Falklands. Most of the Naval Task Force, including the two carriers, sailed from Portsmouth, but passenger vessels were also taken up: the *Canberra*, which sailed on 9 April, and the North Sea ferry, *Norland*, taking troops, and the *Uganda* serving as a hospital ship. Moreover, the *QE2* took 5 Brigade to South Georgia to be transferred to *Canberra* and *Norland* in May. There had been no crowds at Southampton in 1914 or 1939–40. Thus, when *Canberra* returned to Southampton, her welcome certainly rivalled anything seen at the port during the South African War. That moment serves, perhaps, as an appropriate epitaph to all those servicemen who have embarked or disembarked at Southampton in peace and war.

Figure 10 The Picture Palace, Southampton, by permission of Southampton City Council.

Chapter 10: Southampton, the Great War and the cinema

Michael Hammond

There exists in the National Film and Television Archive a short film made in 1898 by the British Bioscope company entitled *Tram Ride Down Southampton High Street*. The film is what was known at the time as a 'phantom ride'. The camera was mounted atop one of the trams and the film begins as it passes through the Bargate moving toward the docks. The picture is first shrouded by the shade of the Bargate and then brightens up as the vista of the High Street unfolds. Unlike other moving-picture films, which depicted movement in front of a stationary camera, here the camera moves and carries the spectator through the space of Southampton High Street. The world that we witness is a poignant reminder of Southampton's status as a palimpsest written over many times by history and memory. This film renders a bustling late 19th-century city centre where people are busily carrying out their daily work, a horse and carriage trots slowly towards the camera, pedestrians cross the tramline, and the street is lined with awnings which indicate the considerable commerce that takes place beneath them.

The tram moves just through the Bargate and past East Street, the site of a concentration of cinema palaces which were to come in the next decade. This film was most likely screened as one of a number of films on a programme at the MacNaughten Palace music hall or at the Philharmonic Hall or at any one of the travelling exhibitions that came to the commons at Shirley or at Margate nearer the town. However, its screening would not have been limited to the local area but would have been screened across the entire nation. This world of everyday Southampton was as exotic to most Britons as it would be to a modern-day viewer, who today looking through the Bargate sees a city, written over by the bombs of the Second World War, the ravages of an ill-considered rebuilding programme, the disappearance of the liner trade and the predictable 'malling' of the High Street.

Consider another British Bioscope film made in the same year, *Savage South Africa Comes to Southampton* (1898), depicting a showman with a travelling show of 'authentic' Zulu warriors just disembarked in Southampton docks who do a brief dance for the camera. Films such as this one had two purposes: to advertise the travelling show and, more subtly, to demonstrate the power of cinema in bringing exotic events, locations, people – in fact the Empire – to the British cinemagoer.[1] These two films, perhaps the only surviving films of Southampton from this period, are a marker of the combined role that cinema and Southampton shared as gateways to the modern world. Perhaps this seems fanciful, but our tramride takes us through the Bargate, down towards a second gate, the docks. This theme is picked up by the second film as the camera, pointing in the same direction as the first film, towards the open water, picks up the arrival of the Zulu warriors, a celebration of Empire and an introduction, by the cinema, to Southampton as point of entry of a changing, fascinating and perhaps dangerous modern world.

While this theme of a parallel existence of cinema and Southampton as gateways is probably not unique to Southampton – recall the close relationship that New York harbour has with cinema of the early 20th century – it may help illuminate the role cinema played in Southampton throughout the First World War. As with the Boer War, for the soldiers of the Great War, Southampton was the port through which they passed on their way to the front, and the newsreel cameras were there to record it. Through the cinema, Southampton during the war took on, perhaps paradoxically, a tangible presence in the popular imagination, the last 'real' space the soldiers saw before going to the hardly imaginable horrors of the Western Front. But also, as in every town in Britain after 1914, the war signalled a basic shift in entertainment practices in which the latest war news and pictures were a necessary part of an entertainment programme. The soldiers return here as ghostly images flickering on the cinema screen.

Partly as 'business as usual', and no doubt to take advantage of the large number of troops passing through, the new cinema palaces catered to dating couples by highlighting the 'cosiness' of the hall. This usually referred not only to the comfort of the seats but also to the practice in some theatres of having segregated boxes, often with curtains for privacy. This, combined with the darkness during screenings, attracted the attention and scrutiny of the Town Council as well as unofficial moral guardians in their many guises. The result of these attentions and the response of exhibitors often gave Southampton centre stage in the national debate on cinema. The resolution of these regulation debates in Southampton anticipated the national industry's generally successful argument for the respectability of cinema as an entertainment. This ultimately resulted in Southampton's growing cinema culture, gaining a permanent place in the social fabric of the town during the war years.

I   August 1914

When war in Europe broke out in August 1914, the cinemas were coming out of the traditionally slow summer season and looking forward to the more lucrative autumn months. As the unsettled political situation led to war in the early days of August, cinema exhibitors became uncertain as to the future of their business. Cinema in Southampton, as elsewhere, faced three challenges at this time: increased competition for audiences, an emphasis on the theatre space as an attraction at least equal to the film, and increased competition for films, and in particular, American product. The boom in cinema-building that began in 1910 had created a condition in the local market that was highly competitive, and this was exacerbated by the uncertainties that accompanied the outbreak of the war. In turn, this prompted exhibition strategies that drew upon house-management traditions of music hall that emphasised the liberality and good citizenship of the manager. All of this took place against the background of the shift from the 'open market' of film-booking where managers had a degree of control to the exclusives method that favoured the production companies and was to eventually result in the advance block-booking policies of the 1920s. Managers were quick to take advantage of the prevailing patriotic climate and worked to incorporate their houses into the local community by holding charity benefits for war aid and providing special concessions and programmes for soldiers and refugees. In this way, local managers were able to use the timeliness of the war to strengthen their case for a positive, and recognised, social function of cinema.[2]

Southampton was typical of most English towns in this respect, and, by August 1914, as in most of the larger towns and cities, the relatively new form had made significant inroads into the established entertainment culture of the town. In line with a nationwide trend, there had been considerable investment in cinemas by local entrepreneurs in the years 1912–14. These speculative enterprises were undertaken by local businessmen such as Percy Vincent Bowyer, whose main interest was in property speculation, and William Dalton Buck, a local builder in the township of Shirley. William Buck built the first purpose-built cinema, the Atherley, in the Southampton area in 1912. He managed the cinema himself, with his wife leading the orchestra. By contrast, Bowyer was typical of the kind of investment interest that fuelled the boom in cinema-building nationally. His family were well known in political and business circles, brother Henry had until recently been Mayor of Southampton, and Bowyer himself was an alderman on the Town Council. He had a number of business interests and property investments, including four cinemas by the autumn of 1914.[3]

While Buck owned and operated his concern, Bowyer, in his role as managing director, brought in showmen from outside the town, such as one Mr George Elliot who had worked as a booking agent with Sanger's Circus, to run these businesses. To attract audiences, cinema managers like Elliot drew upon already existing traditions of showmanship which were tailored to specific markets depending on the cinema's location. Southampton's status as a commercial port meant a considerable turnover of travellers and businessmen, consequently, the cinemas located on or near the High Street in the centre of the city depended on passing trade. The cinemas outside the centre worked to appeal to their local area through programming and house-management strategies designed to maintain audiences and encourage the cinema habit.

Between August and December 1914, business practices shifted dramatically as Southampton changed from a commercial to a military port and became the primary embarkation point for the British forces. Managers and owners also engaged with the complexities of official and unofficial regulation, national and international pressures within the changing production and distribution sectors, and the unpredictability of the changes brought about by the first few months of the Great War. These included temporary but significant local unemployment brought about by the closing of the port's commercial activities in August 1914, which were the town's main form of industry. This situation was soon alleviated, however, by the influx of troops and related industries. Nevertheless, just as the confidence in cinema as an investment was at its height, the situation of the first months of the war cast an air of uncertainty that did not bode well for entertainment of any kind.

II   Competition for audiences

Southampton provides a clear example of the results of the expansion and increase in venues where there was fierce competition at every level for the exhibitor, from securing the most desirable films to providing the kind of environment that would encourage the cinema habit. At the close of 1914, with 16 cinemas open and each playing three programmes a week, the town was well catered for. This also meant that in order to fulfil the image of packed houses, managers had to fill 7,000 seats per day. With the population at 119,000 this meant that potentially 50 per cent of the town's population would have to attend at least once a week in order to keep the cinemas running at a profit. In reality, this was feasible, since most cinema-goers attended at least twice a week; nevertheless, Southampton was considered in the industry at large as being 'a rather congested area'.[4]

As early as March, 1914, a comment on the national craze for cinema-building in the fan magazine *Pictures and the Picturegoer* outlined the problem:

> Every week we hear of new picture theatres just opening or building or about to be built, and unless there be a builders' strike or some sort of stoppage we shall have more tip-up seats than people to sit on them even if we all become picture-goers. Surely in some districts at least a reasonable limit is being exceeded in this mania for 'running up'. We want enough houses to go round, of course, but in some of these newest palaces (each one is better than the last) nothing is wanted except an audience – apparently a secondary matter at the time of building.[5]

This story made tangible the fears expressed by local exhibitors in Southampton the previous December when the Works Committee of the Southampton Council received a letter from Frank Bromley, the Manager of the Kingsland Cinema. Bromley drew the Council's attention to the large number of entertainment venues being granted licences. His letter was 'on behalf of the existing entertainment caterers asking that a deputation be received by committee to consider the position of the present caterers and the advisability of any further licenses being granted for new or proposed houses of entertainment in Southampton'. The Council resolved that they were not prepared to receive a deputation on the matter.[6] This indicated two important factors: the first being that the Council was committed to expansion and development, and the second that the entertainment and leisure business community were anticipating, and perhaps experiencing, market saturation and seeking official regulation. The Council's hands-off attitude had often benefited exhibitors, particularly on the continuing question of Sunday opening, yet this situation placed the cinema managers in the unusual position of arguing for intervention. The onset of the war in August 1914, de facto, gave the exhibitors the regulation they had wanted by virtue of the fact that confidence in the future of the exhibition business faltered, and, in many cases, the building plans for larger palaces were suspended or abandoned altogether.

The cinema boom had also placed local exhibitors in stiff competition for films as well as audiences. The films were the central part of the programme and a highly visible way of differentiating the experience of each specific cinema. This competition for films was primarily a result of 'open market'

film-booking and the number of film theatres situated together in close proximity throughout British towns and cities. With 16 cinemas, the conditions for
exhibitors in Southampton were typical of the kind of concentration of cinemas that the boom years of 1911–14 had produced in similar sized towns and
cities throughout the country.[7] The open-market system had a number of consequences for local exhibitors. The most sought-after films would often be
rented to cinemas in the same districts. (Hence, the use of the term 'exclusive'
in amusement papers such as *What's On* indicates that that cinema is the only
one in town showing that particular film.) The shelf-life of a film was about
90 days, which resulted, as Kristin Thompson has shown, in a pressing requirement for new films as well as an excess in imported films which were not taken
up. The rapid turnover of films created a need for cinema exhibitors to get the
product as quickly as possible, and before their local competitors, as the potential audience for films would rapidly dissipate.[8] The Palace music hall in
Southampton, for example, devoted its entire Sunday-evening programme to
the screening of films that it consistently advertised as 'an excellent programme
of FIRST TIME SCREENED pictures'.[9] Exhibitors regularly advertised their
success in getting the latest films, and managers were often praised for their
ability to do so.

In addition to the competition for films, throughout the war, exhibitors presented their venues as offering a rendezvous point as an accessible public
space, although with varying address to different classes of clientele. The environment of the picture theatre was an important means of product differenti-
ation in the face of the number of venues with which each exhibitor had to
compete. The number of soldiers passing through, as well as the influx of
single women workers replacing men in factories and on public services such
as transport and as clerks in the business district, altered Southampton's regular audience base. This gave rise to exhibitors' engagement with new audiences
and new social formations which required them not only to draw on existing
traditions of showmanship and house hospitality but also to reshape those
traditions. New audience formations of single women and soldiers were
increasingly supplemented by middle-class audiences brought in by news films
of the war and the Official War Films, particularly *The Battle of the Somme* (released
September 1916). Such significant changes in audiences demonstrate how the
social function of cinema-going became acceptable during the war. This was
not, however, a smooth transition, and the tensions that existed between the
Council, moral guardians and cinema exhibitors were considerable at times.
Those points of tension make it possible to trace these debates in order to more
fully understand the development of cinema culture in Southampton.

The attraction of the cinema house as an environment of leisure and entertainment, and within certain limitations, the choice of specific films, was under
the specific control of the exhibitor. The manager as 'showman' was a considerably strong factor in a particular cinema's identity as it was presented to the
public through the local press and expressed in the cinema's decor, its front-of-
house management, the live music and often live acts. Exhibitors distinguished
between a regular clientele and passing trade, and their advertising strategies
and overall presentation differed depending upon which audience they sought
to attract. What follows is an account of two Southampton cinema managers –
George Elliot and Arthur Pickup – and their responses to the challenge facing
the industry during the war years.

III   Wartime and public morals

George Elliot managed two of Percy Bowyer's theatres, the Northam
Picturedrome, in 1914–15, and the Carlton, from 1915 to the end of the war.
In both cinemas, he utilised the existing showman traditions of publicity
and programming as he tried to cope with significant changes in production
and distribution, the demographic shifts brought on by the war and the
changes in the way the cinema was perceived by official, and unofficial, public
institutions.

Elliot seems to have been a particularly astute manager, and, throughout the
nine months of his management of the Picturedrome, he placed ads and commentary in *What's On* that clearly targeted the local populace of Northam.
Recognising his constituency as a potentially 'regular clientele', he appealed
to the working-class audience through emphasising the atmosphere of the
theatre where 'the jaded and worn out worker [can] visit the warm and cosy
Picturedrome'.[10] He attempted to assuage the concern and potential disruption
of the St Augustine Church Council by instigating Sunday-evening concerts
and courted the child audience through Saturday matinees. In his press advertisements, Elliot also began to promote the abilities of his projectionist,
William Brimble, praising him for the quality of the image on the screen. In an
article, typical of the *What's On* style, the author gives an account of a
'perchance' stop at the Picturedrome:

> Passing along the Northam Road the other evening; and having a couple of
> hours to share [*sic*]; the writer popped into the Northam Picturedrome and set-
> tled down snugly in the luxurious easy chair, to witness the programme. I was
> immediately struck with the clearness and steadiness of the pictures and the

sharpness of focus, and what pleased one most, was the quickness in which the change of pictures were [*sic*] made, doing away with the tedious waiting so often experienced at picture halls.[11]

By stressing the cosy atmosphere and the quality of the image, Elliot emphasised the quality of the theatre, and this took precedence over the actual film programme. In addition to the Sunday-evening concerts, and within weeks of his taking the cinema over, he held special shows for the war effort. He entertained Belgian soldiers with cigarettes and chocolate, and 'though some of the Belgians were seriously wounded they seemed to enjoy thoroughly the programme and the reception they received'. On Intercession Day, 2 January 1915, he gave the cinema over to the Vicar of Northam, the Revd Percival Scott, for a special Sunday service, instead of the regular concert programme. In February 1915, an advertisement ran which heralded:

the capital programme [which] made the tired and jaded workers merry and bright and just fit for the next day's work, thus a little pleasure now and then is welcomed by the wisest men and during the war crisis an evening's amusement at the Northam Picturedrome decidedly acts as a sure rest cure to the worried worker.[12]

Highlighting the restorative properties of the cinema for the local working-class audience and holding benefit performances for refugees were exercises in attempting to embed the cinema into the area as an integral part of the local culture.

In the spring of 1915, owner Percy Bowyer moved Elliot and Brimble to his most high-profile cinema, the Carlton, in the more well-to-do area of Carlton Crescent. Here he continued his style of management derived from his time as a showman and influenced by the liberality associated with music-hall managers and publicans. Connecting the tradition of the music-hall manager with the older antecedent of the publican, this intimation of liberality not only recommended the house as a place of comfort and quality but also broadened the appeal of the house by accentuating the social value of the manager. Peter Bailey has shown that the public indulgence of luxury and an impression of 'fulsome provision' were part of the presentation of the music-hall manager as the 'host of a great feast while simultaneously charging for it.'[13]

In the absence of the provision of alcoholic refreshment, the cinema manager's equivalence of this liberal plenitude was the comfort and decor of the hall and the emphasis on the cinema as a place to take non-alcoholic refreshment. Elliot courted the favour of the community through his use of charity and free shows for wounded soldiers. Every Tuesday was set aside for these programmes. An indication of the elaborate nature of the bill is provided in the account of the show of 5 October 1915. As well as showing the full-length British feature film *Harbour Lights* and the usual Chaplins, there was 'excellent singing' by Mrs Moody who sang, 'Somewhere a Voice is Calling', 'The Little Grey Home in the West' and 'Mother Machree' accompanied by Miss Chick, 'a clever pianist'. Significantly, the songs were recent hits, apart from 'Somewhere a Voice is Calling', which was a 'sacred song'. In addition to the unique combination of live performance and films, '[s]everal ladies gave their services and looked after the soldiers' comfort [while] Mrs Moody [. . .] generously gave every soldier a nice cigar'.[14]

Elliot is an example of the way in which cinema managers, with backgrounds as showmen, actively courted particular clientele, and this was based on addressing their audiences through advertising strategy, cinema decor, house management and special events. The desired effect was to give the impression of a hall which is within the predominant taste parameters of the local area. The choice here of making the house distinct in relation to other houses was to pitch the advertising towards the exclusive, high-class audience. The entertainment of troops and the returning wounded as well as charity benefits for particular causes were ways in which cinema exhibitors such as Elliot were able to position their houses as respectable places for friends and families to attend. The war conditions were incorporated into the creation of house identities, and cinema owners utilised the connection with the war as an endorsement of their legitimacy.

These type of events were not limited to the cinema house itself, and exhibitors were often engaged in local patriotic pageantry and community events. In September 1914, Messrs Bacon and Hood, proprietors of the Palladium in the more affluent suburb Portswood, rented premises on Southampton High Street in order to set up a 'cinema rifle range'. Images of German soldiers were thrown on a reversible steel screen . . . and the public was 'invited to get their own in against the Germans!'[15] Obviously, the methods of taking advantage of the war to increase business for exhibitors were numerous, and Southampton exhibitors were in line with practices elsewhere in the country.

The question of Sunday opening had been a consistent debate since the rise of picture palaces in 1911. However, Southampton exhibitors enjoyed the endorsement of the Town Council and were never forbidden to show films on Sunday. Southampton, throughout the war, carried on a practice which was adopted by most towns and cities in Britain. This was to limit screenings on Sunday to the evenings, usually beginning at 7.30 p.m. In discussions in the local press, one of the deciding factors in the debate was the prevalence of soldiers who were billeted on Southampton Common. The cinema offered a regulated, non-alcohol-serving entertainment venue that served the interests of the town in a way that outweighed concerns about the propriety of Sunday opening. Southampton was reported in the *Bioscope* on 11 March 1915 as having led the way by scoring a 'triumph on the question of Sunday opening'. While resistance had been led by the Free Council Church, two letters by Revd N. Lovett, the Rural Dean, and Chief Constable Mr E. W. Jones were thought to have swayed the Works Committee. Revd Lovett wrote, 'I still think that the film and the conduct of a palace may be as much against public morals on the week-day as Sunday and that the right kind of picture palace is not harmful on Sunday after church hours'. While not an endorsement of the moral turpitude of pictures, Lovett's resigned tone was endorsed in more practical terms by Chief Constable Jones:

> Providing [. . .] that suitable pictures are shown, I am of opinion that in the interest of young persons who, but for this form of entertainment, would parade the streets, and others who undoubtedly frequent public houses, it would be a mistake to refuse to license these places on Sunday.[16]

As these arguments began to hold sway in towns like Southampton, they gradually formed a significant plank in the Cinema Exhibitors Association's argument for the relaxation of restrictions in their testimonies for the National Council of Public Morals report on the cinema in 1917.

IV   Exoticism on screen

As welcoming to the new form of entertainment business as Southampton's Council was, and this may or may not have been the result of one of its members, Percy Bowyer, having significantly invested in it, there was an instance where the propriety of the contents of cinema's advertising was brought into question. The practices of the manager of the newly opened Gaiety cinema on the High Street just below the Bargate drew the attention of the Council through complaints received concerning the type of posters he had been displaying in his forecourt and front of house. In summer 1914, one Mr Arthur Pickup had been hired to manage the brand new cinema by an investment group headed by Mr E. S. Edgar and Mr D. L. Elkin. The opening of the cinema, in September 1914, had been a heralded event attended by the Town Sheriff, Councillor G. Etheridge, who in his speech praised the Gaiety's architecture and its contribution to the town's culture by declaring its 'educational value'. This remark was prompted by the Gaiety's 'oriental' style of architecture, and the Sheriff went on to congratulate the architect and builders 'on having provided such a handsome building, remarking that it would have an educational value.'[17]

Despite this warm welcome by the Sheriff, Arthur Pickup was faced with a difficult task. The war had broken out the previous month, and all of his advertising preparations had pitched his cinema towards the businessman: '[c]entrally situated in the High Street the businessman, besides the leisured classes, will occasionally adjourn to find temporary relaxation from the worry and bustle of his daily calling, as the performances will be continuous from 2pm till 10.45 p.m.'.[18] Pickup was faced with not only a dwindling male population but, in the first months of the war at least, there seemed to be no audience to replace them. Judging by his advertising in these months, however, he seems to have determined to target an audience of young women. His change in strategy, which was almost immediate, is instructive in terms of how Southampton exhibitors coped with the changing demographics brought about by the war.

Rather than adopt the showmanship of music-hall management common at the time, as did George Elliot, Arthur Pickup's strategies looked forward to a kind of *cinema* management style which gave less emphasis to his own personality and instead foregrounded the features and exclusives set within the exotic luxury of the hall itself. Consequently, Pickup began to develop a programming style that was dominated by feature films of 'highly coloured' melodramas, or 'pathetics', often with controversial subject matter as their themes. While much of the actual programme was indistinguishable from that of other cinemas, the emphasis in the press, and in the front-of-house display, was on these types of pictures. These publicity practices resulted in a complex set of negotiations with the Council and moral guardians of the town.

The themed architecture of the Gaiety was in line with the wider trend towards the ornate palace throughout the first cinema-building boom that began in earnest in Britain in 1912. The Gaiety's oriental theme had antecedents in theatrical architecture, and the continuing fascination with the 'orient', and Egypt in particular, in the British imperial imagination at the end of the 19th century was one avenue in a discursive paradigm that simultaneously allowed the depiction of eroticism within a framework of education and 'high-art' aesthetics. The fact that the Gaiety's exterior incorporated a mosque theme merely replaced Egypt for another 'distant yet compelling' culture. The building itself, then, functioned as a means of negotiating desire through the associations with eroticism and the 'oriental', on the one hand, and educational uplift on the other. Added to the exoticism of the architecture was the choice of films. Arthur Pickup's advertising strategy was committed to the feature. He advertised them exclusively, highlighting the upcoming features and mentioning briefly a full programme.[19]

The cosmopolitan image of the Gaiety's name made reference to the musical comedy of London's West End, but the films themselves were less lighthearted. The programming strategy of the first few weeks at the Gaiety is revealing. It was characterised by its emphasis on the feature, which was either a 'pathetic' melodrama, or a war subject, normally a drama. The opening feature was the British and Colonial company's feature directed by Maurice Elvy entitled *The Loss of the Birkenhead* (1914). Pickup had secured this as an exclusive and screened it for the first time at Southampton. In line with the patriotic trend of exhibitors, he advertised the film as able to 'arouse not merely their [Britons'] interest and enthusiasm, but their national pride.'[20]

In the following week, Arthur Pickup screened *Dealers in Human Lives*, 'a white slave traffic exposure'. Southampton's status as a port for emigration resonated with the international element of the white-slavery moral panic, as it fed into fears about abduction of English women by foreigners. The Gaiety was located near Canal Walk. This street connected the docks to the town and had become something of a 'sailor's paradise'.[21] The police strength dedicated to this area was three times that of the other areas of the town.[22] Here Southampton's status as a port town was most visible, with a considerable number of lodgings for sailors and the transient population, and it resembled those sexually dangerous settings in the white-slave narratives.

White-slave narratives were crucial to the development of cinema and were at the same time a challenge to the industry's bid for social respectability. The high profile of the white-slave film in Britain tempts a certain equivalence with the reception of these films in the USA.[23] As a rule, the American films which had caused the most concern in Britain were those which showed the activities of criminals. However, exhibitors in Britain were consistently pointing out that criminal activity in the US films rarely, if ever, went unpunished, and they were held up as a positive and indeed educational example to reinforce the British industry's arguments for the acceptance of US films in Britain. Mr John D. Tippett, Managing Director of the Transatlantic Film Company, expressed the sentiments which the industry as a whole utilised to insure social acceptance:

> No manufacturer in his senses would invest money in a picture which was indecent or immoral. Of course we must not be debarred from presenting a powerful story, or facing sex problems of vital import to the future of our race, but it is certain that all this can be done with propriety, decency and proper dignity.[24]

Arthur Pickup had taken a similar tack in his advertising for *Dealers in Human Lives*. As a 'white slave exposure', the film was advertised as educational. Pickup's strategy in exhibiting a white-slave film seems to be trying out product in search of an audience. He had advertised the cinema as a place where a businessman could spend a spare hour, and, indeed, its position in the busiest business district supports that. But as Shelley Stamp Lindsey has suggested, in the USA, the white-slave films were attracting female audiences 'through sensationalism and titillation'.[25] Based on the existing evidence of this performance in the trade press and the local press, it is impossible to determine the kind of audience that attended the Gaiety on that second week of its opening, but there is one scant account of the audience response to the film in the *Bioscope*. The article had been praising the ability of the hall to attract patrons when most of the men had enlisted and then praised the management:

> It is tribute to the wise discrimination of the management in booking to the taste of the public that such success has been achieved. The exclusives screened by Mr. Pickup last week were both intense and realistic dramas – *Dealers in Human Lives* and *Locked in Death*.[26]

The article went on to describe the upcoming feature *The Slave of the Poppy* as 'ruthlessly exposing' the horrors of the opium traffic. The focus on 'intense and realistic dramas' was to become a hallmark of the Gaiety in the next year. Combined with the decor of the hall, the experience of a white-slave film or an exposé of the opium trade was an incitement to desire governed by the rationale of educational value.

Arguably, the morally sensational nature of the subject matter was precisely the aspect of the films that attracted young female audiences, and there is a clear correlation between the availability of these narratives and the increase of young women into Southampton. In May 1915, the Variety Theatre in nearby Eastleigh staged a production of *The White Slaves of London*, 'a story of young girls who are led away by the gaiety and life of a big city'.[27] In the same month, the Grand Theatre staged the play *The White Slave Girl*, which 'shows the perils which beset young girls who have to work for their living in the great cities or even in the country. It deals strongly and yet carefully with this delicate subject'.[28]

The Gaiety's attempt to equate the sensational with the educational became transparent in the following summer of 1915. While in the first few weeks of opening the Gaiety was presented as a culturally enlightening experience where the 'pictures are accompanied by an orchestra who have a capacity for playing high class music with real art', throughout the winter and spring of 1915, the advertisements for the Gaiety began to focus on the sensational elements of the features.[29] In February, the film *Ghurka's Revenge* was advertised as '[s]howing how a German forces his unwelcome attentions on a Ghurka's wife, who finally has the satisfaction of avenging her death'. The advertisements also began to employ the use of sensationalist language. In April, the film *1914*, by 'Rita' (pseudonym for the popular writer Eliza Margaret Jane Gollan), was advertised as a '[w]ar drama palpitating with excitement'. *Woman*, an Italian film which featured '*The Tango of Death*' was the story of a 'princess forced by scandal to dance the Tango of Death on a music hall stage'.[30] In the last week of June, the theme of white slavery returned in *Honour Thy Mother*, with 'vividly realistic scenes in life's underworld'. In July, the advertisement for *Nana of the Moulin Rouge* included a quote from an inter-title: 'In a blind rage I drew my revolver'. *Two Women* was advertised as 'throbbing with human interest and passionate excitement'.[31] *The Evil Men Do* was 'vibrating with heart-stirring problems of passionate emotion'.[32]

As this distinct trend in the Gaiety's advertising was hitting its stride during the summer of 1915, the cinema's use of front-of-house advertising came under official scrutiny. The Southampton City Council Minutes record that on 26 July 1915 it was brought to the attention of the Works Committee that a poster advertising a film was found to be objectionable. Subsequent letters throughout the next two months show that the Works Committee threatened the proprietor E. S. Edgar with non-renewal of the licence. The exact nature of the poster and film is not recorded. Nonetheless, there were two films that the Gaiety screened during the week of 10 July 1915 whose advertising may have been the cause of consternation. They were *The World's Desire*, starring Lillian Braithwaite, advertised as '[v]ibrating with heart-stirring emotion and pathos. The wife's dream is fulfilled but the doctor dare not tell her the truth', and *Her Nameless Child*, a '[p]owerful drama of a brave young wife who kept her marriage a secret – and her child nameless – to save her brother's honour. Throbbing with dramatic moments'. Both films' advertising hinted at two of the 22 grounds for which films had been cut which the British Board of Film Censors had published in its annual report of 1914. These were 'indelicate sexual situations' and 'scenes suggestive of immorality'.[33]

Posters were a potential problem for all cinema exhibitors at this time due to the already established censorship system for poster hoardings overseen by the Billposters' Association. The jurisdiction of this body did not, however, include the front of the picture palace, which was a privately owned space. The Gaiety, located as it was on the High Street at the edge of the shopping district had a larger forecourt where a larger number of posters were displayed. Posters of this kind were artistic renderings of scenes which usually had only tangential links with the film advertised. The object of posters was to catch the eye of passers-by and entice them to enter into the cinema. Trade-press advice about the use of posters tacitly warned against 'suggestive' advertising and generally focused on the 'tasteful' and 'artistic' quality and presentation within the lobby. Nevertheless, the relationship of the front-of-house poster to the film did not simply function to provide a glimpse into the film. The uses of 'lurid colour' and excessive pose or gesture were attractions in themselves. Their position outside of the cinema offered pleasures beyond those of the film. Those pleasures were often coded in ways that attracted the attention of moral guardians, such as Revd N. Lovett, who, in his letter supporting Sunday opening in Southampton, also commented on the use of posters:

> I am inclined to think that pictures are sometimes misunderstood, not only by those rightly jealous for public morality but by dirty-minded onlookers, who express their evil imaginations by sniggling and giggling and deliberately trying to see evil where it is not intended, and who, therefore give to the better minded the more reason to suppose the wrong was intended; but I am bound to say that managers ask frequently for these misinterpretations by the title of their subjects, which they placard outside by posters, etc and with which they seek to attract their audiences. The appeal made to the public by these titles is too often an appeal to the prurient and to those eager for nastiness. I consider the titles are a disgrace to the streets in which they appear and an offence in the eyes of decent minded people who go about their business.[34]

The Dean's letter indicates the sensitivity to the impact on the public space the type of advertising that Arthur Pickup had been engaged in. Within regulating discourses such as that of the Dean's, the prevailing assumption was of the cinema as a proletarian public sphere, yet bound to a code of 'decency' beyond the letter of the law. Moreover, this audience was seen to be predominantly women and children. Further, the nature of the space inside the cinema was contested in profound ways. The experience of the cinema took place in a discursively liminal space between public and private. The poster, in its position as an invitation to that space and articulated in terms of visual representation and with the purpose of solicitation, occupied a site of negotiation between the public and private spheres. Yet the depictions of dramatic moments, spectacularly staged, were directly addressing the private pleasures the cinema offered. These posters represented a gateway not only between the public space of the street and the private space of the auditorium, but were also a window into filmic moments that spoke to the private world of the viewer.

The Gaiety's advertising was toned down to an extent, but the cinema had succeeded in the first year in establishing a clear identity. Through the combination of the architecture, the decor and by emphasising the exclusives on the film programme, Arthur Pickup was able to anticipate and attract audiences in Southampton and to establish a regular clientele. Through these marketing and programming strategies, the Gaiety experience differentiated itself by aiming to attract young working women, particularly those who had newly acquired disposable income through work made available by enlistment and conscription. Throughout the war, the programme was in reality as varied as the programmes of other cinemas, but, nevertheless, two kinds of films consistently appeared throughout the war: the society and crime film and the official war pictures. This specific address to a female audience, balancing sensational and titillating moral and physical danger with education and uplift, lay at the heart of the marketing strategies at the local level as a means of differentiating the Gaiety from other local cinemas as a modern, progressive experience.

Conclusion

To return to the theme of the cinema and Southampton's shared status as portals to new worlds, it is clear that Arthur Pickup's strategy was one foregrounding the experience of the cinema as blurring the boundary between the public experience of a night out and the private pleasures of a cinema informed by suggestion and desire. These narratives were invariably complex, requiring full attention to keep pace with the story. Contrast this with George Elliot's painstaking attempts to make his cinema familiar and acceptable, holding special events and closing on Sunday evenings to allow his workers time to rest on the Sabbath. His clientele shifted between the working-class area of Northam to the middle-class area of Carlton Crescent, but his dependence on the older management style of liberality drawn from music-hall management remained the same. The Northam Picturedrome's management was taken over in 1915 by Jack Mathers from County Armagh in Northern Ireland, another manager with a showman's background. The Northam Picturedrome remained open under various names until 1934. The Carlton was less fortunate and closed in 1922, probably due to having to compete with larger High Street houses like the Gaiety. The Gaiety, however, remained open and independent until the mid-1950s. Percy Bowyer, the local investor, sold his interests in the Carlton in 1917 and appears to have sold off his other interests in cinema ownership by the end of the war. It is probable that he was able to see a strong return on his investment as the war years saw cinema attendances rise to a peak in 1916 which would not be reached again for another ten years.[35] Even with the dip in ticket sales brought about by the introduction of a national entertainments tax in that year, attendances remained buoyant. In light of the fact that cinema ownership by and large gave way to the centralised circuits after the war, Bowyer's retreat was probably prudent.

This tale of the more modern method of cinema management as represented by the Gaiety has a neat parallel with the growing status of Southampton as a port of entry during the first half of the 20th century and, perhaps, a more sombre one as the gateway for the embarking soldiers and returning wounded. The cinema, during the war, became the site of knowledge and visible evidence, however regulated, of the events at the Front, the exotic images of Empire replaced by the horrific images of the war machine.

As exhibitors drew on the traditions of showmanship and theatre management, they also strove to emphasise the special qualities of the cinema by programming newsreels and, from 1915 onwards, official war films. Cinema's role, they argued, was not only as a house of entertainment contributing to the war effort through benefits and charity shows, but through the latest war pictures and official war films such as *The Battle of the Somme* (1916) and *The Battle of Ancre and the Advance of the Tanks* (1917), it was an effective means of educating the populace about the events of the war at the Front. The Official War Films employed techniques developed by actuality film-makers throughout the short history of cinema. Actuality films not only represented national news events, but they had been an important part of the visual representation of the local space. Important events in the local community were often filmed and then screened for audiences by cinema managers. For example, in June of 1914 the managers of the Portswood Palladium, the same group who erected the cinema rifle range, secured the rights to the filming of the Southampton Tudor Pageant which took place at the deanery grounds and screened it for their patrons.[36] Local-interest films such as these, placed alongside the newsreels of national and international news, linked the space to those events. More specifically, the local-news film worked as part of managers' overall strategy of supporting the war effort with depictions of soldiers departing or at drill, or pictures of recruitment centres and the queues outside all serving to knit the local into the national. After the war was over, Southampton continued to appear on both national and local screens as dignitaries and film stars entering England on luxury liners via Southampton were chronicled by the newsreels.[37] Charlie Chaplin's arrival in Southampton in September 1921 was screened the world over, as was the arrival of Douglas Fairbanks and Mary Pickford in 1920. Local films became less concerned with parochial events as Southampton's image once again became more international, and Hollywood's dominance increased. The cinema, like Southampton, had became the image of modernity for Britain.

Chapter 11: A vision unfulfilled

Southampton's ambition for the world's first sea aerodrome

Adrian Smith

Introduction

Surely only the Spitfire enjoys a similar place in the civic psyche of Southampton. Like all great romances, there has been excitement (literally building the aviation museum around a Sunderland) and tragedy (the 1998 sinking of a Catalina with consequent loss of life). The arrival of a seaplane over the Solent will always generate enormous interest, recalling an era when Southampton saw itself as the epicentre of the Empire. It may be a cliché, but flying boats really did signify glamour and romance. On the eve of war, a first-class ticket on a C-Class carrier guaranteed comfort and conviviality all the way to Cairo. Indian Army generals and viceregal advisers eschewed P&O to reach Karachi or Calcutta in less than a week. Indeed, even the least intrepid imperial traveller could fly as far as Sydney, secure in the knowledge that his or her every need would be catered for by an A-team of stewards and a flight crew intent on touching down a mere eight days after leaving England.

Clearly, the great transatlantic liners have a unique place in the history of Southampton, and yet, at the same time, the city has relished its long and often intense love affair with flying boats. These aircraft acquired their own unique mythology and complex set of rituals, the latter embodying modernity *and* maritime tradition. Thus, the flying boats can be seen as simply another stage in a long and proud history of voyage and migration. Prior to the Second World War, this emphasis on continuity, when combined with civic pride and economic expansion, fostered a belief that Southampton could be more than just a convenient departure point for the rich and powerful. The city had an imperial mission, hence the need to consolidate its position as the nation's premier 'marine airport'. In consequence, as early as the mid-1930s, ambitious plans were already being advanced with a view to Southampton acquiring facilities akin to those enjoyed by the major shipping lines following expansion and refurbishment of the port. With the onset of war, such ideas had to be put on hold, but as early as 1942 the initial, highly ambitious blueprint for reconstruction gave qualified support for what became, two years later, a grandiose scheme for a joint sea/land airport on the eastern shore of Southampton Water. This proposal, and its modified successor, were absurdly expensive and wholly unrealistic and were at the expense of a genuinely innovative and potentially more beneficial scheme to improve shopping and recreational facilities adjacent to the Civic Centre.

The Harbour Board's 'land and sea air base' initiative demonstrated perfectly how civic ambition was increasingly out of kilter with national policy, not least the Ministry of Civil Aviation's commitment to land-based long-haul airliners. Yet this is not simply a case of inflated municipal pride. Post-war Southampton's splendidly unrealistic plans have to be seen in the context of the Attlee Administration's similarly blinkered insistence on a 'Fly British' policy. Both central and local government took an unduly long period of time to adopt a sensible and commercially viable perspective on the future of civil aviation in the UK. Nevertheless, after 1948, all parties secured a firmer grasp of reality. By Christmas 1950, the British Overseas Airways Corporation (BOAC) had flown its last flying boat out of Berth 50, and the terminal had closed for good. The maintenance base at Hythe was shut, and plans for a quantum leap in marine aeronautics were quietly shelved – the magnificent SR45 *Princess* was to end her days shrink-wrapped on an Isle of Wight sand bar. The rise and fall of the Southampton 'sea aerodrome' covered less than two decades, but it constituted a discrete chapter in the port's sometimes glorious, sometimes inglorious, history as a gateway to Empire.

I   Southampton and flying boats between the wars

In the early 1930s, a new word – indeed a new concept – crossed the Atlantic. The arrival of the 'airliner' signalled for travellers a seductive combination of the fresh (crossing continents at high speed and great altitude) and the familiar (the indulgence of the most comfortable cruise ship). The Americans, faced with the challenge of traversing a great continental land mass, fused avionics and art deco in strikingly modern passenger aircraft such as the Lockheed Electra. Having jumped a generation in the development of land-based monoplanes, major carriers such as Pan American (Pan Am) promoted ocean-going aircraft as a unique fusion of luxury and long-haul transport. At the same time, the military in Washington saw seaplanes as a vital means of monitoring Japan's naval presence across the vast spaces of the Pacific. The result, by 1939, was Pan Am's hi-tech Clipper fleet and a future icon of the special relationship, the PBY-5 Catalina. The history of the British aerospace industry confirms a similar capacity for ground-breaking design, and yet all too often the initiative has passed to the USA – for example, swing-wing and vertical take-off. Repeatedly, a failure of political will and/or a lack of management competence had seen a programme of research and development denied investment and direction, the latter most visibly in the form of potentially lucrative civil or military contracts. In the late 1930s, the Empire flying boats were to prove a powerful exception to the rule, maintaining a transatlantic technological imperative in at least one aspect of aircraft design. Furthermore, the enduring qualities of the C-Class 'Imperial Flying Boat' became evident in the Second World War through the pivotal role of its military spin-off, the Sunderland.

The C-Class carriers, each with its own brand name and distinctive identity (the record-breaking *Cambria*, the pioneering *Caledonia*, the marooned *Corsair* and so on) marked a huge leap of faith on the part of Imperial Airways.[1] The airline's lumbering biplanes were always woefully underpowered and clumsily built: short production runs necessitated minimal time at the drawing board, in sharp contrast to the American experience. Yet in 1934, the company placed a 1.75-million-pound order with Short Brothers for no less than 28 state-of-the-art flying boats. The priorities were speed (cruising at 200 mph), distance (800 miles non-stop) and sophistication (former Cunard cabin staff serving canapés and cocktails in clubland comfort). The Empire boats were the first civil aircraft in Britain to show a healthy respect for smooth lines and cutting-edge aerodynamics. The absence of a prototype is testimony to the confidence both Shorts and Imperial Airways placed in their joint design team (at the same time in Southampton, the Air Ministry was showing a similar implicit faith in R. J. Mitchell's blueprint for a revolutionary new fighter aircraft). These aeroplanes were unashamedly modern and yet reassuringly secure, contriving to be both streamlined and solid. In this respect, the 'Imperial Flying Boat' sent out a powerful message of Empire: rooted in tradition, and yet eager to embrace modernity. With no clubland class to distract or interfere, the imperial consul could compress the delights of an indulgent sea cruise east of Suez into a matter of days, arriving in Karachi or Cape Town fresh and eager to dispense good government or to furnish sound advice. The C-Class fleet symbolised a forward-looking British Empire and Commonwealth, the latest developments in transport and telecommunications enhancing collaboration and consultation between the 'mother country', her colonial responsibilities and her freshly empowered dominions. Appropriately, the spur to one of the last great imperial initiatives had been guaranteed delivery of the Royal Mail at a flat rate to anywhere in the world flying the Union Flag. The scheme was massively subsidised by both Government and the Post Office, to the tune of around 1.7 million pounds per annum, with the Admiralty sanctioning free provision of launches, refuelling tenders and mooring facilities. The latter was a huge hidden subsidy, which as we shall see, came back to haunt the Treasury after the Second World War.[2] It was the munificence of the Royal Navy which confirmed the case for sea- rather than land-based aircraft, and which brought the C-Class carriers to Southampton Water.

With Shorts concentrating production in first Rochester and then Belfast, either city can claim to be the spiritual home of the flying boat; and yet, by virtue of history and location, Southampton deems itself uniquely qualified to claim the title. This was the case even 70 years ago, when the community saw itself ideally placed to act as host to the new 'air-liner'. After all, Southampton was a port that could effortlessly service the needs of the grandest blue-riband contender. March 1937 marked the inaugural flight from Alexandria of the *Castor*, first of the C-Class fleet. With the Waterloo-bound express waiting outside Berth 50 to whisk them off to the metropolis, the 15 pioneering passengers were given a warm welcome by the harbour authorities and city fathers. Attention then turned to a weary captain, leading his flight and cabin crew ashore with suitable ceremony and decorum (flying *boat* ritual drew heavily upon naval procedure).[3] Yet long before the first Empire boat berthed alongside the great ships which it might one day supersede, the Solent was already seen as synonymous with seaplanes. Supermarine had pioneered floatplane design before and after the First World War, culminating in its triumphant capture of the Schneider Trophy in 1931.[4] The Woolston firm's promotion of cross-channel services to Guernsey and Cherbourg ensured a keen interest in the fortunes of Imperial Airways following its establishment in 1923. Manufacturers such as Supermarine retained a stake in Britain's flagship airline, if only because more routes meant more aircraft. The record-breaking S6B and the prototype Spitfire signalled the future, but for much of the inter-war period, Supermarine relied upon its reputation for building fast and reliable flying boats. Thus, the factory slipway at Woolston retained its dual status as a customs airport until as late as 1934.[5]

Given the rather ad-hoc arrangements for landings and take-offs in the 1920s and early 1930s, it is amazing that there were so few collisions on Southampton Water. Yet well before the arrival of the Empire boats, both the Harbour Board and the Borough Council's Works and Harbour Committee had floated the idea of a permanent 'sea aerodrome'. As with so many municipal initiatives between the wars, principally the new docks (1934), the Civic Centre (1932–9), and the sports centre (1938), the driving force was Alderman Sir Sidney Kimber. With so much of its wealth derived from elite passenger shipping, Southampton weathered the downturn in global trade at the onset of the Depression reasonably well. As J. B. Priestley noted in 1933, the town appeared deceptively prosperous, but once away from the High Street, the 'very poor quarters' of St Mary's and Northam told a different story:

> The only thing to be said in favour of these little side-streets of Southampton is that they did not seem as devastatingly dismal as the slums of the big industrial towns. There was still a sea sparkle in these people's lives. They were noisy and cheerful, not crushed [. . .] It might have been much worse. But it could be – and at first I thought it was – much better.[6]

Priestley highlighted the contrast between the champagne lifestyle of first-class passengers and the conditions of service for those seeking to satisfy their every need.[7] C-Class cabin crew were clearly looked after far better than the chefs and stewards regularly crossing the Atlantic, yet they must have shared that same sense of alienation: nowhere outside the West End was the gulf between rich and poor starker than on a luxury liner or an Empire flying boat. To be fair, had Priestley revisited Southampton a few years later, then he would have seen tangible improvements in the quality of life, not least the impact of grand public works initiated by benevolent authoritarians such as Kimber. The Ratepayers' Party retained municipal power despite the growing challenge from Labour, and Sidney Kimber was the embodiment of Mr Baldwin's paternalistic 'two nations' Toryism.[8] There was also more than a hint of John Maynard Keynes about the council leader, given his preference for local firms when it came to awarding major contracts. Criticism of a lack of transparency in the bidding process was muted so long as the work stayed within what was still a surprisingly close-knit community.[9]

As the council's principal representative on the Harbour Board, Kimber initiated discussions with the Air Ministry and the Director General of Civil Aviation 'as to the future of the port as a civil sea aerodrome'. By the mid-1930s, an area adjacent to Netley Castle had been designated available for future development, and in March 1938 a purpose-built pontoon was established at Berth 107 in the new docks. Later that same year, a transfer to Berth 108 enabled the provision of proper terminal facilities at 'Imperial House' – rarely was a building less appropriately named, being surprisingly modest, and, with its timber construction, appearing both fragile and temporary.[10] Across

Southampton Water, on the western shore, Imperial Airways had established maintenance facilities in the aircraft sheds at Hythe originally built by Supermarine. The demand for space grew dramatically over the next 15 years, and the presence of both the flying boat depot and the highly successful British Powerboat Company made Hythe a major centre of skilled engineering until the demise of both operations at the end of the 1940s. Although some workers lived on what is today known as the Waterside, most mechanics, fitters, and support staff commuted every day from Southampton on the ferry. By 1949, no less than 900 personnel were involved in maintaining the boats, which naturally raises the question of what they all did, given the modest size of the fleet.[11]

Kimber and his colleagues had been spurred into action by the news that Portsmouth councillors were actively promoting Langstone Harbour as a permanent base for Imperial Airways. This was despite the Admiralty's unequivocal opposition and the airline's reluctance to abandon its new home once the 'Empire Air Mail Scheme' was up and running. Throughout the late 1930s, as the aircraft continued to roll off the assembly line, so the network of passenger and mail services extended to the farthest reaches of the Empire: the first flying boat arrived in Auckland no less than eight months after the outbreak of war, albeit courtesy of sister airline Tasman Empire Airways.[12] April 1940 was scarcely an auspicious moment to girdle the globe, but it highlighted the determination of what was now known as BOAC to soldier on through the 'phoney war'.[13] By this time, the Air Ministry and the Harbour Board had secured parliamentary approval to ban shipping from a recognised flight path and to establish the 'Empire Flying Boat Terminal' on a permanent basis – the nation, and indeed the Empire, had its first 'Marine Air Base'.[14]

II   War and reconstruction

With the onset of war, BOAC sought safety in Dorset. Pre-war crashes, requisition by the Royal Air Force (RAF), destruction by enemy action and the creation of a southern hemisphere service based in Durban, meant a much diminished fleet flying out of Poole Harbour.[15] In total, 45 C-Class boats were built, but only 13 survived the war, their losses compensated for by Sunderlands converted to civilian use.[16] BOAC's post-war order for the Solent, the last sea-based passenger aircraft to go into full production, was cut once it became clear that the versatility of the Sunderland and the Catalina guaranteed a surplus not a shortage of flying boats. More crucially, the demand was now for aeroplanes capable of carrying people or freight quickly and cheaply – and therefore in volume – from one particular destination to another. The other great workhorse of the Second World War had been the Douglas DC-3. The ubiquitous, all-purpose Dakota had sent out the clearest message of all – that the future lay with runways.

The level of damage sustained during the Blitz vindicated BOAC's decision to vacate Southampton. The four major raids on the city in the winter of 1940–1 focused upon the port and the central shopping area to the north and south of the medieval Bargate (respectively Above Bar and the High Street). Losing so many shops was critical in terms of future planning, as the Borough Council, lost one-third of its rates revenue. With income from harbour activities negligible, given the continued presence of the military, many councillors insisted on new retail outlets as a priority of reconstruction. Replacing the shops destroyed by the Luftwaffe would create jobs and restore rateable value, particularly Above Bar, where the damage was especially severe.[17] Debate over the future shape of the city centre focused upon whether to rebuild quickly along familiar lines or share the vision of the council's 1942 report, *The Replanning of Southampton*.[18] Generally speaking, the Ratepayers' Party – including Sidney Kimber – argued that shops be rebuilt along a familiar north-south axis, while Labour supported the case for a wholly fresh approach, with major retailers relocating within 'The Circus', a large pedestrian promenade adjacent to the Guildhall.[19]

H. T. Cook, Southampton's first planning officer, had co-authored the 1942 report with Stanley Adshead, a renowned architect, academic and planning guru. 'The Circus' and its complementary traffic-relief scheme were consistent with Adshead's enthusiasm for continental-style plazas. Most councillors gave a cautious welcome to what was a comprehensive and wide-ranging plan for Southampton and its hinterland, noting the authors' detailed proposals for increasing housing and leisure provision and for attracting fresh industry.[20] However, complaints from local traders secured a significant dilution of the original proposals. Above Bar and the High Street remained the principal shopping area once it became clear that after the war new industries would not be located locally: regional development would focus upon those areas most hard hit by the Depression, and so the town needed to protect its major employers. In any case, there was only modest public interest in reconstruction. Thus, although after 1945 Labour controlled the Council, 'The Circus' was quickly forgotten.[21]

The Replanning of Southampton endorsed previous warnings of an over-dependence upon a single source of employment: although 6,000 jobs had been lost between 1930 and 1938, over a third of the working population remained directly engaged in shipping and allied services.[22] The report urged better local amenities, not least because a revival of tourism would generate jobs. Attracted by the idea of reviving long dormant pretensions to be a fashionable spa and seaside resort, councillors saw an important role for flying boats in fostering an image of Southampton as chic, stylish and cosmopolitan. Encouraged by Cook and Adshead's emphasis on the centrality of air transport to post-war prosperity, the planning committee initiated a major consultative exercise in July 1943. Meanwhile, the Harbour Master, his clerk and chief engineer were busy drafting recommendations for a 'combined land and sea air base' to follow hot on the heels of final victory. On 23 September 1943, Sidney Kimber, chairing a specially appointed sub-committee, enthusiastically received the Harbour Board's ambitious proposals – the contrast with his negative approach to reconstruction of the town could not have been more striking.[23] Ironically, this was the one occasion that justified a strong dose of healthy scepticism. A brief glance at the 1942 report suggests enthusiasm for development of a major 'sea aerodrome' on Southampton Water, but closer reading reveals a firm belief that peacetime civil aviation, whether freight or passenger, would be land based: 'It would seem that one effect of the war has been to carry forward the experimental stage of long-distance flights over large expanses of sea and to have established the land 'planes in preference to sea 'planes for services on these routes'. If Southampton was to be a major passenger port and an 'International Air Base', then the aerodrome at Eastleigh should be the focal point for future investment. Southampton Water was an ideal location for flying boats precisely because, unlike Langstone Harbour, an efficient service could be maintained without 'the expenditure of a large sum of money on constructional works'. Focusing BOAC's post-war operation on Hythe would be the cheapest and safest option, negating any need for a specially designated channel along the eastern foreshore.[24]

Neither the Special Air Base Sub-Committee of the Harbour Board, nor that equally august body, the Chamber of Commerce's Post-War Civil Aviation Committee, seem to have heeded the experts' warning. Working in close harmony, the two committees preferred the advice of 'experienced trans-Atlantic air pilots', both of whom, not surprisingly, enthusiastically endorsed the draft 'scheme for a combined water and land base'. A far more cautious response came from the Air Ministry. When lobbied by local dignitaries, Secretary of State Sir Archibald Sinclair suggested that they would be better served making their case to the Director General of Civil Aviation. What is remarkable about the final report, published in mid-January 1944, is how little consultation had in fact been undertaken, given the project's self-declared national and imperial mission. There is a total absence of costings and revenue projections, and yet the accompanying map of the 'finest possible Combined Air Port for the South of England' is strikingly imaginative and inventive – big, bold and undeniably visionary.[25]

Over the next two years, the grand plan slipped down the priority list, not least because of the huge cost implications. However, in January 1946, the Harbour Board commissioned a follow-up report from A. Shaw Maclaren, a civil engineer previously employed by BOAC. The spur to action had been growing evidence that flying boats were no longer welcome in Poole Harbour. While revenue-conscious councillors were relaxed about the rising number of take-offs and landings, local yachtsmen were vocal in their opposition to any suggestion that BOAC's temporary base become permanent. Their annoyance was compounded by the emergency terminal being vacated in favour of one of Poole's largest yacht clubs. The airline's costs escalated as the new arrangement necessitated the maintenance of 12 embarkation launches, manned by around 60 crew members.[26] Furthermore, passengers were complaining about the greater distance by rail from Waterloo, as well as the rather basic customs and immigration facilities. Once BOAC initiated the transfer of its company headquarters to Hythe, it was assumed the whole operation would soon relocate to Southampton Water. Such speculation encouraged the Harbour Board to revisit its proposal for a 'permanent marine air base', hence the decision to recruit a suitably qualified consultant.[27]

BOAC managers arrived on the Waterside early in April 1946, and that same week Maclaren's revised scheme was submitted to the Harbour Board. The Ministry of Civil Aviation (MCA) requested immediate access to the report, although local politicians had no idea why Whitehall deemed the matter so urgent. However, all would soon be revealed. Other than a minor relocation eastwards, the blueprint appeared on the surface to be little different from the 1942 proposal. Wartime experience was drawn upon to dismiss shipping operatives' very real concern that heavy traffic would increase the likelihood of a major collision. Less convincing was Maclaren's attempt to counter the suggestion that four tidal movements a day made Southampton Water unusually exposed to adverse meteorological conditions: the suggestion that only four days a year would be lost to inclement weather was clearly an under-estimate. A major flaw in the plan was redesignation of the complementary land airport as available only for short-haul traffic. Heathrow had been formally opened on New Year's Day 1946. Mclaren rightly envisaged London's new airport as the future focal point for 'trans-continental and trans-oceanic services', but, in so doing, abandoned the original suggestion that Southampton's integrated operation would negate the need for any other international airport. Yet what was the point of establishing this far more modest operation when the proposed railway line would speedily convey new arrivals straight into the heart of London? Furthermore, the region already had an aerodrome with potential for development, at Eastleigh. However, what really sank Maclaren's modified proposal was its cost. He estimated that implementation of the full scheme would require a budget of at least 5.25 million pounds and that the first phase alone would necessitate an immediate outlay of around 3 million pounds.[28] This was in a year when BOAC and its two subsidiary airlines cost the Treasury no less than 10.2 million pounds.[29] The cash-stricken burghers of Southampton, bereft of the bigger picture, blithely assumed such a major project would be funded entirely by central government. Their belief that any final decision therefore lay with the most powerful department in Whitehall was absolutely correct. The mistake was in assuming that there would be real policy debate, rooted in genuine consultation. In reality, the Treasury vetoed the proposal from the outset.

III   The return of peace and the Whitehall view

On 30 May 1946, Lord Winster, Minister for Civil Aviation, invited Lord Pakenham to chair a four-man 'Flying Boat Committee'. Its remit was to take evidence and, inside a months, to identify a permanent home for BOAC's flying-boat operations. Only two weeks late, the final report identified Langstone Harbour as the most suitable site. Immediately, alarm bells rang in the Admiralty, with Andrew Cunningham, the First Sea Lord, insisting Attlee intervene. By the time the report was finally published, in May of the following year, a carefully drafted preface had been added. Pakenham's team acknowledged that it had focused too narrowly upon the needs of civil aviation, at the expense of the defence of the nation.[30] The report was a smokescreen, as the Treasury had already baulked at the MCA's estimates of the various options, noting that both Langstone and Southampton would each cost the Exchequer well over 4 million pounds. Not that Southampton was ever seriously in the frame, as the report made clear: stable, non-tidal conditions were second only to distance from London as a 'critical operational requirement'. This criterion was deemed so vital that Pakenham's committee identified only one alternative to Langstone, namely, an artificial lagoon off the north Kent coast near the village of Cliffe. Rejecting token Treasury advice to explore cheaper options in Essex and West Sussex, the MCA saw no harm in publicly investigating Cliffe's credentials, even if the Minister and his advisers privately conceded that they were merely going through the motions. The Treasury was happy to go along with what it assumed to be a paper exercise, all parties having agreed by the autumn of 1948 that the key question was not if and where a base was to be built, but when was the most opportune time to announce the project's final demise. Blissfully ignorant, and desperately clutching at straws, the *Echo* air reporter saw the arrival of geologists at Cliffe as a real opportunity for Southampton to restate its claim should the new front runner be found wanting.[31] Interestingly, in the light of recent proposals for a new airport on the same site, alluvial deposits on the Thames estuary proved unusually deep, thereby negating any possibility of land reclamation. While noting that the MCA could now offer tangible evidence as to why all three options examined by Pakenham's committee were impractical, the Treasury was furious to learn in January 1950 that payment of the geologists had not been sanctioned.[32] This highlighted a systemic lack of financial accountability, of which one of the clearest beneficiaries was the port of Southampton.

The Treasury had no direct, or even via the MCA, indirect control over spending on civil flying-boat operations. BOAC's budget was discrete, with rent and fees paid direct from the airline to Poole or Southampton Harbour Board, the Southern Railway Company, and any other landlords or service providers. Similarly, capital investment was sanctioned by the Board, without reference to the MCA. At first, the latter appeared quite relaxed about this arrangement, assuming that a generous subsidy was 'essential in the interests of Commonwealth communications'. However, Lord Addison, as chair of the cabinet sub-committee overseeing the Government's civil-aviation programme, increasingly bemoaned mounting costs, particularly with regard to procurement.[33] BOAC's unilateral decision to spend 139,000 pounds on a new terminal at Berth 50, and to construct a control tower and administrative annexe at Netley, was hotly contested inside the Treasury. The decision to cease flying out of Poole was announced in late October 1946, yet as late as July 1947, Whitehall accountants were complaining that they had been kept in the dark over planned expenditure. The complaints focused upon process rather than outcome, as the planned investment was necessary given that so far as the Treasury was concerned, the 'permanent marine air base' would never be built. Thus, in reality, BOAC would be based at Southampton Water for as long as it maintained a flying-boat alternative to the new intercontinental services coming on stream at Heathrow. The 1945 order for a large fleet of Solents had, of course, encouraged an optimistic view – and necessitated further capital investment, with plans to nearly double the size of the maintenance facilities at Hythe.[34] In common with so many building projects immediately after the war, a shortage of labour and materials delayed the refurbishment and expansion of Berth 50. Although the terminal's lounges and waiting rooms were ready, the restaurant was far from complete when the inaugural flight landed on 31 March 1948. Appropriately, the first passenger to disembark was a junior minister at the Colonial Office, Lord Listowel. His arrival allowed the local paper to trumpet the flying boat's 'peculiarly British character, and its obvious suitability for maintaining vital Empire communications'. Here was the last truly romantic way to travel, and what better location than Southampton Water from which to set out on a globe-trotting journey of adventure and discovery?[35]

A fortnight later, Winster's successor as Minister of Civil Aviation, Lord Nathan of Churt, officially opened Berth 50. Amid great civic celebration, the Mayoress christened the latest Solent *Southampton*, pouring 'Empire wine' from an antique silver ewer over the aircraft's hull.[36] In his speech, Nathan was suitably complimentary, massaging the municipal ego and reassuring those present that BOAC was at Southampton for the duration. The real question, however, was how long was the duration, particularly when the Minister himself was asking whether 'passengers would choose the more speedy land planes or the more roomy flying boats'. He also highlighted the very real problem imperial planners faced in finding appropriate locations for 'marine airports' capable of accommodating the next generation of flying boats. The MCA was increasingly thwarted by geography and by the changing face of the Commonwealth. Thus, not only did the Indian sub-continent have no more than three sites suitable for development, but its newly independent nations expressed scant interest in retaining, let alone expanding, a post-colonial flying-boat service. By 1950, BOAC was asking central government to cover the cost of vacating Karachi and Calcutta. Ironically, the airline also appealed to the MCA and the Treasury to take over the leasehold of Berth 50 as part of a phased withdrawal from the Eastern Docks. Lord Nathan's speech had been unusually prescient, but why?[37]

IV   The port and the *Princess*: the end of a dream, 1949–52

The simplest answer was that, even before the first generation of post-war airliners entered service, passengers were increasingly prepared to sacrifice comfort for speed. A month after Nathan delivered his mixed message, the first Solent-class flight to South Africa taxied down Southampton Water, arriving in Vaaldam, near Johannesburg, five days later. The equivalent journey using land-based aircraft, while far less enjoyable, would have arrived in Johannesburg two days earlier and cost significantly less.[38] In Australia, TEA had ceased joint operations with BOAC by 1948 because a shift in demand dictated that it focus solely upon land-based operations. Without its Australian partner to share terminal costs, BOAC's losses became prohibitive, hence the switch to long-haul Lockheed Constellations in May 1949. The adoption of American aircraft marked a triumph for the MCA and BOAC, which throughout the late 1940s fought a bitter battle with the Ministry of Supply to secure the cheapest, most modern and most readily available long-haul aircraft. The airline's partial success in challenging the Government's 'Fly British' policy was to have major implications for both land-and sea-based services. The spring of 1948 marked the peak of BOAC's flying-boat operations, with a total of 16 flights in and out of Southampton each week. However, retrenchment was rapid. By the summer of 1949, the only surviving services were to eastern and southern Africa, and BOAC had switched from buying Solents to trying to sell them.[39]

Like his advisers inside the MCA, Nathan was deeply sceptical about the continued viability of Labour's 'Fly British' policy. Within the Civil Aviation Committee, he questioned the Ministry of Supply's enthusiasm for the Saunders-Roe SR45. This 140-ton super seaplane, like another giant, the Bristol Brabazon, never progressed beyond the prototype stage. Both projects were the result of the Brabazon Committee's insistence on a wholly British fleet of ostensibly state-of-the-art civil airliners, each dedicated to a particular task. The committee's recommendation was adopted by the War Cabinet and consistent with the post-war Government's vision of 'socialised' airlines flying the flag for British aeronautics. Like the Brabazon, the SR45 *Princess* boasted cutting-edge technology, and, in the latter case, this was certainly true. The avionics were pioneering, the dual pressurised cabin decks were unique, and the ten turbo-jet engines generating 35,000 horsepower were a genuinely awesome means of conveying over 100 passengers across the Atlantic or the Pacific.[40] Yet the SR45 was obsolete long before its initial test flight in the summer of 1952. The *Princess*'s two sister aircraft never took to the air but were cocooned at RAF Calshot pending a more powerful version of the Bristol Proteus engine – by the late 1960s, all three aircraft had been despatched to the breakers. The problem was that the SR45 was too big, too expensive and too late. In March 1948, only a month before his visit to Southampton, Lord Nathan recommended that the project be cancelled, pointing out that its projected cost had nearly doubled from an initial estimate of 2.8 million pounds.[41] This was commercial folly, and, anyway, no facilities currently existed to accommodate the three SR45s should they ever become operable. The latter was the main reason why the MCA dragged its feet over announcing that plans had been dropped for a 'permanent marine airport' – so long as there was a slim possibility that the SR45 would enter service then where they could be properly housed remained an issue.[42] In June 1948 the Civil Aviation Committee modified but by no means abandoned its 'Fly British' policy, thereby offering the SR45 a stay of execution. Desperate to find a role for the aircraft in the face of BOAC's accelerating transition to solely land-based operations, the MCA persuaded partner airline British South American Airways (BSAA) to take over the project. For the *Southern Daily Echo*, this was front-page news, confirming Southampton's future status as 'Britain's permanent marine airport', paired with such exotic locations as Montevideo and Buenos Aires. Yet by 1950, BSAA had succumbed to commercial reality, and technically the SR45 was back in the hands of BOAC. The budget was spiralling out of control, and yet, remarkably, the decision to cancel was deferred pending an evaluation of the SR45's military value.[43]

Unlike Howard Hughes's giant seaplane, the Spruce Goose, the *Princess* flew for over 90 hours between August 1952 and its final grounding in 1954. It was a familiar, and at the same time awe-inspiring, sight over the Solent. Long before it first took to the air, Southampton had become particularly proprietorial about the SR45. Built at Cowes on the Isle of Wight, the aircraft was deemed local, particularly as Saunders-Roe looked to the home of Vosper and Supermarine for a regular supply of skilled designers, fitters and engineers. The *Princess* was, in its way, a fantastic technological achievement, which looked splendid as an *Eagle* cut-away drawing or a BOAC Speedbird calendar. It was a unique fusion of the old and the new, imperial splendour and 'new, post-austerity, manufacturing England'. Unashamedly modern, it embodied the extent to which, 'Aircraft were at the very heart of the national technological effort of the post-war years'.[44] Like the Comet or the Mach 1 Fairey Delta, the SR45 confirmed the virtuosity and adaptability of Britain's best designers and development teams – the men and women who built and tested the Spitfire, Mosquito, Typhoon and Lancaster (but *not* the Defiant or the Firefly). The *Princess*'s problem was that its production run was too short, and its manufacturer too small, to secure any economies of scale. It was beautiful, but in an era of Heathrow and La Guardia, it was a white elephant. The most obvious comparison is with the DH89 Comet, the world's first jet airliner, which – to its ultimate cost – flew within three years of De Havilland accepting the Government's challenge to beat the Americans at their own game. The Comet took to the skies in August 1949. The SR45's inaugural flight was not for another four years. By that time, the Comet had already entered service, symbolising BOAC's determination to establish itself as one of the world's premier airlines. Nemesis was only two years away, but nobody foresaw the problems with metal fatigue which would lead to the aircraft being grounded from 1954 to 1958. Indeed, it was evidence of the Comet's potential as a competitive transatlantic carrier that, in 1950, sealed the fate of both the Brabazon and the SR45.[45]

The demise of the SR45 signalled the demise of Southampton as a marine airport. On 12 December 1949, BOAC announced that Berth 50 and the Hythe maintenance base would close within 12 months, with a total loss of around 1,100 jobs. Even in an era of full employment, this was a major blow to the local community. The airline insisted that alternative work would be available for anyone willing to travel, but, in practice, few employees took up this offer. Closure came as an inevitable consequence of BOAC's decision to provide a solely land-based service to Africa. There was no longer any serious pressure from the Government to maintain the loss-making operation in Southampton: the MCA had no fundamental objection; the Treasury felt the decision was long overdue; and the Ministry of Supply was happy to acquiesce once BOAC reluctantly agreed to fly the untried Handley Page Hermes down to Africa, the quid pro quo being Boeing Stratocruisers on its Atlantic routes.[46] In the spring of 1950, the airline's reorganisation raised the faint prospect of a limited operation running out of Hythe. Hopes were swiftly dashed, and, on 3 November, the *Somerset* set off on the final run to South Africa. Eleven days later, the returning Solent appeared over Southampton Water trailing a 20-foot laying-off pennant. The golden age of the flying boat was all but over. Throughout the 1950s, Aquila Airways, a tiny airline born out of the Berlin Blockade, flew affluent holiday-makers down to the Mediterranean. However, the arrival of charter airlines killed off this seat-of-the-pants, swashbuckling enterprise that mimicked but scarcely matched the extravagance of Imperial Airways a generation earlier.[47]

In 1946, the aerodrome at Eastleigh had been dismissed as only a minor player in the grand scheme of regional development. Yet from the late 1950s, tour operators across Britain encouraged the development of underused municipal airfields. The construction of the M27, and the establishment of a purpose-built stopping station on the express service between London and the south coast, signalled Eastleigh's potential as a major regional airport. Package holidays and short-haul scheduled services justified significant capital investment, but it was the arrival of low-price airlines in the mid-1990s which would transform 'Southampton International' into a major capital asset. At the start of the 21st century, scarcely anyone in Southampton could recall post-war plans for a sea aerodrome, and yet every seasoned traveller knew that easy access to Europe was just a ten-minute drive from the city centre.

Conclusion

Dreams of an imperial airways did not die with the demise of the seaplane on the Solent. Twenty years later, and what the flying boat was to the Empire, the Comet was to the Commonwealth. Aspiring fathers of the nation or idealistic aid workers could sit alongside high commissioners and Rhodes scholars, all travelling in relative comfort and at subsonic speed between Heathrow or Gatwick and an ever-lengthening list of ex-dominions and former colonies. Now, of course, British aircraft had to be welcomed into the airports of Nairobi, New Delhi and Nicosia. No longer the imposed timetable, laid down in oak-panelled offices at Croydon or Victoria by retired air commodores oblivious to local needs and sensitivities. Scarlet-splashed route maps were revisited solely to refresh fading memories of colonial cool and mock-Hollywood glamour – a world where the cocktail bar had never deviated from GMT, the 78s had invariably been Noël Coward, and the library had always snubbed the tyro Greene in favour of Somerset Maugham. Once that world had gone, so too had Southampton's aspirations to build a unique imperial portal. The notion of a genuinely integrated land and sea operation was, in one way, brilliant and in another barmy. Such an ambitious prestige project might just have been defensible before the war, but by the mid-1940s it failed every criteria, not least when it came to need and to cost. Ironically, the other grand initiative to emerge from Southampton's blueprint for reconstruction, 'The Circus', did make sense in terms of commercial viability, better facilities and a genuinely pleasing urban landscape. In this respect, Sir Sidney Kimber's flawed judgement, and his manifest failure to back the best course of action, contrast starkly with his leadership and drive a decade earlier. What is astonishing is that so many key players within the Harbour Board and the Borough Council were willing to suppress their natural scepticism and help prolong the fantasy. But then, flights of fantasy are an essential part of the flying-boat mystique – travellers invariably speculated on the exotic nature of their ultimate destination, while even the most jaded crew could believe that east of Suez there still lay adventure and romance. In which case, what was to stop terminal staff imagining themselves guarantors of a seamless transition from the grey, grim reality of the present to the bright future beyond the blue horizon? The Southampton sea aerodrome was truly fantastical, wholly at odds with the harsh reality and prevailing mood of austerity Britain, and yet it is that striking combination of municipal vision and global mission which renders it so attractive to any latter-day student of civic enterprise.

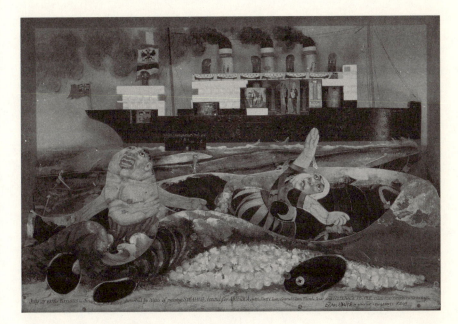

Figure 11 Sam Smith (1908–83), *Bathers in Southampton Water*, 1979 (mixed media). Copyright Southampton City Art Gallery, Hampshire/The Bridgeman Art Library.

Chapter 12: Not that far?

Remembering and forgetting cosmopolitan Southampton in the 20th century

Tony Kushner

Introduction

There is no public space that acknowledges Southampton's integral role as a vital hub in the neglected global story of transmigrancy in the 19th and 20th centuries. Aside from immigrants ranging from Italians at the turn of the 20th century through to Poles and Russians 100 years later, and taking in Caribbean and Asians in between, as well as a range of refugees across the 20th century, Southampton by 1914 was beginning to rival Liverpool as Britain's leading transmigrant port, largely catering for East European Jewry. In less than a five-month period in 1905, for example, 37,285 transmigrants were inspected by the American consular officials in Southampton, of whom half were Russians.[1]

Jonathan Boyarin has argued that it is 'only by having an inkling of at least the *possible* scope of memory that we can sense the "quantity" of forgetting'. The process of forgetting, adds Boyarin, is as complex as that of remembering, and its intensity is often 'localized'.[2] This chapter examines the port of Southampton as a whole and the cultural and ideological factors behind its amnesia of transmigrancy. It will do so particularly through the memory work associated with the world's most famous ship, the *Titanic*, and its most beloved aeroplane, the Spitfire. Both have intimate connections to Southampton, the former being explored elsewhere in this volume. Here, however, the focus will be on the hidden diasporic narratives within these 20th-century British icons.

On the surface, the invisibility of the past reality of migrancy and transmigrancy sits uneasily with contemporary descriptions of Southampton as 'cosmopolitan'. This has been manifest particularly in recent property development, for example, in 'Admiral's Quay', which 'perfectly combines a sailing atmosphere with all the convenience of cosmopolitan living'.[3] In fact, the cosmopolitan tag that is now routinely attached to Southampton in its tourist and commercial literature is both present-centred and superficial. In essence, when clarified, the reference point is the 'world of cuisine including Italian, Thai, Cajun and Indian [restaurants]'.[4] It neither refers to the past, nor to the actual diversity of Southampton's population and certainly not to the inner-city districts where non-white ethnic minorities are concentrated.

A visitor to Southampton in the early 20th century commented how '[i]n the streets near the docks a rare medley of peoples, races, and languages are to be met with. Lascars, Norwegians, Japanese and many others jostle one another, and pass unnoticed – too familiar a sight here to excite remark'.[5] Yet such past diversity has escaped many in the local official heritage world, as exposed in 2001 through a major national web-based exhibition and resource, 'PortCities'. Funded by the New Opportunities Fund, the aim of 'PortCities' was for the visitor to the site to 'explore the diverse history and culture of PortCities UK'. One of five chosen cities, the Southampton section of PortCities promises 'a rich online experience' through what is described as the 'Gateway to the World'. The visitor is encouraged to 'discover the people and port of Southampton', but they will find no references to Jews, and just six items out of the many thousands on the site relate to 'immigrants'.[6]

The denial of historic diversity in Southampton, or rather, the absence of reference to it, has been accompanied by an official version of its past and present as free of racism and prejudice. A guide published in 1979 by Southampton City Council referred to its 'tradition of tolerance'. It added that '[g]ood relations exist between the members of different faiths in Southampton, as befits a port with so many international contacts and a history of religious understanding and tolerance'.[7] Similarly, in 1921, the then Chief Rabbi of Britain and the British Empire, Joseph Hertz, was welcomed back 'home' after arriving in Southampton following a world tour. At the port, he was told by a local dignitary that '[t]hey in Southampton were proud of their Jewish citizens and the finest relations existed between the various religions [in the town]'.[8]

Tolerance, however, does not necessarily imply acceptance of diversity, and less than a year earlier Hertz's arrival, the town had taken Edwin Lutyens' 'neutral' design for its war memorial, a prototype of the cenotaph in Whitehall, and had imposed a 'great cross' on its front, thereby excluding the local Jewish war dead from inscription alongside their Christian counterparts.[9] 'Our Glorious Dead', inscribed on the Southampton cenotaph, does not therefore include its Jewish citizens who lost their lives in the First World War. There was a bitter irony in this exclusion, as the local Jewish community had contributed generously to the subscription funds for the Southampton cenotaph and had been assured that they would be represented within it. Moreover, it had suffered greatly, as a small community, through its war losses, which not only were, proportionally, over double those of the locality as a whole but also represented roughly one in ten of the adult male Southampton Jewish community.[10] Instead, local Jews who died in the conflict would be 'relegated' in memory to the private sphere through plaques in the local synagogue.[11] Only one Jew, Frederick Charles Emanuel, a member of a long-established and prosperous family, is included on the Southampton Cenotaph. Bill Williams has written how the Jews of late Victorian Manchester 'were validated not on the grounds of their Jewish identity, but on the basis of their conformity to the values and manners of bourgeois English society'. He adds that such conditional acceptance remains 'the quintessential means by which British society accommodates ethnic minorities'.[12] Similarly, in Southampton, for the family of Frederick Emanuel, the cost of recognition was being memorialised in an explicitly Christian monument.

Emanuel, a member of the Royal Army Medical Corps, died in 1917, aged 41, at the Royal Victoria Hospital in Netley 'whilst in the service of his country'. The memory of this remarkable hospital on Southampton Water has been wonderfully evoked and analysed by Philip Hoare in *Spike Island* (2001), and in his contribution to this book. Hoare's book has rightly been praised for its 'unique sense of time and place, and a great depth of vision',[13] and it is notable for its multilayered brilliance in connecting the local to the national and the global. Even so, his astonishing memory work does not fully encapsulate the full cosmopolitanism of the Royal Victoria Hospital. There is reference, for example, to E. Mbenyesi, of the South African Native Labour Corps, who is buried in its graveyard,[14] but none to the Indian soldiers and the funeral pyres that would have taken place.[15] Nor does *Spike Island* consider how the exclusion of Emanuel from the Christian cemetery at the hospital led to his burial in Southampton's Jewish cemetery. Emanuel was the grandson of the first Jewish mayor of Southampton. His father, a pawnbroker in the town, had also become Mayor, and the family as a whole had played key roles in the organised Jewish community for close to a century. Where is the place, if not in such a rich and sensitive account of local memory as Hoare's, for the story of those immigrants and minorities that lived in or passed through Southampton? Memory, suggests Boyarin, is much more demanding than forgetting and 'may perhaps be served only at the cost of diminished ambitions'.[16] By exploring particular places and their meanings within Southampton, such costs, in the form of exclusion, will form the substance of this chapter.

I   Ocean Village

'[T]he fascination of watching the ships and the sea is always present on our waterfronts; it is an integral part of the life of Southampton'.[17] Elsie Sandell, talented local historian and populariser of Southampton's past, was in no doubt that the 'watchers of the tideway' were a constant feature of the town from Roman times onwards. Equally, she was aware that the function and nature of such 'watching' had changed markedly over the ages, encompassing the Saxon ' "look-out" for the advent of possible foes' through to the Victorian observatory used to check the movement of commercial ships in the burgeoning port.[18] Nevertheless, writing in 1953, she surely would have been surprised by the new meanings and memory work associated with its historic dockland waterfront half a century later.

The summer 2004 launch edition of the Hampshire magazine, *Aspire*, featured an article on the new housing project in the old dock area, renamed 'Ocean Village' in an earlier redevelopment. In attacking the further development of luxury apartments on the site, *Aspire's* leading writer overflowed with nostalgia for 'Ocean Village':

> Since my first visit to Southampton about seven years ago, there is one image that has always stuck with me; sitting on the waterfront in the glorious sunshine at Ocean Village, a cool Pimms in hand watching the world go by. It was one of the main factors that influenced my decision to move here. Not only did Southampton offer all the modern amenities you would expect from an up and coming city, but also a wonderful seafront haven where you could be transported away from the hustle and bustle of urban life. With one of the world's great maritime playgrounds spread before you, it seemed a gateway to another, more appealing, way of life.[19]

Building work on Ocean Village began in the mid-1980s and was one of a series of redevelopments of rundown dockland areas in Britain's leading ports – part of a wider global trend in waterfront transformation. The surplus land, formerly the Princess Alexandra Dock (the original Outer Dock), consisting of 75 acres, was sold by Associated British Ports, to be transformed into shops, offices, leisure facilities and marina. In relation to public access, the hope of Southampton City Council's Planning Committee was that '[v]iews to and across the harbour will be planned so that the water will again be visible from Canute Road as it was at the inception of the docks in the 1840s'.[20] Canute Road, named in honour, as the local heritage industry would have it, of the place where, in 1028, the King tried to turn back the tide,[21] was dominated throughout much of the 19th and 20th centuries by a 'rich diversity of buildings' – seamen's missions, shipping companies and foreign consuls.[22] Melding references to heritage, consumerism, Englishness and commerce, the main shopping area of 'Ocean Village' was named 'Canute's Pavilion'.

Unfortunately, the planned Maritime Museum in the former cross-channel passenger ferry never materialised, and a sense of historical place in the new development was manifest only through small display boards in Canute's Pavilion. Here, the emphasis was on the story of the *Titanic* and the Spitfire, with passing references to the development of the docks. By the late 1990s, most of the shops in Canute's Pavilion had closed. In 2002, it was commented that parts of Ocean Village looked 'dowdy and run down compared with other waterfront developments throughout the world'.[23] The following year, work began in demolishing Canute's Pavilion to make way for further luxury apartments, with, as we will see, their own sense of history.

But back to the vision of *Aspire*: Ocean Village has already developed its own mythology with resultant confusion of time and place. Roger Harvey, a man who had 'lived in the city for over 40 years' recalled how he 'loved going down to Ocean Village when I was young [. . .] it was like an insight into how the other half (the upper class) lived. Watching the yachts sail to and fro on the Solent was like a portal into another world'.[24] Southampton, it should be remembered, throughout the 20th century and into the 21st was, and is, one of the world's busiest commercial ports. The idea of Southampton being a Pimms-fuelled 'gateway to another, more appealing, way of life' is a remarkable image and one, returning to Sandell, which was a world away from that of the immediate post-war years. More typical was the powerful narrative of the town's history provided by Bernard Knowles, the Secretary of its Chamber of Commerce, in his *Southampton: The English Gateway* (1951).

Commissioned locally, it contained a foreword by the popular historian, Arthur Bryant, reinventing himself after 1945 as the great British patriot and conveniently forgetting his close involvement with the anti-Semitic, pro-Nazi extremist peace movement in Britain during the 1930s and early years of the Second World War.[25] Bryant stressed how Knowles's main theme was the story of the town's

endurance, resilience and splendid fortitude in the great war against Nazi Germany and the Fascist Axis. In doing so, in his detailed record of the men and women of Southampton during the agonized months of the Blitz and the long, strenuous, dogged years of preparation for the liberation of Europe, he has added something to the history of England.[26]

The emphasis in the book was how Southampton's geographical location made it 'destined to play a key part in the military history of England'. Trade also had its place in Knowles's account, but it was largely subsumed in favour of the military invasions, inward and outward, which had been channelled through the port of Southampton. Rather than the town and its port acting as a focal point for emigration and immigration, of world trade connections and a hub of empire, Knowles's lyrical prose highlighted Southampton as a crucial dam helping to preserve 'an island fortress'. Knowles's Southampton was inward looking and victorious: 'Whatever else had vanished amid the holocaust of war, the English vision – the breath of England's being – had survived'.[27]

Yet, however disparate are Knowles's post-war insular version of Southampton's past and *Aspire*'s 'yuppie' vision of its port as a post-industrial, post-commercial playground, they have, in common, a failure to confront one of the city's inherent characteristics throughout the ages: its cosmopolitanism. Sometimes that cosmopolitanism has been blatant, attracting contemporary comment, positive and negative. More frequently, it has been unacknowledged, reflecting several recurring and powerful themes. First, it reflects an unwillingness to accept the reality of Southampton's diversity – a local variation on a national lacuna. Visiting the Ellis Island Immigration Museum in New York in the early 1990s, Rob Perks pondered whether '8,000 pounds could be raised in Britain for a museum about immigration, let alone the 80 million pounds raised for Ellis Island'. The failure to raise even modest funding of such a project, the Heritage Centre, in Spitalfields, East London, over a decade later, has proved that Perks, a major oral historian of the immigrant and refugee experience in Britain, was proved right.[28] The Caribbean writer and literary critic, Michael Gilkes, makes a telling cross-Atlantic comparison: 'John F. Kennedy spoke proudly of the United States as "a nation of immigrants". To say that today about Britain might give offence'. The failure to acknowledge a tradition of immigration is, however, particularly telling in a port such as Southampton which has seen so many inflows and outflows of population.[29] Second, the denial of cosmopolitanism has been a feature of Southampton's (again denied) role as gatekeeper, and the confinement and subsequent invisibility of its 'foreign' population. Both these tendencies of denial and concealment are apparent in the amnesia surrounding the transmigrant presence in the town from the late 19th century through to the inter-war period.

II   *Titanic* years

In the years before the First World War, Southampton emerged as a rival to Liverpool in the lucrative and fast-expanding trade in transmigrancy.[30] Many of these transmigrants, largely Jews from eastern Europe, were sent to the town in sealed train carriages and then temporarily housed in hostels near the docks.[31] From there, after a matter of days or weeks, they recommenced their journeys to North and South America, South Africa and other parts of the globe. A stone's throw from Ocean Village is the site of the former Atlantic Hotel, which, in spite of its promising appellation, was close to being a doss-house for the transmigrants. Opened in 1893 as the 'Emigrants' Home' (and later renamed), its creation and building involved close cooperation between the American consul in Southampton, the major shipping companies and the port health authorities. It reflected their shared fear that transmigrants would 'float' round the town and, especially, the concern of the spreading of infectious diseases, particularly cholera after the Continental epidemic in the early 1890s.[32]

To an extent isolated from the rest of the port, few in the town would have had everyday contact with Atlantic Hotel. An exception was Albert Gibbs, who was at school with two sons of the owners of the enterprise, the Dolings. His testimony, recorded in the 1980s, provides an evocative portrait of Atlantic Hotel. It highlights the 'otherness' and confusion caused to a young boy confronting the surrounds of Atlantic Hotel and its residents, still resonating three quarters of a century later as he constructed his life story:

> Now the Immigrants' Home was a home that used to accommodate the people that were coming from Middle Europe as immigrants to go to a new life in America. Accommodation was very poor, they used to go to sleep on concrete floors with just the coats they came in. They always looked grubby and poor and normally the men had huge beards, I think there was a very big proportion of Jews among them, because they were mostly the people that were exported from Europe, even in those days ... [T]hey were sleeping in the basement usually and I used to go down below with the Doling brothers and stand looking at them and [...] of course [...] as a boy I didn't know what to think about it.[33]

What is significant about this testimony is its subsequent primary utilisation *not* to highlight the importance of transmigrancy in the economy of late Victorian and Edwardian Southampton but to add to the memory store of the hegemonic *Titanic*. Mrs Doling was on board the *Titanic*, and survived, yet her journey was not for pleasure but to develop her family's transatlantic transmigrancy business further.[34] Similarly, in Manchester, Kovno-born Jacob Farber had established a successful travel business in 1887 with agents in Liverpool, Manchester and Southampton providing access to the major transatlantic liners such as the *Mauretania* and the *Lusitania*. As part of this enterprise, the agency sold tickets on the *Titanic*'s maiden voyage to eastern European Jews who had first settled in Britain and were now hoping to try their luck in America.[35] Included in this category was a relative of the author, Joseph Abraham Hyman, one of the fortunate few of those travelling steerage who survived. He returned to Manchester and set up a still-flourishing Jewish delicatessen and catering business, named (in perverse gratitude as well as recognition of the moniker given to him by the local press) 'Titanics'. It is significant, however, that there is no place for this family story in Southampton's existing heritage and history world. Instead, it has been told through the testimony of Joseph Hyman's great-grandson, Richard, proprietor of a delicatessen in Cheetham Hill, Manchester – one that still bears the ship's name. Richard's family history features amongst a bank of video testimony that greets the visitor at the start of Manchester's controversial museum of urban living, 'Urbis'. Alongside it are the brief life stories of a gay couple who have settled in the city, a young Afghan refugee whose family live in its Moss Side district and the trials and tribulations of a Manchester tattoo artist. For all its limitations, 'Urbis', using Manchester as its major template, at least has relished and emphasised the plurality of voices and diversity, as well as the shock of arrival and importance of migration and immigration, that make up the modern city experience.[36]

In contrast, returning to the Atlantic Hotel and Southampton, those developing the site as 'luxury' accommodation and renaming it 'Atlantic Mansions' (after the First World War it became offices before falling into dereliction in the 1990s) have highlighted the *Titanic* connection. The letting agency responsible for its apartments have been eager to point out that Atlantic Hotel had been used by second-class passengers prior to departure on the *Titanic*. The grim description offered by Albert Gibbs presumably has no place in selling 21 units which would '[i]deally suit [a] professional person or couple', whereas the (contrived) association with a ship now associated with the glamour and romance of James Cameron's film stars, Leonardo DiCaprio and Kate Winslet, certainly has.[37] It is sad but revealing that one of the rare public acknowledgements of Southampton's role in transmigrancy, the foundation stone for the 'Emigrants' Home' unveiled in November 1893 by Mrs Eliot Yorke (a member of the Rothschild family), is now totally hidden from view by industrial-size rubbish bins, fenced in to further reduce access and visibility. The imaginative journey from a re-remembered Atlantic Hotel, catering for *Titanic* passengers, to the upmarket Atlantic Mansions is not long. That from the grim Emigrants' Home to city-living professionals is figuratively huge. Physically, from the Emigrants' Home to Atlantic Mansions is 'not that far'. Indeed, it is no distance at all. But surely the task of those working towards inclusiveness and equality, whether through a position of cultural authority – historians, writers, educators, curators, politicians, journalists and so on – or as ordinary citizens, is to make such connections between people and places, and past and present? As Jonathan Boyarin writes,

> [t]he fact that conventional delimitations of space entail collective representations implies a measure of identification among those who live within or whose ancestors have within a given space. The degree to which this identification fails to ground active empathy is [a] litmus test for the presence of forgetting.[38]

In the local Southampton heritage industry, through the contribution of its oral history unit, the transmigrant function of Atlantic Hotel has not been totally obliterated, and connections have been made. Whilst it is true that Albert Gibbs's testimony has been instrumentalised primarily in relation to the *Titanic*, it has, nevertheless, been given prominence, helping to emphasise that '[m]any of the third class passengers were emigrants bound for Ellis Island in the United States' and Southampton's 'link with this trade'.[39] Elsewhere, another fragment of surviving memory connected to the building has appeared in a series of local publications – a postcard of the Atlantic Hotel sent by a man to his mother in London the day after the First World War started. It was presumably on the eve of his (intended) departure. John Doling had these postcards made for publicity and advertising, attempting to establish his business as truly international. Teasing out the significance of the subsequent labelling of this much-reproduced postcard is itself revealing. Who the emigrants utilising Atlantic Hotel were is never referred to. The reproduction of the message on the back of the postcard – '[t]his is a photo of where we are living. I have 3 suits, 15 ties, 2 dozen collars, 3 hats, 1 pair of boots, 5 shirts and sundry other articles – and don't forget the bicycle . . . Complete we are!' – suggests British rather than foreign composition. This wonderfully ordinary and 'English' list has been juxtaposed with comments on the adjoining property, that of Eli Loftus, who, from 1902, traded there as a money-changer and outfitter. References are made to this shop's 'polyglot notices' and how '[i]t is interesting that the sign-writing [. . .] is in a language other than English'.[40] The 'exotic' nature of Loftus's shop places it 'other' to the Southampton experience. In fact, its proprietor, Eli Loftus, was a long-standing member of the town's Jewish community, and his pre-war business an indication of how important transmigrancy was to the local economy.[41]

Returning to the *Titanic*, memory of the ship has been strongly contested, becoming an academic growth industry.[42] For example, at a local level, the huge loss of life of the Southampton-based crew has been highlighted against the fate of the rich and famous who have captured the wider imagination relating to those on the ship – it has been estimated that of the 900 crew members, 699 were from Southampton and only 170 survived.[43] Nevertheless, the place of transmigrants on board, who, alongside the crew, suffered the highest death rate, has been marginalised, as has, until recently, that of the Southampton connection. Steven Biel's *Down with the Old Canoe: A Cultural History of the Titanic Disaster* (1996), the leading study, makes no mention of the town whatsoever. Biel's statement that '[n]o matter how many books I read, I can't keep track of who was where when' explains his unfortunate oversight.[44] The positive critical reception of this book, in spite of, or perhaps even because of this local lacuna is indicative of the failings of cultural history when it dwells on the history of representation and shows no interest in or knowledge of the history of the event itself. Nevertheless, Biel is aware of the racialisation of the disaster both at the time and subsequently. He highlights how the bravery of the 'Anglo-Saxon' first-class passengers, obeying the moral code of 'women and children first' was contrasted in contemporary reporting and later representation to the stories of panic and selfishness attributed to the racially inferior types travelling steerage.[45] The alleged last command of Captain Smith, '[b]e British!',[46] soon used as the lyrics of a charity record sold locally for widows and orphans of the crew,[47] fitted comfortably into such race discourse.

To his credit, Biel has examined the American, Finnish, Czech, Irish, Italian and Jewish newspapers and does not ignore the impact of the disaster on immigrant and minority communities. By reproducing headlines such as 'Finnish Passengers on the "Titanic"'; 'Irish Victims on the Titanic', and 'Many Jews were Passengers on Ill-Fated S.S. Titanic', Biel recognises that the 'ethnic press constituted its readers as communities of mourning and gave identity and dignity to the nameless "foreigners" in the conventional narrative'.[48] Yet not going further and failing, as have other cultural-studies interpretations of the *Titanic*, to recover and analyse the memories and life stories of those transmigrants travelling steerage on the ship, is to continue their unsavoury image and discriminatory treatment in 1912. The *Titanic* memory and heritage industry, whether focusing on specific British places, such as Southampton or Belfast, has forgotten or marginalised those immigrants travelling steerage. When the focus has been international, the attention has been on the rich and famous, and those travelling steerage are only signicant as being represented as 'other' to the first-class passengers, rather than as individuals with lives of equal worth and interest.

The power of exclusive narratives, both then and now, and the subsequent effort required to humanise those in the lower decks is neatly illustrated through the career of Southampton-born artist, Sam Smith. Smith was born in 1908, and it has been suggested that '[c]hildhood experiences of the City were to have a lasting influence on his work', especially 'watching liners and their impressive funnels drawing in and out of the docks':

> Ours was a seaport town. Funnels of great ships dominated the town; and the first drawings I remember attempting were of liners, with rows of wavy decks [...] I was a bit of a funnel snob – believing that the bigger they were and the more of them, the greater the distinction that must fall, by some means of associated magic, on those who sailed with them. I loved looking at boats, and picked up all manner of clichés about them. Terms like 'Atlantic Greyhound', 'Blue Riband' and 'Britannia's Bulwark' were with me before I ever got onto 'God Save the King'. The sight of Cunarders and their sisters filled me with pride, which must have spawned from the rather heady patriotism rampant at the time.[49]

The young Smith, however, was also alienated from confronting, at a distance, such evidence of wealth. He remembers feeling that 'such beauties were above my station'. In a work entitled *Bathers in Southampton Water* (1979), Smith revisited his earlier understanding of the liners making linkages that had earlier eluded him.[50] The work is labelled 'July 27 1908 [the birth date of the artist]: BATHERS in Southampton Water disturbed by Wash of passing STEAMER, bound for AMERICA, with First Class, Second Class, Third Class and STEERAGE PEOPLE'. In his notes on the work, Smith wrote that '[t]he interior of the liner illustrates the class-system afloat, where money bought space, unlimited helpings and better-sprung bunks. Down in the steerage are the real people'. Two years earlier, Smith had drawn a set of sketches, 'Immigrant Studies', reflecting his desire to make visible and humanise those located in the depths of the liners. These studies were, in part, inspired by Smith's increasing interest in and recognition in the USA and, in particular, by visits to Ellis Island. On the top decks of *Bathers in Southampton Water*, colourful couples in first class are shown dancing and dining in luxury. Just below the waterline and just visible in their darkened and overcrowded hold are those travelling steerage, drawn largely in shadow. Smith labels them with Emma Lazarus's words from the Statue of Liberty as the 'huddled masses yearning to breathe free'. In his sensitivity to the reality of the immigrant experience, it is perhaps not surprising that Sam Smith 'obtained a substantial and dedicated following in America but recognition in his own country came more slowly'. Smith said of his own work that it was 'about situations between, or about, people. An idea can present a theme which I will work on until I can do no more. All my pieces have a strong story line. The pieces are made to be looked into and not looked at'.[51]

It has taken the artistic imagination of Sam Smith, or, in literature, Antony Sher, in *Middlepost* (1988), with his east European Jewish character 'Smous' who travels from Lithuania to Cape Town via the Hampshire port, to reconnect Southampton to its intimate relationship with transmigrancy in the late Victorian and Edwardian eras.[52] There are, thus, fragments of memory work that avoid the surface bedazzlement of the *Titanic* or the more mundane expansion of a southern coastal town to reveal fluidity as central to the Southampton experience in the years before the First World War. Rather than being marginal to the town, transmigrants were present in huge numbers – if rarely seen or heard. Move beyond 1918, however, and the transmigrant becomes even more obscure within Southampton's collective memory. Ironically, however, the town, or rather its outskirts, was at the heart of international developments in immigration policy. Atlantic Park, situated several miles south of its docks, became a symbol, and perhaps the largest physical manifestation of it on a global scale, of the restriction of movement faced by immigrants and refugees after the First World War.

III   The last of the few: Atlantic Park versus the Spitfire

I have written elsewhere about the internal history of and national and international politics surrounding Atlantic Park, which came into existence in 1922 and finally closed down as a transmigrant camp in 1931, but here the focus is on its subsequent memory. At its peak, several thousand transmigrants were housed there in a huge site of 33 acres. Atlantic Park was run by a consortium of the major shipping companies operating through Southampton, including Cunard, Canadian Pacific and the White Star Line. With a capacity of 5,000, and with an investment of 650,000 dollars, the intention was to provide facilities for transmigrants waiting for ships out of Southampton to take them to the 'new world'. For the shipping companies and the American authorities, Atlantic Park was to serve two functions: commercial for the former and a means of control, and particularly medical screening, for the latter. Control became the dominant feature, however, as the American 1921 and 1924 immigration quotas almost totally excluded entry of those nationalities likely to pass through Atlantic Park. Heavily racialised and based on the assumption of 'Anglo-Saxon' superiority, the quotas acted as a barrier to east Europeans, especially Jews attempting to escape the brutality of war, civil war, revolution, counter-revolution, famine and persecution. Britain, through the Aliens Restriction Act of 1919, had introduced immigration policies which were both earlier and even more restrictionist than those in the USA. In a world of increasing nationalism and racism, western countries such as France that maintained a commitment to refugee asylum and a (partial) welcome to newcomers were the exception rather than the norm. As a result, Atlantic Park became a holding station for transmigrants with no place left to go. The lucrative enterprise hoped for by the shipping companies failed to materialise, and it became a drain on their resources.[53]

Scale, and the link to international politics – several major conferences were held near the site to discuss the plight of transmigrants in the 1920s – make it surprising that public manifestations of Atlantic Park's memory have been so minimal. Indeed, the ease of amnesia in this case requires thorough explanation. The most obvious point is that the site was, similar to its earlier and much smaller counterpart, Atlantic Hotel, away from the public eye – although it was next to the London–Southampton railway line, it was a mile from the nearest town, Eastleigh. In terms of immediate contact, it is significant that the few scraps of local autobiographical writing referring to the camp have come from a schoolteacher who worked with the children of the camp and from a man whose first job was delivering vegetables to the kitchens.[54]

Yet the physical obscurity of the camp as the explanation for its subsequent absence within national and local collective memory is not fully convincing. The case of the schoolteacher points to the fact that the children were (highly successfully) integrated into Eastleigh schools: 'The children were lively and intelligent and very quickly learnt to express themselves in English. I remember that the teenagers, having little else to do, used to write extremely long essays as homework, making many hours of marking for their teachers!'.[55] Many local youngsters would have come across these transmigrant children through their education. There were also a set of sporting teams created at Atlantic Park which played in local leagues. Further pointing towards local knowledge and integration, in the mid-1920s, a float created by the residents of Atlantic Park won second prize at the Eastleigh Carnival. In many respects anticipating the work of Sam Smith, the transmigrants' entry was a ship dominated not by its physical size but by its passengers. Yet, unlike Smith's later *Bathers in Southampton Water*, it is the immigrants who are on the top deck, representing the myriad nationalities that had made up, and, they hoped, would continue to make up, the American population.[56]

A surviving photograph of the Atlantic Park float shows the transmigrants dressed up in various 'authentic' ethnic outfits.[57] Playing on stereotypes, the ship *Atlantic Park* was both a parody of ethnicity as well as of the racial essentialism that had excluded them from the USA.[58] There was also a great subtlety at work using comedy to undermine the prevailing beliefs in national-racial certainties. In its quiet way, by presenting themselves, the victims of what, at the end of their century, would be referred to as 'ethnic cleansing', and part of what would be the world's largest refugee crisis until the Second World War, as clichéd immigrants, the float challenged the humour of their competitors, past and present, who freely indulged in such 'blacking up'. Such crude representations had long roots in local culture. Specifically relating to the transmigrants, E. Temple Thurston's play, *The Wandering Jew*, was staged at Eastleigh's Variety Theatre in 1924. Based on the early modern image of the Jew who endures perpetual exile through his refusal to accept Jesus, the play starts with the message: 'To each his destiny – to each his Fate. We are wanderers in a foreign land between the furrow and the stars'.[59] The transmigrants on the Atlantic Park float were, at one level, pandering to local prejudices but at another turning round assumptions of them as eternal and damned nomads or as itinerant and dubious traders. Furthermore, whilst the good ship *Atlantic Park* is being steered westwards across the Atlantic, America, and its integration of immigrants, is not presented as unproblematic. Two figures dominate the top deck. One is a kindly and jovial captain – perhaps a tribute to the sensitivity shown to the transmigrants by the multilingual and culturally adept superintendent of Atlantic Park, Colonel Barbor. The other is a well-drawn impersonation of Charlie Chaplin in his comedy, *The Immigrant* (1917), a film highlighting the limitations, loss and pathos of arriving in the 'promised land' as well as the hardship and dislocation of the journey itself.[60] The multilayered meanings revealed in this float show the sophistication and knowledge of the transmigrants and the complex political messages that can underpin apparently straightforward local activities as manifested in this case by carnival. The rival Eastleigh Carnival floats presented by large capital in the area may have engaged satire, but they were hardly subversive. That of Atlantic Park temporarily brought the camp from the margins as the world's 'unwanted' into the heart of local society and put their plight of statelessness into the public domain.

The USA was not alone in imposing racist restrictionism in the 1920s. Similar exclusionary processes had been at work in the British case, leading to the absolute refusal of the Home Secretary, William Joynson-Hicks, to let the transmigrants settle (as had been requested by several more progressive Anglo-Jewish organisations).[61] Nevertheless, the transmigrants exempted their temporary host government from overt criticism. The transmigrants on the carnival ship represented themselves as a microcosm of the League of Nations with a plethora of flags displayed (and, significantly, without the Stars and Stripes). But by far the most prominent and numerous was the Union Flag, which festooned the ship and was worn with apparent pride by the various ethnicities on board. Such a manifestation of patriotism could be dismissed as a necessary gesture away from internationalism in order to curry favour in the carnival competition by emphasising local loyalty and thereby counter prejudice against them as utterly alien. There is, however, no evidence of any animosity shown by the transmigrants towards the British State or British culture as a whole throughout Atlantic Park's existence.

In January 1925, there was a hunger strike against the monotonous food in the camp, which was surely one of the shortest but most effective fasts in the 20th century. It ended at tea when peckishness overcame principle. Remarkably, in spite of only missing breakfast and lunch, the transmigrants managed to get their grievances aired across the world's media. As Colonel Barbor, ever sympathetic, suggested, the hunger strike was not, at root cause,

> a question of fish and eggs. To my mind it is much more a matter of psychology. These unfortunate people, for whom I have a very real sympathy, have been here over a year, and naturally despairing of ever reaching their goal – the United States.[62]

As manifested in the carnival float and the hunger strike, it was America and not Britain which was the major source of the transmigrants' anger, and it was hoped that the latter would force the former into accepting their entry. In June 1924, an international delegation visited Atlantic Park and was met by 'two humorously-garbed transmigrants [. . .] with placards on their backs announcing themselves as "Lord and Lady Ellis Island"'.[63] In contrast to their dismay at America – many had been turned back on reaching Ellis Island – there seems to have been genuine affection for Barbor and, more generally, for Britain and British culture as a whole amongst the transmigrants. Proving that the game has no natural boundaries, Barbor, a Dubliner, successfully introduced cricket to the Ukrainian Jews, Menonites and other nationalities and minorities that made up Atlantic Park.[64]

The surviving schoolbooks from Atlantic Park of Liza Schlomovitz, then a 13-year-old orphan of Ukrainian pogroms, included the lovingly copied words of Wordsworth's poem 'Lucy'.[65] Liza's engagement with the English education she experienced at Atlantic Park clearly mattered to her – indeed, she kept her school notebooks for the rest of her life. It has been suggested that at Atlantic Park the transmigrants 'adopted a British way of life', amongst other things visiting the shops [and] going to the pictures'.[66] This is certainly true, although it needs to be set alongside other layers of identity made manifest through the transmigrants' strong interest in, amongst others, Russian, Jewish and American cultures.

It is clear from their Carnival Float, hunger strikes and protests to international delegates that the transmigrants were far from passive victims, no matter how tedious their years in the camp. They did their best to make the most of their time in Atlantic Park and took with them positive memories of the place alongside the frustrations they undoubtedly experienced. Births, marriages and deaths took place in the camp, and bonds were formed that lasted beyond Britain. When the camp was officially closed in 1931, it was reported that '[a]fter reaching the States, the immigrants formed the Atlantic Park Club of New York, where they held periodical reunions'.[67] It is ironic that the memory of the camp should have been concentrated in the country that had attempted to exclude the transmigrants rather than the country that had provided them with a home for the better part of a decade. Subsequently, its memory has rested in piecemeal form through the individual detective work of the diasporic descendants of Atlantic Park who managed to find refuge in countries such as Canada and South Africa.[68] In Britain, locally and nationally, there has been almost total silence, reflecting a resistance to fit the history of Atlantic Park within wider narratives. A further irony is provided in Atlantic Park's labelling both at the time and subsequently as the 'British Ellis Island' or 'An "Ellis Island" in Hampshire'.[69] Accurate in its way, such naming has *not* been to expose immigration control and restriction in Britain during the 1920s but to highlight that of the USA. Within its dominant narrative, Britain is a country without immigration, but, because of its self (and external) image as fair and decent, one also without discriminatory immigration control, part of the 'myths we live by'.[70]

When reference has been made to Atlantic Park in 'official' local memory, the inaccuracies in detail have been revealing. Two more prominent examples will be analysed to reveal how they have been geographically accurate but chronologically out of time. The first is through the autobiography of Sir Sidney Kimber, a figure who dominated the political life of inter-war Southampton and who more than anyone, shaped its development and direction before the town was wrecked by the Blitz. Published in 1949, Kimber devoted one chapter to the development of the municipal airport during the 1930s. In what was a chronological and apparently factual narrative, Kimber stated that

> In 1931, the Corporation was offered the 30 acres adjoining the Aerodrome and, known as Atlantic Park Hostel, which had been used by the Cunard and White Star and other shipping companies as a transmigrant station during the war, and was complete with hangars and other buildings.[71]

The second example comes half a century later, when Eastleigh Borough Council's Highways and Works Committee agreed to call a small street in a new housing estate close to the airport 'Atlantic Park'. In explaining the naming, the Council explained that 'Southampton International Airport was originally known as Atlantic Park during the war when Spitfires were actually constructed there and it was thought appropriate that as the airfield could be seen from the estate, that name should be used'.[72]

Maurice Halbwachs, when exploring 'localization' within his seminal *On Collective Memory*, argued that:

> What makes recent memories hang together is not that they are continuous in time: it is rather that they are part of a totality of thoughts common to a group, the group of people with whom we have a relation at the moment [. . .] To recall them it is hence sufficient that we place ourselves in the perspective of this group, that we adopt its interests and follow the slant of its reflections.

As Halbwachs adds, '[e]xactly the same process occurs when we attempt to localize older memories'.[73] Atlantic Park has a place in local collective memory, but it is not because of its internationally significant role as a transmigrant camp. Instead, the site of the camp is referred to as part of the history of the airport, and, more specifically, its importance relates to the relationship to the Spitfire fighter plane which was first flown from what was still known as Atlantic Park in 1936. For Kimber, placing the transmigrant camp in the First World War removed any need to see it as part of the 'normal' peacetime world of Southampton in which he made such an impact. For those responsible in the ever-controversial task of local street-naming, it was easier to subsume Atlantic Park into the overwhelming narrative of the Second World War and the pivotal role of the Spitfire within it. In both processes, the need for chronological cohesion within local memory work has been at the expense of the actual history and significance of Atlantic Park.

What is particularly fascinating in the case of the street-naming is how two icons of local memory became interwoven and confused and that other possible readings of local history and memory were not considered. The goal of the local West End Parish Council was to have names that recognised 'the proximity of the Airport' or to have 'a West End and seafaring connection'. The naming was thus divided into two. First, 'ATLANTIC PARK was the original name of the Airport and MITCHELL, SPITFIRE, MERLIN and BROWNING are in recognition of the Spitfire which was built there'. Second, 'West End has a seafaring connection with the *Titanic* disaster. The captain of the CARPATHIA the ship which rescued many of the survivors,

Captain ROSTON, is buried in West End. Captain SHAW was in command of the Titanic'.[74] That Atlantic Park had an intimate 'seafaring connection' was lost on the local council. Such active processes of forgetting takes us back to the testimony of Allen Robinson, the grocer's delivery boy of the 1920s. Robinson also remembers the child refugees from the Spanish Civil War, who, in 1937, were settled in a camp a short walk from Atlantic Park. At the end of his brief memoir, he concludes that '[t]here is so much history in the Eastleigh and Bishopstoke districts and we older people like to look back on it all. The Russian and Basque refugees are just part of that history'.[75] Alas, when Atlantic Park's origins are forced into the Second World War, its history and local memories, such as those of Allen Robinson, are denied. Even the international diplomatic connections of Atlantic Park have been lost sight of. The Townhill Park estate had been bought by Lord Swaythling, Liberal politician and prominent member of British Jewry, in the late 19th century. In 1924, the second international conference on post-war migration was hosted by the Swaythlings at Townhill Park, which included a visit to Atlantic Park. A year later, the second Lord Swaythling's wife wrote an open letter of protest to the American President protesting about the continued refusal to let the transmigrants of Atlantic Park into his country. The transmigrants responded to this gesture in deep gratitude and pathos: 'you were the first to call upon the conscience of the people who inconsiderately caused us so much pain and grief and made us spend a considerable portion of our lives in great agony and despair'.[76] The street-naming in 1990 reflected the last opportunity to reflect the history of Atlantic Park and the presence and activities of the Swaythling family, as it was 'the final area on [the] Townhill Farm Estate [that was] now under construction'.[77] But the very idea of connecting up, through the common theme of refugee movements and transmigrancy, the story of the *Titanic* with that of Atlantic Park was (and continues to be) too alien to have been considered, let alone accepted. The memory work directly associated with Southampton International Airport confirms such processes of inclusion and exclusion.

In 1994, the new airport building in Southampton was officially opened. The old hangars which had housed first the American airforce, then the transmigrants and, finally, the Municipal Airport, were demolished. All traces of the transmigrant camp were thus destroyed, although there was brief mention of its existence in an exhibition area created in the new airport building and located in the viewers' gallery:

1921: The buildings were acquired by a shipping consortium, renamed Atlantic Park Hostel, and used by European migrants bound for the USA. By the late

1920s national interest in municipal airports was growing. Southampton City Corporation purchased 100 acres of land adjacent to the Hostel and officially opened the Airport in 1932.[78]

The majority of the display, however, was devoted to the development of the Spitfire in the 1930s. The brainchild of Reginald Mitchell, Chief Engineer of the Southampton company, Supermarine, its test flight took place in Atlantic Park in 1936. A year later Mitchell, who had been seriously ill when the Spitfire was first flown, died of cancer. After his death, the Spitfire was constructed at the Supermarine works in the suburb of Woolston, overlooking Southampton's outer docks. Since the late 1990s, the historical display at Southampton International Airport has been withdrawn and replaced by memorials and original documentation relating only to the Spitfire. In autumn 2003, a replica Spitfire was unveiled just outside the airport in a roundabout on its approach road, Mitchell Way. The replica attested to the plane's dominance in local memory and the literal wiping out of any other histories of the site that might have complicated the narrative of the Spitfire.[79] In proposals to develop the airport site in the late 1980s, the slogan 'Pride in the Past, Confidence in the Future' was coined – the 'past' being illustrated by a Spitfire.[80] The hegemonic status of Spitfire memory more generally in Southampton was confirmed in 2000 with the 60th anniversary commemorations of the Battle of Britain. Southampton pronounced itself as 'Proud Home of the Spitfire: Famous throughout the world as the "Port of Ocean Queens", the City [. . .] is also rightly proud of being the home of the nation-saving Vickers-Supermarine Spitfire'.[81] In June 2000, 'Sea Wings', the climax of local commemorations of the Battle of Britain, was attended by over one 100,000 visitors with an estimated 250,000 people seeing the display. The central feature was the presence of 13 Spitfires, which had taken off from their spiritual home in the airport, the display concluding with a solitary fly-past accompanied by a requiem.[82]

Southampton's identification with the Spitfire and R. J. Mitchell is not surprising: in the words of the first semi-official account of its history, written by John Taylor and Maurice Allward, and published in 1946: 'This is the story of the most famous aeroplane the world has ever known'. But, as they added, '[i]t is also the story of the achievement of a great people walking together in the greatest of all causes – the cause of freedom and justice'.[83] As with the *Titanic*, the local impact of the Spitfire has been highlighted in memorialisation in Southampton and its region. This memory work has been partly made through the recognition of the devastating air raid on the Supermarine factory in September 1940 that left over 100 of its workers dead. It has mainly been manifest, however, through the Mitchell connection. The Southampton Hall of Aviation was originally titled the R. J. Mitchell Museum, and the memorial function to Mitchell is still dominant within it. Mitchell moved to Southampton during the First World War and spent the rest of his life there. He died and was buried in the town. In spite of his Potteries roots, as the local newspaper has stated, '[h]e has good claim to being the greatest ever Sotonian'.[84]

The Mitchell story and that of the Spitfire generally have intense mythical power and resonance. It was recognised during the war itself in the film *The First of the Few* (1942), directed by Leslie Howard and with the director as the hero, R. J. Mitchell. Mitchell's self-sacrifice and gentle patriotism were the main focus of the film. Indeed, in *The First of the Few*, he becomes symbolic of the later Battle of Britain – physically weak, he is mentally strong and 'always fighting' and ultimately victorious, even in death. The film also included explicit references to Southampton – no town, as the local newspaper emphasised 'has a more intimate interest'.[85]

Spitfire narratives have often incorporated a spiritual and often explicitly Christian discourse: 'The Spitfire Funds were like altars at which the man, woman and child in the back lines could light a candle for the men fighting in the nation's fight in the front line'.[86] Mitchell has been portrayed as Christ-like in his self-sacrifice, dying to make the world a better place and as an example to others: 'He has the finest memorial any man could wish for, he lives in the minds of those among whom and for whom he lived'.[87] In Knowles's *Southampton: The English Gateway*, its role is both God-given and described as being part of a seamless garment of quintessential Britishness. In the dark days of 1940:

> as every Englishman realized, the time had now come when that particular responsibility must be borne in part by the little Southampton-built fighter-'plane. Because of this, the *Spitfire*, like the Navy, touched 'mystic chords in the English breast that went deeper than reason'. Like the sight of a rolling Jack Tar or of a grey battleship at sea, the spectacle of a *Spitfire* in flight had for the Britisher 'the power of a trumpet call'.[88]

But Knowles's national-religious framing of the Spitfire went alongside an equally powerful evocation of an essential nautical reading of the British past which was added to the mythologising of the plane.

It has been stressed that 'maritime identities have been painstakingly constructed and reinvented over the centuries as part of that complex creature that is "Britishness"'.[89] The Spitfire, with its roots in Mitchell's earlier design work in developing the sea plane, could be incorporated into an older mythology as well as bringing its own unique history into play. The complexity of melding sea, land and air was achieved by instrumentalising the historic maritime place identities of Southampton's recent and distant past:

> The waters from Southampton down to the Solent, which had seen so much historic progress – from the oak ships of Buckler's Hard [where Henry VIII's fleet was built] to the liners of the thirties – were now to cradle the finest and fastest flying machine ever built by man.[90]

So far, however, there has been no space within the narrative of this legend – internationally, nationally or locally – to include either the close pre-history of Atlantic Park in which it was first flown, and, thereby, a direct link to the trans-migrants of inter-war Southampton, or the dubious anti-alien origins of Supermarine through the figure of its founder, Noel Pemberton-Billing, described in local heritage as 'eccentric'[91] but more accurately labelled by Philip Hoare as a 'proto-fascist'.[92] Ultimately, the myth of the Spitfire concerns an intense battle over memory and identity. Knowles used the example of Southampton's Spitfire to show that 'personal, even mystic, sense of duty which is part of the Englishman's heritage', highlighting his theme further through utilising Wordsworth:

> It is not to be thought of that the Flood
> Of British freedom, which, to the open sea
> Of the world's praise, from dark antiquity
> Hath flow'd, with pomp of waters, unwithstood
> ... We must be free or die, who speak the tongue
> That Shakespeare spake; the faith and morals hold
> Which Milton held. . .[93]

Through Atlantic Park, however, and the schoolbooks of a young girl, Liza Schlomovitz, who had witnessed the massacre of her parents and the harshness of a post-war world in which there was no place for the dispossessed, we have seen how Wordsworth's poetry could reach an audience and have a resonance that Knowles's insular vision of Englishness simply could not imagine.

Conclusion

On one level, Southampton's collective forgetting of migration and transmigrancy within its past simply mirrors that on a national level. Yet, at another, the very richness and, indeed, in the case of Atlantic Park, the uniqueness of this past points towards a particularly local process of amnesia. It might be suggested that Southampton, which experienced fast growth from the 19th century but lacked the internal capital to develop a strong civic culture and historical infrastructure, has not had the self-confidence to embrace past heterogeneity. Instead, it has embraced and instrumentalised the memory of the iconic *Titanic* and Spitfire narrowly and exclusively as its principal blocks of memory-building. In turn, the absence of physical reminders of migrancy and transmigrancy has hindered more inclusive memory work. As black British artist, Lubaina Himid has stated, with regard to her attempts to commemorate slavery at a national and local level:

> I was trying to find a way to talk of a thing that is not there, sort of *Inside the Invisible* if you like. I am interested in the politics of representation, how when something is there you can talk about it, write about it, paint about it, but when something isn't there what can you say, how can you make something of it, how can it not have been in vain, if you like … [My] idea for memorialising came from trying to visualize the invisible.[94]

Returning to Philip Hoare, the most sophisticated interpreter of local memory in the Southampton region, it highlights again the obscurity of Atlantic Park, as he himself notes elsewhere in this volume. Indeed, the memory of the *American* Ellis Island *is* called upon throughout *Spike Island*. At one point, Hoare makes a direct comparison between the Royal Military Hospital and Ellis Island:

> The great brick hospital on the shore had become an imperial processing plant, its raw material – its patients – arriving by sea to be admitted into its interior, like the red-brick buildings of Ellis Island in New York Harbour, to which it bore both stylistic and functional similarities. Both were insular buildings invested with hope and fear, fraught with medical and bureaucratic decisions on human destinies; individuals catalogued and assessed as they arrived from foreign lands.[95]

Hoare's inability to make a more straightforward comparison between a site of memory in Hampshire and Ellis Island – that of Atlantic Park – reflects not individual failure: *Spike Island* is a work of great subtlety. Instead, it exposes the exclusionary power of national mythologies and the absence of a sociology and anthropology of knowledge that could bring Atlantic Park alongside Royal Victoria Military Hospital or its near neighbour, Netley Abbey, into shared landscapes of memory.

This essay has been equally, if not more, concerned about the processes of amnesia as those of remembering. 'Forgetting', as Jonathan Boyarin reminds us, can be 'a technique of the dominated, used to enable memory'.[96] Boyarin suggests that 'more has been forgotten in and about the Jewish Lower East

Side than virtually any other place or time in America'.[97] Southampton was never the East End of London, let alone the Lower East Side of New York, yet it still has played a crucial role in the history of world migration and settlement. But, finally, the analysis of local memory work reveals how it is not so much the past that is exposed as a foreign country. It is more that foreignness itself has been perceived as alien to the past.

Notes

Chapter 1

1. Duffy, Michael, 'World-Wide War and British Expansion, 1793–1815', in Marshall, P. J., ed., *The Oxford History of the British Empire*, Vol. II, *The Eighteenth Century* (Oxford, 1998), p. 184. For Britain and the French Revolutionary and Napoleonic Wars, see Black, Jeremy, *Britain as a Military Power, 1688–1815* (London, 1998); Stone, Lawrence, ed., *An Imperial State at War: Britain from 1689 to 1815* (London, 1994); Guy, Alan James, ed., *The Road to Waterloo: The British Army and the Struggle against Revolutionary and Napoleonic France* (Stroud, 1990); Emsley, Clive, *British Society and the French Wars, 1793–1815* (London, 1979); Glover, Richard, *Britain at Bay: Defence against Bonaparte, 1803–14* (London, 1973).
2. Davies, J. Silvester, *A History of Southampton* (Southampton, 1883), p. 505.
3. Patterson, A. Temple, *A History of Southampton, 1700–1914*, Vol. I, *An Oligarchy in Decline, 1700–1835* (Southampton, 1963), pp. 41–2; Stovold, Jan, *Minute Book of the Pavement Commissioners for Southampton, 1770–1789* (Southampton, 1990).
4. Patterson, *A History of Southampton*, pp. 42–4, 57–9; Oldfield, John, *Printers, Booksellers, and Libraries in Hampshire, 1750–1800* (Winchester, 1993), pp. 17–18, 20, 23–5. For local theatres, see Ranger, Paul, *The Georgian Playhouses of Hampshire, 1730–1830* (Winchester, 1996), pp. 17–18.
5. Patterson, *History of Southampton*, p. 57; *The Directory for the Town of Southampton* (Southampton, 1803), pp. 3–6. All figures cited here are extracted from the 1803 *Directory*.
6. Patterson, *History of Southampton*, pp. 75–7; Oldfield, J. R., *Popular Politics and British Anti-Slavery: The Mobilisation of Public Opinion against the Slave Trade, 1787–1807* (Manchester, 1995), p. 66n.
7. Patterson, *History of Southampton*, p. 95. For émigré French priests, see Bellenger, D. A., *The French Exiled Clergy in the British Isles after 1789* (Bath, 1986), especially pp. 2–3.
8. Southampton City Archives, Town Clerks Papers, Box 4/14/7, List of French émigrés in Southampton, n.d.; *Hampshire Chronicle*, 23 June, 4, 11, 18 August 1794, 25 May, 8 June, 20 July 1795.
9. Patterson, *History of Southampton*, p. 95; *Hampshire Chronicle*, 18 February 1793.
10. *Hampshire Chronicle*, 4 February, 18 March 1793; Southampton City Archives, SC 2/1/12, Corporation Minutes, 1783–1807, entries for 30 January and 17, 20 February 1793. Moreover, in November, the Mayor and Corporation proposed and opened a subscription for furnishing warm clothing for the British Army

serving under the Duke of York. See also *Proceedings of the General United Society for Supplying the British Troops upon the Continent with Extra Clothing* (London, 1798), p. 17 and Appendix XXXV.

11. *Hampshire Chronicle*, 29 April, 17 June 1793.

12. National Archives [hereafter TNA], WO 17/239, returns of various regiments and detachments under the command of the Earl of Moira, December 1793 to August 1795, in Guernsey, Cowes, Lyndhurst, Netley Camp and Southampton; Patterson, *History of Southampton*, p. 95.

13. *Hampshire Chronicle*, 7 April 1794. Local sources refer to a number of barracks in Southampton, including those at Chapel and a large block of cavalry barracks built in the early nineteenth century 'near the entrance of the avenue' (later the site of the Ordnance Survey). See Davies, *A History of Southampton*, p. 131; Hearnshaw, F. J. C. and Clarke, F., *A Short History of Southampton* (Oxford, 1910), p. 118. Nevertheless, the pressure on local inhabitants, especially publicans, was sometimes intense. In 1813, for instance, the cavalry barracks in Southampton were 'appropriated to the use of infantry detachments, in order to relieve the publicans from the billet'. See *Hampshire Courier*, 4 October 1813.

14. *Hampshire Chronicle*, 4 February, 24 March, 7 April 1794; Patterson, *History of Southampton*, p. 95; South, Mary L., 'Epidemic Disease, Soldiers and Prisoners of War in Southampton, 1550–1800', *Proceedings of the Hampshire Field Club and Archaeological Society*, 43 (1987), pp. 185–96. As South makes clear, the blankets used by the soldiers in the hospital were later sold to the townspeople during the harsh winter of 1795, with the result that the typhus fever continued until June of that year.

15. Patterson, *History of Southampton*, p. 95; *Hampshire Chronicle*, 23 June 1794.

16. *Hampshire Chronicle*, 23 June 1794.

17. TNA, WO 17/239. Here, again, the number of troops who were sick is striking. In August 1794, 266 out of approximately 2,892 men were listed as sick. As of 1 September, the corresponding figures were 559 and 3,864.

18. *Hampshire Chronicle*, 18 August, 1, 15 September, 20, 27 October, 1, 15 December 1794.

19. WO 17/239; *Hampshire Chronicle*, 17 August 1795. Nursling Common is some-times confused with Shirley Common, but local maps make it clear that the camp was in Nursling. Also see Bullar, John, *A Companion in a Tour round Southampton* (Southampton, 1819), pp. 139–40.

20. Douch, Robert, ed., *Southampton, 1540–1956: Visitors' Descriptions* (Southampton, 1961), p. 22.

21. Hampshire Record Office, Winchester, 52 M81/PR 2, Register of births, deaths, and marriages, St Boniface's Church, Nursling.

22. *Hampshire Chronicle*, 10, 24 August, 7, 14, 26 September 1795.

23. *Hampshire Chronicle*, 3 October 1795.

24. *Hampshire Chronicle*, 21 November 1795.

25. Patterson, *History of Southampton*, p. 97; TNA, WO 17/234, returns of various regiments and detachments under the command of Major-General Doyle, at sea, at Île d'Yeu and Southampton, September 1795 to January 1796.

26. *Hampshire Chronicle*, 12, 19 March, 2 April, 25 June, 30 July 1796.
27. Patterson, *History of Southampton*, pp. 97–8; *Hampshire Chronicle*, 18 February, 18 March, 1797; 31 March, 28 April, 9 June, 18 August 1798.
28. Glover, *Britain at Bay*, pp. 43–4; *Hampshire Chronicle*, 10 June 1799; 9 June 1800.
29. *Hampshire Chronicle*, 13 May, 8 July 1799. On this occasion, the camp was on Shirley Common and not in Nursling.
30. *Hampshire Chronicle*, 15, 22 July, 18 November 1799.
31. Lewin, T. H. ed., *The Lewin Letters: A Selection from the Correspondence and Diaries of an English Family, 1756–1884*, 2 vols (London, 1909), Vol. I, p. 130. Significantly, Lewin added that traces of these pits could still be seen on Netley Common as late as 1839.
32. *Hampshire Chronicle*, 19 May, 23 June, 7, 21 July, 4, 11 August 1800.
33. *Hampshire Chronicle*, 4 August 1800. The *Hampshire Chronicle* reported the following week (11 August) that the Government had 'very liberally ordered each woman to be paid a guinea, and every child five shillings to defray their expenses home'.
34. Douch, *Southampton, 1540–1956*, p. 21; South, 'Epidemic Disease, Soldiers and Prisoners of War in Southampton', p. 194 (Table 4).
35. *Hampshire Chronicle*, 24, 31 May 1802.
36. Patterson, *History of Southampton*, pp. 99–100; *Hampshire Chronicle*, 22 August, 3 October 1803.
37. *Hampshire Chronicle*, 14 November 1803, 7, 14, 21 May 1804, 10 June 1805.
38. *Hampshire Chronicle*, 14 May 1804.
39. These troop movements can be traced through local newspapers. In 1814, for instance, the 'gallant' 23rd Regiment, which had been serving with 'the immortal Wellington', marched through Southampton where it was greeted with cheers and a ringing of bells. See *Hampshire Courier*, 18 July 1814.
40. Patterson, *History of Southampton*, p. 100; Glover, *Britain at Bay*, p. 47.
41. *Hampshire Chronicle*, 17 July, 19 August, 4 September 1809; *Hampshire Courier*, 19 April, 20 September 1813.
42. Quoted in Knowles, Bernard, *Southampton: The English Gateway* (London, 1951), p. 71.
43. Knowles, *Southampton*, pp. 78–9; Holland, A. J., *Buckler's Hard: A Rural Shipbuilding Centre* (Emsworth, 1985), pp. 43, 77, 223.
44. National Archives, ADM 49/102, lists of ships built and repaired in merchants' yards, 1801–17.
45. *Hampshire Chronicle*, 20 May, 17 June 1805, 13 July, 10 August, 26 October 1808; ADM 49/102; TNA, ADM 95/7, estimates for building ships, 1791–1807.
46. Holland, *Buckler's Hard*, p. 223.
47. ADM 95/7; ADM 95/8, estimates by contracts, 1807–16. Quite apart from the costs of materials and labour, the Navy also 'inflicted' heavy penalties, sometimes running into thousands of pounds, for work that was late. See ADM 49/102.
48. ADM 95/7; *Hampshire Chronicle*, 26 October 1807, 4 July 1808, 7 June 1813.
49. John, Second Lord Montagu of Beaulieu, *Buckler's Hard and its Ships: Some Historical Reflections* (London, 1905), p. 36.
50. Douch, *Southampton, 1540–1956*, pp. 23–4.

51. *Hampshire Chronicle*, 27 June, 4 July 1814; *Hampshire Courier*, 4 July 1814.

52. *Hampshire Courier*, 19 September, 20 November 1814, 26 June 1815.

53. *Hampshire Courier*, 19 June 1809.

54. *Hampshire Courier*, 23 June, 21, 28 July 1794, 6 July 1795, 24, 31 December 1798, 23 September 1799.

55. Patterson, *A History of Southampton*, p. 107. For the resumption of trade with France after July 1814, see *Hampshire Courier*, 8 August, 19, 26 September, 19 December 1814.

56. Patterson, *History of Southampton*, p. 110; *Hampshire Chronicle*, 23 December 1799, 13 January 1800; Wells, Roger, *Wretched Faces: Famine in Wartime England, 1793–1801* (Gloucester, 1988), pp. 128, 131, 180.

57. Hearnshaw and Clarke, *A Short History of Southampton*, p. 11; *The Southampton Guide* (Southampton, 1816), pp. 48–9, 57. Building and development did not come to a complete halt, however. In 1798, the *Hampshire Chronicle* reported that Southampton was 'greatly improved with a number of new places', among them 'a new square called Red-lion square, Maria-place, Albion-place, Cumberland-place, St Mary's place, Orchard-place, and St James'-parade' (*Hampshire Chronicle*, 11 August 1798). Also, see *Hampshire Courier*, 10 May, 7 June 1813.

58. *Hampshire Chronicle*, 30 July 1796.

59. Patterson, A. Temple, *Southampton: A Biography* (London, 1970), p. 97.

60. *The Southampton Guide* (Southampton, 1804), pp. 24–5; TNA, WO 17/219, monthly returns of His Majesty's 97th Regiment of Foot, commanded by Lieutenant Colonel Denzil Onslow, 1 August 1794.

61. Patterson, *A History of Southampton*, pp. 102–3.

Chapter 2

1. Carnarvon Papers, British Library, Add. Ms. 60,781, fols. 167–8, Private Secretary to Canadian visitors, 12 October 1858.

2. Hardinge, A. H., *Life of Henry Howard Molyneux Herbert, Fourth Earl of Carnarvon, 1831–1890* (3 vols, Oxford, 1925), Vol. I, pp. 72–3.

3. Carnarvon, 'Later History of Hampshire' (1857) in Herbert, *Essays, Addresses and Translations*, Vol. I, p. 77.

4. Hardinge, *Life*, Vol. III, p. 300.

5. Carnarvon, 'Early History of Hampshire' (1856), in Herbert, *Essays, Addresses and Translations*, Vol. I, p. 46.

6. Carnarvon, 'Early History of Hampshire', p. 22.

7. Carnarvon, 'Lucius Carey, Lord Falkland' (1878), in Herbert, *Essays, Addresses and Translations*, Vol. I, pp. 337–8.

8. Carnarvon, 'A Word to Country Gentlemen' (unpublished, 1886), in Herbert, *Essays, Addresses and Translations*, Vol. II, p. 70.

9. Carnarvon, 'A Word to Country Gentlemen', pp. 47–8.

10. Carnarvon, 'A Word to Country Gentlemen', p. 55.

11. See his four major publications on the subject: 'Prison Discipline: A Report Adopted at the Hampshire Quarter Sessions' (1864); 'Special Report of the

Visiting Justices of the Southampton County Prison' (1870); 'Presidential Address to the International Prison Congress' (1872); 'Address on Prison Management' (1878), in Herbert, *Essays, Addresses and Translations*, Vol. II, pp. 218–318, and a large section of his 'Address on Social Science' (1868), in Herbert, *Essays, Addresses and Translations*, Vol. II, pp. 169–218.

12. Carnarvon to Aberdeen, 12 January 1854, Aberdeen Papers, BL, Add. Ms. 43,252.

13. Hardinge, *Life*, Vol. I, p. 83; Carnarvon to B. Pinniger (Steward of the Manor), 16 February 1858, BL, Add. Ms. 60,875, fols. 12–14.

14. Carnarvon to Derby, 25 February 1858, BL, Letterbook C7; Carnarvon to Spencer Walpole, 25 February 1858, BL, Letterbook C7; Carnarvon Diary (Notes on the past six months), 12 August 1858, Add. Ms. 67,428, fols. 22–36.

15. St Augustine's College, Canterbury, Occasional Papers, nos. 233–4 (1883); see also, Coleridge's proposal for the foundation of the College, in Coleridge to Gladstone, 21 August 1843, Gladstone papers, BL, Add. Ms. 44,137.

16. Hardinge, *Life*, Vol. I, Chapter 3; Carnarvon, Hansard, 3rd ser., Vol. CXXX, col. 9 (31 January 1854) his maiden speech; Vol. CXXXVI, cols. 2071–3 (1 March 1855); Vol. CXLV, cols. 1650–2 (12 June 1857).

17. As late as 1867, he told the British Minister in Washington that if Canada should 'choose to separate, we on this side shall not object: it is they who protest against the idea. In England separation would be generally popular'. Stanley to Sir F. Bruce, 25 January 1867, National Archives of Canada, Ottawa, MG 27 I A5.

18. Carnarvon Diary, August 1858, BL, Add. Ms. 67,428, fols. 22–36; Hardinge, *Life*, Vol. I, pp. 45–6. Carnarvon continued close relations with Mansel: in 1859 he offered his old tutor the living of Burghclere (near Highclere), Carnarvon to Mansel, 15 January 1859, BL, Add. Ms. 60,875, fols. 37–8. See also Carnarvon's tribute to Mansel in his 'Introduction to Dean Mansel's "Gnostic Heresies"' (1874) in Herbert, *Essays, Addresses and Translations*, Vol. II, pp. 3–21.

19. Minute, 27 October 1858, TNA, Kew, CO 323/252, fols. 419–20; Carnarvon Diary, 12 August 1858 BL, Add. Ms. 67,428.

20. See, for example, those in the Carnarvon papers, National Archives, PRO30/6/132–3; Carnarvon to Seymour Fitzgerald (Under-Secretary, Foreign Office), 14 September 1858, BL, Add. Ms. 60,786.

21. See Mitchell, Leslie, *Bulwer Lytton: The Rise and Fall of a Victorian Man of Letters* (London, 2003); Snyder, Charles W., *Liberty and Morality: A Political Biography of Edward Bulwer-Lytton* (New York, 1995); Brown, Andrew, 'Lytton, Edward Bulwer, 1st Baron Lytton', *Oxford Dictionary of National Biography* (Oxford, 2004).

22. Disraeli to Derby, 25 February 1858, in Monypenny, W. F., and Buckle, G. E., *Life of Benjamin Disraeli, Earl of Beaconsfield* (6 vols, London, 1910–20), Vol. IV, p. 118. Cf. Disraeli's later reference to the 'ci devant Cabinet Minister wh[ich] I had made him': 'Observations', n.d. (c. 1865), Disraeli Papers, Bodleian Library, Oxford, A/X/A/26.

23. Mitchell, *Bulwer Lytton, passim*. However, for favourable views of Lytton's political qualifications, see 'The Right Hon. Sir Edward Bulwer Lytton. His Career, his

Genius, and his Writings', *Dublin University Magazine*, 52 (July 1858), pp. 34–56; *Saturday Review*, 18 September 1858, pp. 285–6.

24. Cf. Mitchell, *Bulwer Lytton*, pp. 209, 217: he was 'a very effective administrator'. Lytton was not shy of praising himself as a minister: Lytton to Derby, 16 December 1858, 14th Earl of Derby papers, Liverpool Record Office, box 162/1.

25. Godley to Adderley, 21 August 1858, in Childe-Pemberton, W. S., *The Life of Lord Norton (Right Hon. Sir Charles Adderley), 1814–1905* (London, 1909), p. 172.

26. Lansbury, Coral, *Arcady in Australia: The Evocation of Australia in Nineteenth-Century English Literature* (Melbourne, 1970), p. 80; Cell, J. W., *British Colonial Administration in the Mid-Nineteenth Century: The Policy-Making Process* (New Haven, Conn. and London, 1970), p. 6. Carnarvon did not, however, as has been alleged (Mitchell, *Bulwer-Lytton*, p. 219) become 'a sort of acolyte' to Lytton.

27. Cannadine, David, *Ornamentalism: How the British Saw Their Empire* (London, 2001), p. 30.

28. Lytton, *The Caxtons: A Family Picture* (1849; Knebworth Edition, London, 1874), Part XII, Chapter 6, especially p. 326.

29. Lytton, *The Caxtons*, p. 327 (emphasis added).

30. Minute for draft to Governor Douglas, 15 September 1858, CO 305/9, fols. 151–7; Lytton to Col. Moody, 29 October 1858, CO60/3, fols. 388–410.

31. Minute, 29 March 1858, CO323/253, fol. 267.

32. Foster-Fitzgerald to Carnarvon, 31 March 1858, 8 April 1858, BL, Add. Mss. 60,786, 60,787.

33. Minute, 10 April 1858, CO323/253, fols. 292–4; cf. Cannadine, *Ornamentalism*, p. 144, for an attenuated rendition of this. On this aspect of the subject, see also, Knox, B. A., 'Democracy, Aristocracy and Empire: The Provision of Colonial Honours, 1818–1870', *Australian Historical Studies*, 25 (1992), pp. 244–64.

34. Derby to Malmesbury, 17 August 1858, 14th Earl of Derby papers, Letter Book 185/2.

35. Lord Malmesbury (attending the Queen in Potsdam) to Derby, 13 August 1858, 14th Earl of Derby papers, box 144/2.

36. See Martin, G., *Bunyip Aristocracy* (Sydney, 1986).

37. See, for example, Lytton to Derby, 15 September 1858, 14th Earl of Derby papers, 162/1; Lytton to Barkly, 22 November 1858, Lytton papers, Hertfordshire Record Office, Letterbook D/EK 028/1; Lytton to Carnarvon, n.d. (October 1858), BL, Add. Ms. 60,780, fol. 43. For attacks on Smith, see CO309/47, fols. 372–497 and BL, Add. Ms. 60,782, fols. 6–15.

38. Lytton to Prince Albert, 30 December 1858, Royal Archives, Windsor, M54/117; Circular, 6 January 1859, CO323/261, fols. 75–81.

39. Carnarvon to Lytton, 11 August, 14 September 1857, 2 November 1857, Lytton papers, D/EK C11.

40. Carnarvon to Mr Arundell, 27 April 1858, BL, Add. Ms. 60,786, fols. 59–61; Hardinge, *Life*, Vol. III, p. 97. Letter and Minute, 2 October 1858, CO201/507, fols. 658–65.

41. Carnarvon to G. Cartier, 8 September 1859, BL, Add. Ms. 60,877, fols. 15–16.

42. See Knox, B., *The Queensland Years of Robert Herbert* (St Lucia, Queensland, 1977).

43. Lytton, *The Caxtons*, p. 328.

44. Letters to family, 17 January, 18 October 1865, 21 May 1866, cited in Knox, *Herbert*, pp. 108, 131, 169.

45. Sir G. Bowen to Lytton, 28 September 1860, Lytton Papers, D/EK C5.

46. Knox, *Herbert*, pp. 36–9. Minute by Sir Frederic Rogers (Permanent Under-Secretary, Colonial Office), 20 April 1866, CO234/15, fol. 108; Carnarvon Diary, 16 August 1868, 30 January 1869, 17 March, 14 April 1870, 13–16 March 1873, BL, Add. Ms. 60,900, 60,901, 60,902, 60,905.

47. Jowett, B., *Lord Lytton: The Man and the Author* (London, 1873), pp. 5–6.

48. Gladstone to Sir James Graham, 7 February 1859, Gladstone Papers, BL, Add. Ms. 44,551, Carnarvon, notes on work as under-secretary (1858), BL, Add. Ms. 60,892, fols. 68.

49. 'I wish to establish a much more courteous attention to Colonists on the part of the Colonial Minister than has yet been practised': deleted passage in Lytton's draft of instructions to the Hon. George Dundas as Lieutenant Governor of Prince Edward Island, 7 January 1859, CO226/90, fols. 295–303; Hardinge, *Life*, Vol. I, p. 124; Escott, T. H. S., *Life of Edward Bulwer, 1st Baron Lytton* (London, 1910), p. 303, citing an interview with Lord Carnarvon; Skelton, O. D., *The Life and Times of Sir Alexander Tilloch Galt* (Toronto, 1920), pp. 246–8; Saunders, E. M., ed., *The Life and Letters of the Rt. Hon. Sir Charles Tupper* (2 vols, London and Toronto, 1916), Vol. I, p. 61; Charles Fisher to Lytton, 6 November 1858, CO188/131, fols. 609–10.

50. Carnarvon's minute (copy) on Sir G. Grey's South Africa proposal, 7 January 1859, PRO30/6/133, fols. 39–48; Godley to Lytton, 29 July 1858 (with Lytton's annotations), CO6/26, fols. 102–7; Childe-Pemberton, *Life of Lord Norton*, p. 172; cf. Lytton to the Queen, 25 January 1859, RA B17/107.

51. Minute, 17 July 1858, CO6/29, fols. 342–53. Minutes, 15 December 1858, CO60/1, fols. 245–74; 18–22 January 1859, fols. 379–88.

52. Minute by Lytton, 20 February 1859, TNA FO12/35, fols. 117–29.

53. Cf. Mitchell, *Bulwer Lytton*, p. 218: the 'submissions' mentioned must be his cabinet papers, which were much more concise than his despatches.

54. Carnarvon to G. Cartier, 8 September 1859, BL, Add. Ms. 60,877, fols. 15–16.

55. Knox, B., 'Conservative Imperialism, 1858–1874: Bulwer Lytton, Lord Carnarvon, and Canadian Confederation', *International History Review*, 6 (1984), pp. 333–57.

56. Carnarvon to George Verdon, 23 March 1867, PRO30/6/157. Verdon was Treasurer of Victoria, in London to negotiate on defence questions.

57. For example, Carnarvon Diary, 9 July 1867, BL, Add. Ms. 60,899; Carnarvon to Sir William Heathcote, 20 February 1868, Add. Ms. 61,071.

58. *Hansard*, 3rd ser., Vol. CXCIX, cols. 193–233, (14 February 1870); BL, Add. Ms. 60,902, Carnarvon Diary, 19, 22, 25 February 1870; Carnarvon to Sir J. A. Macdonald, 10 February 1870, Macdonald papers, National Archives of Canada, Vol. 372, pp. 15,6613–16; Macdonald to Carnarvon, 14 April 1870, Vol. 517 (Letterbook 14); Sir Francis Hincks (Finance Minister, Canada) to Carnarvon, 27 June 1870, PRO30/6/171.

59. Hardinge, *Life*, Vol. II, pp. 29–31; Carnarvon Diary, 13–16 March 1873, BL, Add. Ms. 60,905. Carnarvon was on a cruise for his health; his correspondent and adviser by telegraph to Gibraltar was R. G. W. Herbert.

60. Carnarvon Diary, 5 May, 13 July 1873, BL, Add. Ms. 60,905; Buckle, *Disraeli*, Vol. V, p. 272; Hardinge, *Life*, Vol. II, p. 58.

61. Wilson to Carnarvon, 9 February 1874, BL, Add. Ms. 60,854; Carnarvon's reply (draft) follows. Wilson was disappointed in Carnarvon; after his resignation, one of his associates referred to 'the miserable Carnarvon (whether creature or inspirer of Herbert's)', see G. Serle, 'New Light on the Colonial Office, Sir George Bowen and the Victorian Constitutional Crises', *Australian Historical Studies*, 13 (1969), pp. 533–8.

62. Herbert to Carnarvon, 9 February 1874. BL, Add. Ms. 60,791.

63. Rogers to Carnarvon, 5 October, 21 December 1866, PRO30/6/154. See also Rogers' 'Rough Notes on Colonial Relations with Reference to Mr. Torrens' Motion', CO885/3, Confidential Print, 25 April 1870.

64. Herbert to Carnarvon, 13 August 1874, BL, Add. Ms. 60,791. He urged annexation of part of New Guinea on account of the Australian colonies (Herbert to Carnarvon, 10 April 1874, BL, Add. Ms. 60,791), but he despised colonial democracy for having made responsible government in Australia 'a ghastly farce' (Minute, 2 June 1876, CO48/478). Observing the plans for Victoria's grand parliament buildings, he remarked, '[t]he cage will be much finer than the animals contained in it' (30 October 1877, CO309/115, fol. 385).

65. Disraeli to Lady Bradford, 27 September 1878, in Buckle, *Disraeli*, Vol. VI, p. 420. For a more extended opinion by Lord Derby, see Vincent, J., ed., *A Selection from the Diaries of Edward Henry Stanley, 15th Earl of Derby, between September 1869 and March 1878* (London, 1994), p. 485 and *passim*. On Herbert, see chapter in T. H. S. Escott, *Pillars of the Empire* (London, 1879), especially pp. 120–1.

66. M. Corry to Sir Henry Ponsonby, 13 May 1878, in Buckle, *Disraeli*, Vol. VI, pp. 419–20; Disraeli to the Queen, 6 October, 3 November 1877, RA, B53/19, 36, (Cabinet Reports of Prime Ministers to the Crown 1868–1916, microfilm, Harvester Press, 1974); *Hansard*, 3rd ser., Vol. CCXXVII, cols. 20–1 (8 February 1876).

67. See, for example, Froude to Carnarvon, 4 March 1874, in Hardinge, *Life*, Vol. II, p. 176; Carnarvon Diary, 30 April, 3 May, 24 June 1874, BL, Add. Ms. 60,906; Derby to Carnarvon (with note of Disraeli's agreement), 22 June 1874, BL, Add. Ms. 60,765; Marindin G. E., ed., *Letters of Frederic Lord Blachford* (London, 1896), p. 364.

68. Carnarvon Diary, 29 September 1874, 20 August 1874, BL, Add. Ms. 60,906; Memorandum by Sir G. Duffy, 16 September 1874, BL, Add. Ms. 60,812, fols. 193–213; R. Herbert to Carnarvon, 25 September 1874, BL, Add. Ms. 60,791, fols. 123–31.

69. Cf. Note 7 above; Carnarvon 'Lucius Carey, Lord Falkland', pp. 338–9.

70. Carnarvon Diary, 22 July 1887, BL, Add. Ms. 60,929.

71. *Spectator*, 5 July 1890; *Saturday Review*, 5 July 1890.

Chapter 3

1. Amongst the many works analysing Livingstone – the life and the myths of the life – the following offer a number of short cuts: Jeal, Tim, *Livingstone* (London, 1973); Holmes, Timothy, *Journey to Livingstone: the Exploration of an Imperial Myth* (London, 1993); Driver, Felix, *Geography Militant: Cultures of Exploration and Empire* (London, 2001), pp. 68–89. See also: Livingstone, David, *Missionary Travels in South Africa* (London, 1857), and Stanley, Henry M., *How I Found Livingstone* (London, 1872).

2. After his initial glories following his explorations, which included the sighting and naming of the Victoria Falls (in what is now Zambia), Livingstone returned home a hero. He called upon his fellow men to keep to the spirit of the age and to help him open up Africa to Christianity and commerce so that the scourge of slavery could be forced out. He published an account of his travels which became a best-seller. His second set of explorations – no longer in the employment of the London Missionary Society but as H.M. Consul – was a failure on all these grounds.

3. For example, the *East Kent, Faversham and Sittingbourne Gazette* published these details in February 1874. This newspaper provided particularly prominent coverage of the reception.

4. Mackenzie, John M., 'David Livingstone: The Construction of the Myth' in Walker, Graham and Gallagher, Tom, eds., *Sermons and Battle Hymns: Protestant Popular Culture in Modern Scotland* (Edinburgh, 1990), pp. 24–42.

5. Wolffe, John, *Great Deaths: Grieving, Religion and Nationhood in Victorian and Edwardian Britain* (Oxford, 2000), pp. 138–45.

6. See Lewis, Joanna, 'Laying to Rest a Victorian Myth: The Death and Memorialisation of David Livingstone', (unpublished seminar paper, 2003).

7. See Temple Patterson, A., *A History of Southampton, 1700–1914* (3 vols, Southampton, 1975), Vol. III.

8. See his obituary in the *Hampshire Independent*, 1 August 1896, and miscellaneous local reminiscences: Edwin Jones file, Southampton City Archives.

9. *Hampshire Advertiser*, 1 April 1874.

10. According to local historian, Genevieve Bailey, most of the council were Freemasons at this time (private information, April 2002).

11. Council Minutes, 1 April 1874, Southampton City Archives.

12. See Jeal, *Livingstone*, pp. 277–92.

13. See the discussion in Lewis, 'Laying to Rest a Victorian Myth'.

14. *Hampshire Advertiser*, 4 April 1874.

15. *Southampton Times*, 11 April 1874. Disraeli had requested Gurney to give proper notice of his question in the Commons: *Hansard*, 3rd ser., Vol. CXVIII, cols. 486–8 (31 March 1874).

16. See Wolffe, *Great Deaths*, pp. 140–1.

17. *Hampshire Advertiser*, 11 April 1874.

18. *Hampshire Advertiser*, 18 April 1874.

19. *Southampton Times*, 11 April 1874.

20. *Southampton Times*, 11 April 1874.

21. *Southampton Observer*, 18 April 1874.

22. *Daily News*, 16 April 1874.

23. *Southampton Observer*, 18 April 1874.

24. *Hampshire Advertiser*, 18 April 1874.

25. *East Kent, Faversham and Sittingbourne Gazette*, 18 April 1874; *Southampton Observer*, 18 April 1874.

26. *East Kent, Faversham and Sittingbourne Gazette*, 18 April 1874.

27. 'Livingstone Memories', letter from F. G. Mouncher to *Southampton Evening Echo*, 22 September 1930. Mouncher had played the bugle in the band: Livingstone file, Southampton City Archives.

28. 'Livingstone Memories', letter from H. C. Ashdown to *Southampton Evening Echo*, 19 September 1930, Livingstone file.

29. *Daily News*, 15 April 1874.

30. Photocopy of ledger, courtesy of Genevieve Bailey.

31. 'Drove the Hearse', letter from Mrs L. J. Duffy to *Southampton Evening Echo*, 22 September 1930, Livingstone file.

32. *Hampshire Chronicle*, 18 April 1874.

33. *Southampton Observer*, 18 April 1874.

34. *Southampton Observer*, 18 April 1874.

35. *East Kent, Faversham and Sittingbourne Gazette*, 18 April 1874.

36. *Southampton Observer*, 18 April 1874.

37. *Hampshire Chronicle*, 18 April 1874.

38. Lemon, Sir James, *Reminiscences of Public Life in Southampton, 1866–1900*, (2 vols, Southampton, 1911), Vol. I, p. 74. Minutes of RGS Council, 11 May 1874, RGS Archives, London.

39. *Southampton Observer*, 18 April 1874.

40. *Southampton Times*, 18 April 1874.

41. Reprinted in the *East Kent, Faversham and Sittingbourne Gazette*, 18 April 1874.

42. *Hampshire Chronicle*, 18 April 1874.

43. *Southampton Observer*, 18 April 1874.

44. Minutes of Finance Committee Meeting, 28 May 1874, Southampton City Archives.

45. Minutes of Finance Committee Meeting, 11 June 1874.

Chapter 4

1. Herkomer, Sir Hugh, *The Herkomers* (2 vols, London, 1910), Vol. I, p. 82.

2. Millais was born in Portland Terrace, Southampton, on 8 June 1829 into an old Jersey family. His family departed the city by the time he was four.

3. 'Southampton College of Art, Roy Hattersley Opens', *Southern Evening Echo*, 18 March 1974; 'College of Art: Cost about 720,000 pounds', *Southern Evening Echo*, 19 May 1983.

4. 'Our Weekly Illustrated Feature No. 23: The School of Art', *Southampton and District Pictorial*, 18 September 1912, p. 5.

5. Crawford, Alan, ed., *By Hammer and Hand: The Arts and Crafts Movement in Birmingham* (Birmingham, 1984).

6. 'The School of Art', p. 5.

7. Lambourne, Lionel, *Victorian Painting* (London, 1999), p. 41.

8. Horowitz, Helen Lefkowitz, *Culture and the City: Cultural Philanthropy in Chicago from the 1880s to 1917* (Chicago, Ill. and London, 1976).

9. Curtis, Penelope, ed., *Patronage and Practice: Sculpture on Merseyside* (Liverpool, 1989), p. 8.

10. Lambourne, *Victorian Painting*, p. 41.

11. Anderson, A., *H. R. Hartley* (Southampton, 1987).

12. The Hartley Institute was situated on the Lower High Street, below Holy Rood, and contained a lecture hall seating 2,100 people. In 1902 it became the Hartley University College, and in 1919 moved to Highfield, becoming, in 1952, the University of Southampton.

13. Wright, Christopher, *Renaissance to Impressionism: Masterpieces for the Southampton City Art Gallery* (London, 1998), p. 6

14. Lambourne, *Victorian Painting*, p. 37.

15. Lambourne, *Victorian Painting*, p. 37.

16. Lambourne, *Victorian Painting*, p. 41.

17. Lambourne, *Victorian Painting*, p. 41.

18. Millais formed with William Holman Hunt and Dante Gabriel Rossetti the nucleus the Pre-Raphaelite Brotherhood from 1848 to 1853. Millais went on to become the most famous Victorian portrait painter. Funnell, Peter and Warner, Malcolm, eds., *Millais: Portraits* (London, 1999).

19. Billcliffe, Roger, *The Glasgow Boys: The Glasgow School of Painting, 1875–1895* (London, 1985).

20. Mann, John Edgar, *Southampton People* (Southampton, 1989), p. 22–3.

21. Stewart, Brian, *William Shayer Senior, 1787–1879* (Exhibition Catalogue, Southampton, 1987), p. 4. See Stewart, Brian and Cutten, Mervyn, *The Shayer Family of Painters* (London, 1981).

22. The Buchan family certainly did not desert Southampton. Henry Buchan's son, Henry Joseph (1813–93) was Mayor of Southampton in 1871. But his fortune did not come from dealing in art; rather, it came from ready-mixed paint, as he was a partner in Peacock and Buchan of Southampton (1860–1960).

23. Stewart, *William Shayer Senior, 1787–1879*, p. 6.

24. Stewart, *William Shayer Senior ,1787–1879*, p. 6.

25. Sir Walter Gilbey, quoted in Stewart, *William Shayer Senior, 1787–1879*, p. 8.

26. Stewart, *William Shayer Senior, 1787–1879*, p. 8.

27. For the support of British artists working in Rome, see Curtis, *Patronage and Practice: Sculpture on Merseyside*.

28. For an account of Hicks's life and work, see Allwood, Rosamund, *George Elgar Hicks: Painter of Victorian Life*, (Exhibition Catalogue, London, 1983).

29. Allwood, *George Elgar Hicks*, citing the *Art Journal*, (1863), p. 111.

30. Lambourne, *Victorian Painting*, p. 371.

31. Allwood, *George Elgar Hicks*, p. 11.

32. Allwood, *George Elgar Hicks*, p. 52.

33. Allwood, *George Elgar Hicks*, p. 52

34. Hicks, G. E., *Guide to Figure Drawing* (London, 1853), p. 30n.

35. Herkomer, Hubert, *Autobiography of Hubert Herkomer* (London, 1890), p. 11.

36. Herkomer, *Autobiography*, p. 36.

37. Edwards, Lee MacCormick, *Herkomer: A Victorian Artist* (Aldershot, 1999) p. 29.

38. 'Madame Herkomer, who has so successfully laboured in the town during the past seventeen years as a professor of music, is about to leave Southampton in order to take up residence with her son [. . .] near London. While here she has gained the respect and love of her pupils and a large circle of friends [. . .] Mr Hubert Herkomer has already attained high honours as an artist, and they hope he will shine still further and become one of the stars in the art of painting'. Cited in Edwards, *Herkomer: A Victorian Artist*, p. 18.

39. Engel, Louis, *From Handel to Halle; with Autobiographies by Professor Huxley and Professor Herkomer* (London, 1890), p. 153.

40. Mann, *Southampton People*, p. 92.

41. Herkomer, *The Herkomers*, p. 43.

42. 'This introduction to formal training was a disaster, and in later life he often criticized the crippling academic methods to which he was exposed as a young art student', Edwards, *Herkomer: A Victorian Artist*, p. 20.

43. Baldry, Alfred Lys, *Hubert von Herkomer, RA* (London, 1901), p. 16.

44. Mills, J. Saxon, *Life and Letters of Sir Hubert Herkomer C.V.O, RA: A Study in Struggle and Success* (London, 1923), p. 44.

45. Baldry, *Hubert von Herkomer*, p. 16.

46. As Herkomer later recalled, 'In the evenings young mechanics or school teachers would come to the school to do chalk drawings from casts and I was always amazed to see the points they made on their chalks – masterpieces in themselves and then stipple, stipple, stipple, night after night [. . .] at one piece of ornament [. . .] the result of which would be duly sent to headquarters and awarded a medal or what not', Herkomer, *Autobiography*, p. 20.

47. Saxon Mills, *Life and Letters of Sir Hubert Herkomer*, p. 37.

48. The Bushey School of Art was under his leadership from 1883 until 1904 and then continued under Lucy Kemp-Welch, a former pupil, from 1905 until 1911.

49. Herkomer, *Autobiography*, p. 19.

50. von Herkomer, *The Herkomers*, p. 52.

51. von Herkomer, *The Herkomers*, p. 91.

52. von Herkomer, Hubert, *My School and My Gospel* (London, 1908), p. 21.

53. von Herkomer, *The Herkomers*, p. 101.

54. von Herkomer, *The Herkomers*, p. 104.

55. von Herkomer, *The Herkomers*, pp. 103–4. Wiseman was a framemaker and picture dealer.

56. Engel, *From Handel to Halle*, p.170.

57. 'Artist's Gift to the Town He Loved', *Southampton Evening Echo*, 1 June 1983. Although born in Ottery St Mary, Devon, Williams spent at least the last 25 years of his life in Bath Cottage, Bitterne. The Southampton City Art Gallery holds 123 watercolours by this prolific and talented artist, the bulk presented by Mr and Mrs Alfred Fellows to the Corporation Library in 1895.

58. Willis, John, *The Williams Bequest* (Southampton, 1895), p. 10.

59. von Herkomer, *The Herkomers*, p. 132.

60. von Herkomer, *The Herkomers*, p. 135.

61. *Hampshire Independent*, 29 May 1869.

62. *Times*, 1 April 1914.

63. Edwards, *Herkomer: A Victorian Artist*, p. 28.

64. Engel, *From Handel to Halle*, p. 180. Gregory was elected a member of the Royal Institute in 1876 and was its President from 1898 to 1909.

65. Edwards, *Herkomer: A Victorian Artist*, p. 30.

66. Wedmore, Frederick, 'E. J. Gregory, A.R.A', *Magazine of Art*, 7, (1884), p. 354.

67. Wedmore, 'E. J. Gregory', p. 359.

68. Cited in Morris, Edward, *Victorian and Edwardian Paintings in the Lady Lever Art Gallery* (London, 1994), p. 43.

69. *Academy*, 51 (1897), p. 527.

70. *Boulter's Lock* was purchased by C. J. Galloway, Gregory's most important patron. He bought about one-third of the artist's paintings.

71. 'The School of Art', p. 5.

72. Ovenden, Graham, *James Sellars: Artist-Writer-Teacher* (Bodmin, 2003).

73. Moore, Jerrold Northrop, et al., *The Brotherhood of Ruralists: A Celebration* (Bodmin, 2003).

Chapter 5

1. Kermode, Frank, *The Sense of an Ending: Studies in the Theory of Fiction* (Oxford, p. 58.

2. (Fourth Estate, 2001). 'Spike Island' is the nickname acquired by Netley's neighbouring suburb of Sholing, where I grew up. The most likely derivation of the name comes from an increasing mid-19th-century population of Irish workers and navvies, employed in Southampton Docks and on the railways. The reference was to the original Spike Island in Cork Harbour, a penal colony since Cromwellian times, and was thus a slur on these itinerant gaol-fodder. The original Spike Island was well known to 19th-century readers of *The Times*, as displayed by an article in its edition for 10 June 1878, noting a mutinous disturbance 'among the convicts belonging to Spike Island', giving no further explanation of the then well-known 'convict station'. But other explanations cite the area known as Botany Bay – home of other itinerants, the Gypsies who had historically horse-traded with the military camps on the site – and the story chained transportees said to have been held on the area's heathland, like some semi-rural purgatory, in readiness for their transit to the New World. Further claims came from the geography of the vaguely

spike-shaped peninsula as defined by the Itchen and Hamble rivers or from its profusion of gorse bushes, now rapidly being uprooted as the town moved eastwards in its own act of colonisation, its suburbs edging towards Netley itself.

3. Similarly, the historian Henry Knighton of Leicester had claimed that the bubonic plague epidemic of 1348 entered England through Southampton. It is estimated that half the port's population succumbed to that outbreak. See Bullar, John, *Historical Particulars Relating to Southampton* (Southampton, 1820), p. 23.

4. Defoe, Daniel, *A Tour through the Whole Island of Great Britain* (London, 1986), p. 154.

5. Anon., *Guide to Southampton* (Southampton, 1796), p. 67.

6. Lewis, W. S., ed. *The Yale Edition of Horace Walpole's Correspondence*, (48 vols, Oxford and New Haven, Conn., 1948), Vol. XXXV, p. 249.

7. Lewis, *Correspondence of Horace Walpole*, Vol. XIV, p. 58.

8. Lewis, *Correspondence of Horace Walpole*, Vol. XXXV, p. 249.

9. Courtesy of Deirdre Le Faye, Kent County Archives.

10. Cobbett, William, *Rural Rides* (London, 1967), Vol. II, p. 470.

11. *Passages from the English Notebooks of Nathaniel Hawthorne* (2 vols, London, 1870), Vol. II, pp. 106–7.

12. Brannon, Philip, *The Picture of Southampton: A Stranger's Guide* (Southampton, 1845), p. 17.

13. *Vanity Fair*, 31 July 1875, p. 67.

14. *Report on the Site, etc, of the Royal Victoria Hospital, near Netley Abbey* (London, 1858), p. 40.

15. *Woodbridge Reporter & Aldeburgh Times*, 17 August 1871.

16. Freeman, M. D. and Percival, E. F., 'The Royal Victoria Hospital, Netley: A Horrid Example of Nineteenth-Century Hospital Construction', *Hampshire Magazine*, 20 (June 1980), pp. 61–8.

17. Woodham Smith, Cecil, *Florence Nightingale* (London, 1950), p. 276.

18. Spencer-Silver, Patricia, *Pugin's Builder: The Life and Work of George Myers* (Hull, 1993), p. 141.

19. *Lancet*, 9 May 1868.

20. T. R. W. Longmore, letter to the author, 14 September 2000. Nurses' rooms in the hospital were also initially designed without doors, supposedly to prevent illicit assignations between staff and patients.

21. It has also been suggested that this raised embankment, which became the route to the military cemetery, was planned to take a branch line of the Southampton-to-Portsmouth railway line (itself constructed to serve Netley hospital) directly into the site. This was not achieved until 1900, however, when a line was built from Netley station to the rear of the main building.

22. Pevsner, Nikolaus and Lloyd, David, *The Buildings of England: Hampshire and the Isle of Wight* (London, 1967), p. 351.

23. *Illustrated London News*, 9 May 1863.

24. *Southern Evening Echo*, 2 August 1985.

25. Conan Doyle, Arthur, *A Study in Scarlet* (Oxford, 1993), p. 15.

26. Postcard album, 1914–1918, Park Office Archives, Royal Victoria Country Park, Netley.

27. *Southampton Times*, 16 January 1875.

28. An estimated 80,000 British troops suffered shell shock, more than half being treated in the field, if at all. In his book, *War of Nerves* (London, 2000), Ben Shephard recommends that, due to the Army's reluctance to diagnose the condition, the total figure should be multiplied by at least three.

29. Owen, Harold and Bell, John, eds, *Wilfred Owen: Collected Letters* (Oxford, 1967), p. 470.

30. Hurst, Dr Arthur, and Symns, Dr J. L. M., with the Royal Army Medical Corps, the Medical Research Committee and Netley (Hampshire) and Seale Hayne (Devon) Military Hospitals, *War Neuroses*, 1917, Royal College of Physicians/Wellcome Trust, 16 mm film, 22 minutes. See also Hurst and Syms, 'The Rapid Cure of Hysterical Symptoms in Soldiers', *Lancet*, 3 August 1918.

31. I am grateful to Tony Kushner for drawing my attention to this story. 'The scale of the Atlantic Park Hostel [. . .] to say nothing of the length of its history, make [. . .] its near-total obscurity in both national *and* local history surprising. At its peak, for example, it had half the population of Eastleigh and one-twentieth of that of Southampton'. See Kushner, Tony and Lunn, Ken, 'Memory, Forgetting and Absence: The Politics of Naming on the English South Coast', *Patterns of Prejudice*, 31 (2), 1997, p. 38. In this essay, Kushner and Lunn also argue the link between Atlantic Park and the proto-fascist founder of the Supermarine company, Noel Pemberton Billing, the subject of my own *Wilde's Last Stand: Decadence, Conspiracy and the First World War* (London, 1997).

32. Quoted in Mullan, Bob, *R.D. Laing* (London, 1999), p. 54.

33. Miller, Jonathan, dir., *Alice in Wonderland*, BBC 1966, 72 minutes (BFI DVD, 2003).

34. Press release, 16 September 1966, *Southern Daily Echo* library.

35. Hardy, Thomas, *The Mayor of Casterbridge* (London, 1981), p. 152.

36. Sebald, W. G., *Austerlitz* (London, 2001), pp. 23–4.

Chapter 6

1. Fearon, Daniel, 'General Gordon's Khartoum Star', *British Numismatic Journal*, 34, (1965), pp. 162–5; Behrman, Cynthia F., 'The After-Life of General Gordon', *Albion*, 3, (1971), pp. 47–61; Johnson, Douglas H., 'The Death of Gordon: A Victorian Myth', *Journal of Imperial and Commonwealth History*, 10 (1982), pp. 285–310; Judd, Denis, 'Gordon of Khartoum: The Making of an Imperial Martyr', *History Today*, 35 (1985), pp. 19–25; Rattue, James, 'The "Cult" of Gordon', *Royal Engineers Journal*, 112 (1998), pp. 182–9; Wolffe, John, *Great Deaths: Grieving, Religion, and Nationhood in Victorian and Edwardian Britain* (Oxford, 2000), pp. 145–53.

2. Strachey, Lytton, 'The End of General Gordon' in his *Eminent Victorians* (London, 1918); Porter, Bernard, *The Absent-Minded Imperialists: What the British Really Thought about Empire* (Oxford, 2004), pp. 166–7; Andrew Porter, *Religion versus Empire: British Protestant Missionaries and Overseas Expansion, 1700–1914* (Manchester, 2004), pp. 222–3; Davenport-Hines, Richard, 'Gordon, Charles George', in Matthew, H. C. G. and Harrison, B. H., eds, *Oxford Dictionary of National Biography* (Oxford, 2004).

3. Douch, Robert, *Monuments and Memorials in Southampton* (Southampton, 1968), pp. 32–3.

4. *Southampton Times*, 14 February 1885, p. 4.

5. *Hampshire Advertiser*, 7 February 1885, p. 8; Trench, Charles Chenevix, *Charley Gordon: An Eminent Victorian Reassessed* (London, 1978), pp. 54–5; Leonard, A. G. K., 'Gordon's Southampton Home', *Hampshire: The County Magazine*, 21, (1981), pp. 56–9; Leonard, A. G. K., *More Stories of Southampton Streets* (Southampton, 1989), pp. 157–60.

6. *The Times*, 14 February 1885, p. 8, 28 February 1885, p. 6.

7. Charles H. Allen to Augusta Gordon, 6 June 1885, Gordon papers, BL, Add. Ms. 51,300, fols. 133–4; *The Times*, 30 March 1885, p. 6.

8. *The Times*, 16 March 1885, p. 10.

9. For example, *The Times*, 9 April 1885, p. 10.

10. Hill, G. B., *Colonel Gordon in Central Africa, 1874–9* (London, 1881), p. vi.

11. *Letters of General C. G. Gordon to his sister, M. A. Gordon* (London, 1888), p. ix.

12. Lilley, W. E., *The Life and Work of General Gordon at Gravesend* (London, 1885); *Observations on the Holy Communion by General Gordon* (Southampton, 1885); Montague, C. J., *Sixty Years in Waifdom; or, the Ragged School Movement in English History* (London, 1904), pp. 132–42.

13. Over the following years, Augusta turned her home in Rockstone Place into a shrine to her dead brother. See the account in *Chambers's Journal*, 18 November 1893, pp. 732–5.

14. Barnes, R. H. and Brown, C. E, *Charles George Gordon: A Sketch* (London, 1885). Barnes was the vicar of Heavitree, near Exeter, with whom Gordon stayed prior to his departure for the Sudan in January, 1884.

16. *The Times*, 16 March 1885, p. 10; H. W. Gordon to Lord Napier of Magdala, n.d. (March, 1885), Gordon papers, BL. Add. Ms. 52,401, fols. 80–1. Sir Henry Gordon later claimed that subscriptions dwindled when the Mansion House committee decided on the Port Said project, but given that 8,500 pounds was raised before the decision was taken, and a further 9,500 pounds afterwards, that is arguable. Gordon, H. W., *Events in the Life of Gordon from its Beginning to its End* (London, 1886), pp. 441–2.

16. F. Lake to H. W. Gordon, 25 March 1885, Gordon papers, BL, Add. Ms. 52,401, fols. 180–1.

17. *The Times*, 10 April 1885, p. 7, 27 May 1885, p. 9; Montague, *Sixty Years*, p. 453.

18. *The Times*, 13 June 1885, p. 11, 2 July 1885, p. 8; *Illustrated London News*, 14 January 1885, pp. 49–51.

19. Although Sir Henry Gordon did complain that the new boys' school was too devoted to military training: Gordon, *Events*, p. 442.

20. Council Minutes, 11 March 1885, p. 458, Southampton City Archives, SC2/1/27; *Southampton Times*, 14 March 1885, p. 3.

21. *Southampton Observer*, 21 March 1885, p. 3.

22. *Southampton Times*, 28 March 1885, p. 5; *Southampton Observer*, 28 March 1885, pp. 4–5.

23. *Southampton Observer*, 21 March 1885, p. 3, 28 March 1885, p. 5, 18 April 1885, p. 4.

24. *Southampton Observer*, 4 April 1885, p. 5; cf. Note 16 above.

25. *Friends' Quarterly Examiner*, April 1885, pp. 272–85.

26. *Southampton Times*, 2 May 1885, p. 5, 9 May 1885, p. 7. Later in the year, Revd Henry Solly led a service at the town's Unitarian Church of the Saviour, his subject being 'General Gordon's last words from Khartoum', *Southampton Times*, 26 September 1885, p. 5.

27. *Southampton Observer*, 16 May 1885, p. 4. Captain Eyre Crabbe was also President of the North Stoneham, Chilworth and Portswood Conservative Association. He eventually returned to Southampton in July.

28. Council Minutes, 13 May 1885, pp. 496–8, 17 June 1885, p. 506, 8 July 1885, p. 518; *Southampton Times*, 20 June 1885, p. 3; *Southampton Observer*, 11 July 1885, p. 8.

29. *Southampton Times*, 27 June 1885, p. 5.

30. Council Minutes, 15 October 1885, p. 559; *Southampton Times*, 17 October 1885, p. 8.

31. Council Minutes, 28 October 1885, p. 560. These spears seem either to have been sent back, or returned to Augusta at a later date, for they were back at Rockstone Place by 1893: *Chambers's Journal*, 18 November 1893, p. 732.

32. Patterson, Alfred Temple, *A History of Southampton 1700–1914, 3: Setbacks and Recoveries, 1868–1914* (3 vols, Southampton Records series, 18, Southampton, 1975), p. 72; cf. Warren Hannah, 'Southampton and the Boer War', (unpublished M.Phil. dissertation, University of Southampton, 2004).

33. *Southern Echo*, 11 August 1889, pp. 2–3; *Official Programme of Proceedings in Connection with the Laying of Foundation Stone by HRH Princess Beatrice, of the Gordon Boys' New Home, etc* (Southampton, 1889).

34. *Southern Echo*, p. 3; Council Minutes, 10 August 1889, pp. 301–2.

35. Leonard, *More Stories of Southampton Streets*, p. 160

36. Leonard, 'Memorials of Mementoes of Gordon'; St Luke's Vestry Minutes, 31 March 1910, Southampton City Archives, PR 20/6/1.

Chapter 7

1. See, in particular, Mackenzie, John, *Propaganda and Empire: The Manipulation of British Public Opinion 1880–1960* (Manchester, 1984).

2. See, for example, Thompson, Andrew S., 'Tariff Reform: An Imperial Strategy, 1903–1913', *Historical Journal*, 40 (4) (1997), pp. 1033–54; Richards, Thomas, *The Commodity Culture of Victorian England: Advertising and Spectacle, 1851–1914* (Stanford, Calif., 1990); Summerfield, Penny, 'Patriotism and Empire: Music-Hall Entertainment, 1870–1914', in Macdonald, John M., ed., *Imperialism and Popular Culture* (Manchester, 1986); Richards, Jeffrey, ed., *Imperialism and Juvenile Literature* (Manchester and New York, 1989); Castle, Kathryn, *Britannia's Children: Reading Colonialism through Children's Books and Magazines* (Manchester, 1996).

3. For details of which, see Yorke, Barbara, 'The King Alfred Millenary in Winchester, 1901', *Hampshire Papers*, 17 (October 1999); Bowker, Alfred, *The King Alfred Millenary* (London, 1902).

4. See, for example, *Hampshire Chronicle, Hampshire Observer, Hampshire Independent, Southampton Times* and *Southern Daily Echo* for September 1901.

5. *Southern Daily Echo*, 21 September 1901, p. 2; *Hampshire Observer*, 21 September 1901, p. 8.

6. 'The Alfred Millenary', printed MS, Hampshire Record Office (HRO), 117M88W/68(13).

7. *Hampshire Independent*, 28 September 1901, p. 7.

8. HRO holds examples of such material. See, for example, 117M88W/68(19).

9. *Daily Mail*, 18 September 1901, p. 3.

10. Simmons, C. A., *Reversing the Conquest: History and Myth in Nineteenth-Century British Literature* (New Brunswick, NJ, 1990), pp. 198–9.

11. *Hampshire Observer*, 21 September 1901, p. 5.

12. Creighton, Mandell, *Historical Lectures and Addresses* (London, 1903), pp. 262–3.

13. Bowker, *Millenary*, 126.

14. Lecture by York-Powell, HRO, 71M89W/5.

15. Although, see Ryan, Deborah Sugg, 'Staging the Imperial City: The Pageant of London, 1911' in Driver, Felix and Gilbert, David, eds, *Imperial Cities: Landscape, Space and Identity* (Manchester, 1999), and also her ' "Pageantitis": Frank Lascelles' 1907 Oxford Historical Pageant, Visual Spectacle and Popular Memory', *Visual Culture in Britain* (forthcoming, 2007).

16. Withington, Robert, *English Pageantry* (2 vols, Cambridge, Mass., 1918–20), pp. 194–5, 299.

17. *Southampton Times*, 22 June 1907, p. 3; *Hampshire Chronicle*, 22 June 1907, p. 5.

18. Even the dress rehearsal drew an audience of more than 3,000 (*Southampton Times*, 22 June 1907, p. 3).

19. *Hampshire Chronicle*, 8 June 1907, p. 11; *Southampton Times*, 6 July 1907, p. 9.

20. *Hampshire Chronicle*, 22 June 1907, p. 5.

21. Minutes of Finance Sub-Committee, HRO, 179M84W/1.

22. Minutes of Grand Stand and Seating Sub-Committee, 6 November 1907 (HRO, 179M84W/2); Cast Book (HRO, 179M84W/7).

23. *Hampshire Independent*, 20 June 1908, p. 11, 27 June 1908, p. 12. As early as mid-January 1908, 2,500 seats had already been booked (Minutes of Grand Stand and Seating Sub-Committee, 13 January 1908, HRO, 179M84W/2).

24. Meeting of the Executive Committee of the Winchester Pageant, reported in *Hampshire Independent*, 6 June 1908, p. 8. Three-quarters of the seats for the evening performances were offered at 1 shilling, with children admitted at half-price.

25. *Hampshire Independent*, 4 July 1908, p. 9.

26. *Southampton Times*, 29 June 1907, p. 9.

27. Parker, Louis N., *Several of My Lives* (London, 1928), pp. 283–4.

28. *Southampton Times*, 22 June 1907, p. 3; *Hampshire Chronicle*, 29 June 1907, p. 10.

29. *Hampshire Chronicle*, 29 June 1907, pp. 10–11; *Southampton Times*, 29 June 1907, p. 9

30. *Romsey Millenary Celebration: Words and Music* (Romsey, 1907), p. 15; *Hampshire Chronicle*, 29 June 1907, pp. 10–11.

31. Memo to Costumes Sub-Committee, HRO, 179M84W/9.

32. Minutes of Costumes Sub-Committee, 21 October 1907, HRO, 179M84W/5.

33. A large majority of the 1,200 performers were local people; the total population of Romsey was about 4,000 (*Southampton Times*, 22 June 1907, p. 3).

34. Minutes of Staging and Music Committee, 16 September 1907, HRO, 179M84W/4.

35. Minutes of Costumes Sub-Committee, 7 October 1907, HRO, 179M84W/5.

36. A representative sample of names and addresses was used here, but it must be stressed that cross-referencing in this way only provides an approximate idea of the social background of pageant performers. After all, the census was conducted seven years before the pageant, and a number of people – particularly working-class people – would have moved house or changed jobs in the interim. Despite the element of approximation, however, the overwhelming impression given is one of cross-class community participation. The sources used for this survey were the 1901 Census, Section Book for Stage Management, HRO, 179M84W/8; Cast Book, HRO, 179M84W/7; Performers' Address Book, HRO, 179M84W/6.

37. *Southampton Times*, 27 June 1908, p. 6.

38. In his article, even Hill felt the need to include summaries of the historical events featured in the pageant, as well as quotations from the lines spoken by some of the leading characters.

39. For which see, for example, *Southampton Times*, 22 June 1907, p. 7.

40. Quiller-Couch, Arthur, *Brother Copas* (London, 1911), pp. 335–6.

41. For Winchester examples of such material, see *Souvenir of the Winchester National Pageant* (Winchester, 1908), HRO, W/C1/5/871; Lewis, J. F., *Short Historical Notes on the Winchester Pageant* (Winchester, 1908), HRO, 169M84W28.

42. *Southampton Times*, 29 June 1907, p. 9.

43. *Southern Daily Echo*, 22 June 1908, p. 2.

44. At least 40 books on Alfred were published between 1898 and 1902 (Yorke, 'Millenary', p. 18).

45. Plummer, Charles, *The Life and Times of Alfred the Great* (Oxford, 1902), p. 8.

46. Chapman, Raymond, *The Sense of the Past in Victorian Literature* (London, 1986), pp. 187–9; Harris, Jose, *Private Lives, Public Spirit: Britain 1870–1914* (London, 1994), pp. 32–6; Mandler, Peter, *The Fall and Rise of the Stately Home* (New Haven, Conn., 1997), pp. 109–17; Blaas, P. B. M., *Continuity and Anachronism: Parliamentary and Constitutional Development in Whig Historiography and in the Anti-Whig Reaction between 1890 and 1930* (The Hague, 1978), pp. xiv, 10–11, 32–3, 195–218; Lowenthal, David, *The Past is a Foreign Country* (Cambridge, 1985), pp. 97–102.

47. Harris, *Private Lives*, p. 33.

48. Chapman, *Sense of the Past*, p. 102.

49. Mandler, *Fall and Rise*, pp. 109–17.

50. Scrapbook of press cuttings, HRO, 71M89W/5.

51. *Hampshire Independent*, 27 June 1908, p. 6.

52. Parker, *Several of My Lives*, p. 279.

53. *Warwick Advertiser*, 30 June 1905, p. 5.

54. *Hampshire Independent*, 29 June 1907, p. 12.

55. Minutes of Staging and Music Committee, 10 May 1907, 18 October 1907, HRO, 179M84W/4.

56. *Romsey Millenary*, p. 11.

57. Cutting from *Hampshire Observer*, 14 July 1906, HRO, 179M84W/9.

58. *Southern Daily Echo*, 24 June 1908, p. 2.

59. *Romsey Millenary*, p. 42.

60. *Romsey Millenary*, pp. 11–12.

61. Snell, K. D. M., 'The Culture of Local Xenophobia', *Social History*, 28 (2003), pp. 1–30.

62. Snell, 'Culture of Local Xenophobia', p. 18, n. 108.

63. See Readman, Paul, 'The Conservative Party, Patriotism and British Politics: The Case of the General Election of 1900', *Journal of British Studies*, 40 (2001), pp. 107–45.

64. *Southern Daily Echo*, 21 September 1901, p. 4.

65. Bowker, *Millenary*, pp. 126–7.

66. For example, Bowker, *Millenary*, pp. 109–12; Speech of Shaw Lefevre, 11 March 1899, scrapbook, HRO, 71M89W/5.

67. Bowker, *Millenary*, p. 5.

68. *The Times*, 28 October 1901, p. 10, 29 October 1901, p. 8.

69. *Southampton Times*, 21 September 1901, p. 10; *Southampton Observer*, 21 September 1901, p. 8; *Southern Daily Echo*, 21 September 1901, p. 4.

70. *Hampshire Independent*, 24 August 1901, p. 3.

71. Bowker, *Millenary*, p. 187.

72. For example, those at Oxford (1907), Cheltenham (1908) and Scarborough (1912).

73. *Winchester National Pageant: The Book of the Words and Music* (Winchester, 1908), p. 17; *Southern Daily Echo*, 26 June 1908, p. 2.

74. *Winchester National Pageant*, p. 76, cf. p. 73; Lewis, *Short Historical Notes*, p. 8; Oaten, F., *Characters of the National Pageant* (St Albans, 1908), HRO, 184M84W/1.

75. Wiener, Martin J., *English Culture and the Decline of the Industrial Spirit, 1850–1980* (Cambridge, 1981); cf. Mandler, Peter, 'Against "Englishness": English Culture and the Limits to Rural Nostalgia', *Transactions of the Royal Historical Society*, 6th ser., Vol. VII (1997), pp. 155–75.

76. Bowker, *Millenary*, p. 110.

77. Bowker, *Millenary*, pp. 109–11.

78. Harrison, F., 'Alfred as King', in Bowker, Alfred, ed., *Alfred the Great* (London, 1899), p. 42.

79. *Romsey Millenary*, pp. 11–12; *Winchester National Pageant*, preface.

80. *Romsey Millenary*, p. 42.

81. *Winchester National Pageant*, pp. 79 ff.

82. *Romsey Millenary*, p. 83.

83. *Winchester National Pageant*, p. 25.

84. *Romsey Millenary*, p. 33.

85. *Romsey Millenary*, p. 38.

86. *Romsey Millenary*, p. 33.

87. *Hampshire Chronicle*, 29 June 1907, p. 10.

88. *Hampshire Chronicle*, 29 June 1907, p. 10.

89. Harrison, F., 'The Millenary of King Alfred', in Harrison, F., *George Washington and Other American Addresses* (London, 1901), p. 64.

Chapter 8

1. Williams, David L., *Southampton* (Shepperton, 1984), p. 4.
2. Hoare, Philip, *Spike Island: The Memory of a Military Hospital* (London, 2001), p. 35.
3. Williams, *Southampton*, p. 6.
4. Hoare, *Spike Island*, p. 35.
5. Rance, Adrian, *Southampton: An Illustrated History* (Portsmouth, 1986), p. 133.
6. For other studies of the myth and memory of the sinking of the *Titanic*, see Barczewski, Stephanie, *Titanic: A Night Remembered* (Hambledon and London, 2004); Bergfelder, Tim and Street, Sarah, *The Titanic in Myth and Memory: Representations in Visual and Literary Culture* (London, 2004); Biel, Steven, *Down with the Old Canoe: A Cultural History of the Titanic Disaster* (New York and London, 1996); Foster, John Wilson, *The Titanic Complex: A Cultural Manifest* (Vancouver, 1997); Guimond, James, 'The *Titanic* and the commodification of Catastrophe', in Gray, Peter and Oliver, Kendrick, eds, *The Memory of Catastrophe* (Manchester and New York, 2004), pp. 79–90; and Howells, Richard, *The Myth of the Titanic* (New York, 1999). For more on the 1997 film directed by James Cameron, see Lubin, David M., *Titanic* (London, 1999) and the essays in Sandler, Kevin S. and Studlar, Gaylyn, eds, *Titanic: Anatomy of a Blockbuster* (New Brunswick, NJ, 1999).
7. Rance, *Southampton*, p. 101.
8. The American Line had previously moved to Southampton in 1893.
9. White Star's head office remained in Liverpool, and, therefore, that city's name was emblazoned on the *Titanic*'s stern.
10. The move bumped Murdoch to First Officer and Charles Lightoller, who had been First Officer, to Second Officer. The original Second Officer, David Blair, was forced to relinquish his berth. Blair wrote to his sister that he was 'very disappointed' not to make *Titanic*'s maiden voyage. Hyslop, Donald, Forsyth, Alastair, and Jemima, Sheila, *Titanic Voices: Memories from the Fateful Voyage* (Stroud, 1997), p. 36. This book is invaluable to anyone interested in the *Titanic*'s connection to Southampton, and I owe its authors a considerable debt.
11. Hyslop, et al., *Titanic Voices*, p. 46.
12. Hyslop, et al., *Titanic Voices*, pp. 44–54.
13. Hyslop, et al., *Titanic Voices*, p. 18.
14. I am grateful to T. P. Henry of the Totton and Eling Historical Society for the information from the Northam School log books.
15. Twenty-three of *Titanic*'s 898 crew members were female.
16. Hyslop, et al., *Titanic Voices*, pp. 36, 84.
17. Hyslop, et al., *Titanic Voices*, pp. 67–8.
18. Hyslop, et al., *Titanic Voices*, p. 64.
19. Hyslop, et al., *Titanic Voices*, p. 82.
20. Hyslop, et al., *Titanic Voices*, p. 82.
21. Hyslop, et al., *Titanic Voices*, p. 169.
22. *Southern Daily Echo*, 17 April 1912.
23. *Daily Chronicle*, 17 April 1912; *Daily Chronicle*, 18 April 1912.
24. *Daily Chronicle*, 19 April 1912.

25. *Daily Mirror*, 18 April 1912.
26. An undated copy of this article was shown to me by Brian Ticehurst, the President of the British *Titanic* Society.
27. *Southern Daily Echo*, 17 April 1912.
28. *Southern Daily Echo*, 17 April 1912.
29. Hyslop, et al., *Titanic Voices*, p. 171.
30. Hyslop, et al., *Titanic Voices*, p. 172.
31. See Note 15 above.
32. *Daily Mail*, 19 April 1912.
33. *Daily Chronicle*, 20 April 1912.
34. *Daily Chronicle*, 20 April 1912.
35. Hyslop, et al., *Titanic Voices*, pp. 168–9.
36. Massey, Anne and Hammond, Mike, '"It was true! How can you laugh?": History and Memory in the Reception of *Titanic* in Britain and Southampton', in Sandler, Kevin S. and Studlar, Gaylyn, eds, *Titanic: Anatomy of a Blockbuster*, (New Brunswick, NJ, 1999) pp. 250, 260.
37. Personal interview with Lindsay Ford, 22 June 2001.
38. Personal interview with T. P. Henry, 23 June 2001.
39. Personal interview with Nigel Wood, 23 June 2001.
40. Personal interview with Kevin White, 23 June 2001.
41. The musicians' memorial was destroyed in the Second World War. A replica was placed on the same site in 1990.
42. King, Alex, *Memorials of the Great War in Britain: The Symbolism and Politics of Remembrance* (Oxford, 1998), pp. 184–7.

Chapter 9

1. Headrick, D. R., *The Tools of Empire* (New York, 1981); Headrick, D. R. *The Tentacles of Progress* (New York, 1988); Headrick, D. R., *The Invisible Weapon: Telecommunications and International Politics, 1851–1945* (New York, 1991).
2. Churchill, Winston S., *The River War* (London, 1949), p. 162.
3. Syrett, David, 'The Navy Board and Transports for Cartagena, 1740', *War in History* 9 (2) (2002), pp. 127–41; Rogers, H. C. B., *Troopships and their History* (London, 1963), p. 60.
4. Trooping Programmes for 1867–8 and 1868–9, the TNA, MT23/15, T3351–2 and 3504.
5. *Rudyard Kipling's Verse: Inclusive Edition, 1885–1918* (London, n.d.), pp. 478–9.
6. Rogers, *Troopships*, pp. 161–2.
7. Tulloch, Sir A. B., *Recollections of Forty Years' Service* (Edinburgh, 1903), p. 232.
8. Roberts, Field Marshal Lord, *Forty One Years in India* (London, 1898), pp. 1–2; Harrison, General Sir Richard, *Recollections of a Life in the British Army* (London, 1908), p. 100; Hunter, Archie, *Kitchener's Sword-Arm: The Life and Campaigns of General Sir Archibald Hunter* (Staplehurst, 1996), p. 6.
9. TNA, MT23/102, T42943.

10. TNA, MT23/102, T3981.

11. TNA, MT23/102, T3941.

12. Trustram, Myna, *Women of the Regiment* (Cambridge, 1984), p. 170; Vetch, R. H., *Life, Letters and Diaries of Lieutenant-General Sir Gerald Graham* (Edinburgh, 1901), p. 10; Rogers, *Troopships*, pp. 116–17; Taylor, P. J. O., *A Companion to the Indian Mutiny of 1857* (Delhi, 1996), p. 286.

13. Tulloch, *Recollections of Forty Years' Service*, p. 233.

14. War Office Intelligence Branch, *Narrative of the Field Operations Connected with the Zulu War of 1879* (London, 1881), p. 154; Anglesey, Marquess of, *A History of the British Cavalry*, (8 vols London, 1982), Vol. III, 1872–98, p. 273; Rogers, *Troopships*, p. 147.

15. Laband, John and Knight, Ian, *The War Correspondents: The Anglo-Zulu War* (Stroud, 1997), pp. 120 and 126; Wood, Field Marshal Sir Evelyn, *From Midshipman to Field Marshal* (2 vols London, 1906), Vol. II, p. 95.

16. Maurice, J. F., *The Campaign of 1882 in Egypt* (London, 1887), pp. 108–10.

17. Proceedings of the Confidential Mobilisation Committee, Minutes of 118th Day, 12 February 1885, NA, W033/47, A75. For the Suakin and Nile expeditions generally, see Robson, Brian, *Fuzzy Wuzzy: The Campaigns in the Eastern Sudan, 1884–5* (Tunbridge Wells, 1993), pp. 98–105; Robson, Brian, 'Mounting an Expedition: Sir Gerald Graham's 1885 Expedition to Suakin', *Small Wars and Insurgencies*, 2 (2) (1991), pp. 232–9; Colvile, H. E., *History of the Sudan Campaign* (London, 1889), Vol. I, pp. 176–7 and Vol. II, pp. 317–19.

18. Pollock, John, *Gordon* (Oxford, 1993), pp. 47, 100, 121, 129, 206 and 266.

19. Bailes, Howard, 'Technology and Imperialism: A Case Study of the Victorian Army in Africa', *Victorian Studies*, 24 (1) (1980), pp. 83–104; Beckett, I. F. W., 'The South African War and the Late Victorian Army', in Peter Dennis and Jeffrey Grey, eds, *The Boer War: Army, Nation and Empire* (Canberra, 2000), pp. 31–44; Stone, Jay, 'The Anglo-Boer War and Military Reform in the United Kingdom', in Stone, Jay and Schmidl, Erwin, eds, *The Boer War and Military Reforms* (Lanham md., 1988), p. 25; Amery, Leo, *The Times History of the War in South Africa, 1899–1902* (7 vols, London, 1909), Vol. VI, pp. 282–96.

20. Chapman-Huston, Desmond and Rutter, Owen, *General Sir John Cowans* (2 vols, London, 1924), Vol. I, pp. 103–13; NA, MT23/123, T12958; Maurice, Sir Frederick and Arthur, Sir George, *The Life of Lord Wolseley* (London, 1924), p. 319; *Appendices to the Minutes of Evidence taken before the Royal Commission on the War in South Africa* (London, 1903) Cmd 1792, Appendix III, pp. 17–19; Wilson, H. W., *With the Flag to Pretoria* (2 vols, London, 1900–1), Vol. I, pp. 61–4; NA, MT23/106, T6466, T6598 and T5974.

21. Melville, C. H., *Life of the Rt. Hon. Sir Redvers Buller* (2 vols, London, 1923), Vol. II, pp. 34, 264–5; Pakenham, Thomas, *The Boer War* (London, 1979), pp. 113–14, 156; Symons, Julian, *Buller's Campaign* (London, 1963), pp. 92–3; James, David, *The Life of Lord Roberts* (London, 1954), p. 369; Wilson, *With the Flag to Pretoria*, Vol. I, pp. 219, 225; Wilson, *With the Flag to Pretoria*, Vol. II, p. 525; Cassar, George, *Kitchener: Architect of Victory* (London, 1977), p. 137.

22. Anglesey, *History of British Cavalry* (London, 1986), Vol. IV, 1899–1913, pp. 300–2; Amery, *History of War in South Africa*, p. 293; Moody, Bert, *A Pictorial History of the Southampton Docks* (Settle, 1998), p. 14.

23. Amery, *History of War in South Africa*, Vol. VI, p. 296.

24. Radcliffe, Sir Percy, 'With France: The 'WF' Plan and the Genesis of the Western Front', *Stand To*, 10 (1984), pp. 6–13, reproducing NA, WO106/49A/1; Deedes, Sir Charles, 'The View from the War Office' *Stand To*, 10 (1984), pp. 14–16; Chapman-Huston and Rutter, *Cowans*, Vol. I, p. 264; Callwell, C. E., *Field Marshal Sir Henry Wilson: His Life and Diaries* (2 vols, London, 1927), Vol. I, pp. 149–50.

25. Henniker, A. M., 'To War by Timetable', *Stand To*, 10 (1984), pp. 28–9; Chapman-Huston and Rutter, *Cowans*, Vol. I, pp. 270, 280; Admiralty to War Office, 20 September 1911, NA, MT23/329, T14819; War Office to Admiralty, 18 April 1912, WO32/7102; War Office to Admiralty, Rail Tables, WO33/665; Williamson, Samuel, *The Politics of Grand Strategy* (London and Atlantic Highlands, NJ, 1990), pp. 312–16; Henniker, A. M., *Transportation on the Western Front* (London, 1937), pp. 1–25.

26. Radcliffe, 'With France', pp. 6–13; Scott, Peter, 'Port R Rouen – August 1914', *Stand To*, 11 (1984), pp. 28–31; Chapman-Huston and Rutter, *Cowans*, Vol. I, pp. 280–6; Corbett-Smith, A., *The Retreat from Mons* (London, 1916), pp. 5–6; Anglesey, *History of British Cavalry*, Vol. VII *The Curragh and the Western Front, 1914* (Barnsley, 1996), p. 62; NA, MT23/310, T7665.

27. Dunn, J. C., ed., *The War the Infantry Knew, 1914–19* (London, 1987), p. 8; Hooper, H. J., 'The Diary of an Old Contemptible', *Stand To*, 11 (1984), pp. 40–3; Grounds, N. B. C. B., 'A Diary of the Retreat from Mons', *Stand To*, 11 (1984), pp. 44–9; Franklyn, G. E. W., 'From Deepcut to France', *Stand To*, 11 (1984), pp. 18–22.

28. Deedes, 'View from War Office', *Stand To*, 11 (1984), pp. 6–17; Blake, Robert, ed., *The Private Papers of Douglas Haig, 1914–18* (London, 1952), pp. 72–3; Beckett, Ian F. W., *Johnnie Gough VC* (London, 1989), p. 176.

29. NA, MT23/329, T14819.

30. NA, MT23/309, T7277/1914; NA, M23/17/614–88; MT23/239, T14819; Chapman-Huston and Rutter, *Cowans*, Vol. II, pp. 217–18, 248; Gleaves, Albert, *A History of the Transport Service: Adventures and Experiences of US Transports and Cruisers in the World War* (New York, 1921), p. 97; Moody, *Pictorial History*, p. 17.

31. Chapman-Huston and Rutter, *Cowan*, Vol. II, p. 218; NA, MT25/29; NA, MT23/17/614–88; Western Front Association, *Bulletin*, 62 (2002), p. 23.

32. See <http://members.aol.com/troopships/shipli44.htm>.

33. Rogers, *Troopships*, p. 214.

Chapter 10

1. The spectacle of Empire was a popular subject from the earliest period, and films of this type were not limited to being made by British film companies. See McKernan, Luke, *Topical Budget: The Great British News Film* (London, 1992). See also Musser, Charles, *Before the Nickelodeon: Edwin S. Porter and the Edison*

Manufacturing Company (Berkeley, Calif., 1991); Brown, Richard and Anthony, Barry, *A Victorian Film Enterprise: The History of British Mutoscope and the Biograph Company, 1897–1915* (Trowbridge, 1999). For a contemporary account of filming the Boer War, see Dickson, W. K. L., *The Biograph in Battle: Its Story in the South African War Related with Personal Experience* (1901) facsimile edn, ed. Brown, Richard (Trowbridge, 1995).

2. Hammond, Michael, *The Big Show: British Film Culture in the Great War* (Exeter, 2005). From the outset of the war, the trade press had recommended that exhibitors incorporate patriotic events such as recruitment drives, entertaining wounded soldiers and refugees, charity benefits and official war films as part of their overall house management. See also DeBauche, Leslie Midkiff, *Reel Patriotism: The Movies and World War I* (Madison, Wisc., 1997), Here, De Bauche uses a phrase from a US trade paper to describe the approach exhibitors took in supporting the war effort through special programmes and bond drives as 'practical patriotism'.

3. 'Southampton Shows', *Bioscope*, 16 April 1914.

4. 'Southampton Shows', *Bioscope*, 17 December 1914.

5. 'Screen Gossip', *Pictures and the Picturegoer*, 14 March 1914.

6. 'Works Committee', March 1914, Minutes of the Proceedings of the Council and Committees from 9th Nov. 1913 to 9th Nov. 1914 (Southampton, 1914), p. 110.

7. The number of cinemas are based on those listed in the Southampton Council Minutes from 1914 to 1918. The population figures are from the 1911 census. See Patterson, A. Temple, *A History of Southampton, 1700–1914* (3 vols, Southampton, 1975), Vol. III, p. 115.

8. Thompson, Kristin, *Exporting Entertainment* (London, 1985), p. 29.

9. *What's On in Southampton*, 14 November 1914.

10. *What's On in Southampton*, 26 December 1914.

11. *What's On in Southampton*, 23 January 1915.

12. *What's On in Southampton*, 9 January 1915.

13. Bailey, Peter, 'A Community of Friends' in Bailey Peter, ed., *Music Hall: The Business of Pleasure* (Milton Keynes, 1986), p. 35.

14. *What's On in Southampton*, 23 October 1915.

15. *Bioscope*, 10 September 1914.

16. 'Sunday Opening at Southampton: Rural Dean's Criticisms', *Bioscope*, 11 March 1915.

17. 'Southampton's Fine New Hall', *Bioscope*, 1 October 1914.

18. *What's On in Southampton*, 2 October 1914.

19. For a detailed discussion of the historical relationship between Egyptology, 'Egyptomania' and silent cinema, see Lant, Antonia, 'The Curse of the Pharaoh, or how Cinema Contracted Egyptomania', in Bernstein, Matthew and Studlar, Gaylyn, eds, *Visions of the East: Orientalism in Film* (London, 1997), p. 90.

20. *What's On in Southampton*, 2 October 1914.

21. Monkhouse, F. J., *A Survey of Southampton and its Region* (Southampton, 1964), p. 242.

22. 'Watch Committee', Southampton Council Minutes, 2 March 1914, p. 280, Southampton City Archives.

23. There has been a significant body of work on these films in the USA. For an overview, see Lindsey, Sheley Stamp, '*Traffic in Souls* and the White Slavery Scare', *Persistence of Vision*, 9 (1991), pp. 99–102, and Lindsey, Sheley Stamp, 'Is Any Girl Safe? Female Spectators at the White Slave Films', *Screen*, 37 (1) (1996), pp. 1–15; Sloan, Kay, *The Loud Silents: Origins of the Social Problem Film* (Chicago, Illo., 1988), pp. 80–6; Brownlow, Kevin, *Behind the Mask of Innocence: Sex, Violence, Prejudice, Crime: Films of Social Conscience in the Silent Era* (New York, 1990).

24. National Council of Public Morals, *The Cinema: Its Present Position and Future Possibilities* (London, 1917), p. 60.

25. Lindsey, 'Is Any Girl Safe?', p. 2.

26. *Bioscope*, 22 October 1914.

27. *What's On in Southampton*, 3 April 1915.

28. *What's On in Southampton*, 29 May 1915.

29. *What's On in Southampton*, 12 December 1914.

30. *What's On in Southampton*, 1 May 1914.

31. *What's On in Southampton*, 31 July 1914.

32. *What's On in Southampton*, 14 August 1914.

33. *Southampton Times*, 10 July 1915.

34. 'Sunday Opening at Southampton: Rural Dean's Criticisms', *Bioscope*, 11 March 1915.

35. For a helpful overview of national audience attendance figures during the war and into the 1920s, see Hiley, Nicholas, 'The British Cinema Auditorium', in Dibbets, Karel and Hogenkamp, Bert, eds, *Film and the First World War* (Amsterdam, 1995), pp. 160–70.

36. 'Southampton Shows', *Bioscope*, 18 June 1914.

37. McKernan, *Topical Budget*, pp. 109–15.

Chapter 11

1. Much of this paragraph draws upon Coster, Graham, *Corsairville The Lost Domain of the Flying Boat* (London, 2000), pp. 89–97.

2. A major factor was the business acumen and political clout of the airline's chairman, ex-cabinet minister Sir Eric Geddes. With prior approval from the Chancellor of the Exchequer, he could present the Post Office with a fait accompli. Thus, Neville Chamberlain not only sanctioned Imperial Airways' 1923 creation and 1938–9 nationalisation but also, in 1933–4, facilitated its finest hour.

3. A twice-weekly train service conveyed departing passengers from Waterloo (later Victoria) in two designated Pullman cars, plus, in the brake van, an Imperial Airways clerk to weigh the baggage and complete the relevant flight's load sheet: Coster, *Corsairville*, p. 95; Rance, Adrian, ed, *Sea Planes and Flying Boats of the Solent* (Southampton, 1981), pp. 36, 43.

4. On the early history of the Supermarine Aviation Company, see Rance, Adrian, *Fast Boats and Flying Boats: A Biography of Hubert Scott-Paine Solent Marine and Aviation Pioneer* (Southampton, 1989), pp. 12–37.

5. Supermarine valued its links with the local community, and vice versa. While the Spitfire later became symbolic of that close relationship, between the wars it was seaplanes, witness the civic gift of a shield to be affixed to the Sea Eagle flying boat, 'Southampton No. 1'. 'Town's Flying-Boat Shield', *Hampshire Advertiser*, 14 March 1925.

6. Priestley, J. B., *English Journey* (London, 1987), p. 21.

7. Priestley, *English Journey*, pp. 20–1.

8. The Ratepayers' Party was a Liberal-Conservative coalition which, although polling less votes than Labour in the 1938 local elections, retained control of the borough council.

9. Private information. The population in 1939 was a not insubstantial 180,000, but the rivers Itchen and Test encouraged concentration of dwellings on the urban peninsula, with a heavy focus upon the old town and port, plus, after 1918, Shirley. Suburban development east of the Itchen was largely a phenomenon of the 1930s, prompted by the end of toll charges on the Northam Bridge. Adshead, S. D. and Cook, H. T., *The Replanning of Southampton* (Southampton, 1942), p. 10.

10. The original moorings were at Hythe (and Marchwood in bad weather), with fast tenders conveying the passengers across Southampton Water to the Southern Railway terminal at Berth 50. From March 1938, the flying boats still landed off the western shore but then taxied to Berth 107, later Berth 108. Kimber, Sir Sidney, *Thirty-Eight Years of Public Life in Southampton, 1910–1948* (Southampton, 1949), p. 176; Rance, *Fast Boats and Flying Boats*, p. 44.

11. Rance, *Fast Boats and Flying Boats*, p. 37.

12. QEA, the future Qantas, remained a partner until 1947. Rance, *Fast Boats and Flying Boats*, p. 36.

13. BOAC was more than just a relaunch of Imperial Airways. The Cabinet had endorsed Sir John Reith's critical view of the airline's working practices following his appointment as Chairman in 1938 and agreed to a takeover of the original British Airways prior to the merged company becoming a public corporation. McIntyre, Ian, *The Expense of Glory: A Life of John Reith* (London, 1993), pp. 244–9.

14. Southampton Harbour Board Act 1939; Kimber, *Thirty-Eight Years*, pp. 177–8.

15. The transatlantic terminal was Foynes in the Irish Free State, with a shuttle service to Poole. The importance of the wartime service necessitated BOAC's purchase from Boeing of three Clipper boats, flown in tandem with Pan Am by crews retaining pre-war conditions of service. Hill, Norman, *Flying Boats of the Solent: A Portrait of a Golden Age of Air Travel* (Southampton, 1999), p. 57.

16. Hill, *Flying Boats of the Solent*, p. 58; Rance, *Fast Boats and Flying Boats*, pp. 36–7.

17. Hasegawa, Junichi, *Replanning the Blitzed City Centre: A Comparative Study of Bristol, Coventry and Southampton 1941–1950* (Buckingham, 1992), pp. 26–9, 48.

18. Adshead and Cook, *The Replanning of Southampton*, passim.

19. Hasegawa, *Replanning the Blitzed City Centre*, pp. 52–64.

20. Hasegawa, *Replanning the Blitzed City Centre*, pp. 50–5; 'Men Behind the Scheme' in *The New Southampton: A Summary of the Official Town Planning Report* (Southampton, 1942), p. 3.

21. Hasegawa, *Replanning the Blitzed City Centre*, pp. 65–8, 100.

22. Hasegawa, *Replanning the Blitzed City Centre*, p. 20; Adshead and Cook, *The Replanning of Southampton*, p. 6.

23. Kimber chaired the Council's Works and Harbour Committee. He was Deputy Chairman of the Harbour Board, but for the Special Air Base Sub-Committee he persuaded the Chairman to swap roles, i.e., his role was pivotal. Adshead and Cook, *Replanning of Southampton*, pp. 6, 9, 26–7; Town Planning and Development Committee, 28 July 1943, in *Minutes of the Proceedings of the Councils and Committees from the 9th November 1942 to 9th November 1943* (Southampton, 1943), p. 555; 'Southampton's Post-War Air Base Plans', *Southern Daily Echo*, 24 September 1943.

24. Adshead and Cook, *Replanning of Southampton*, pp. 26–7.

25. 'Post-War Development of Southampton', *Southern Daily Echo*, 3 January 1944; Special Air Base Sub-Committee, *A Scheme for a Sea Aerodrome and Air Base Combined with a Land Aerodrome at the Port of Southampton* (Southampton, 1943), p. 4.

26. The tile company, which in 1940 leased its premises to BOAC for an emergency headquarters and terminal, would not renew the lease. The level of overmanning was as great at Poole as in Hythe, witness the Ministry of Civil Aviation maintaining its own fleet of 14 launches, with a similar complement of crew. 'Flying Boat Services from Southampton', *Southern Daily Echo*, 3 December 1947.

27. 'Headquarters of the BOAC return to So'ton Water on Saturday', *Southern Daily Echo*, 3 April 1946.

28. 'Proposed Airport – Southampton Water Master Plan of Development, Scheme 2', summarised in 'Proposed Air Base in Southampton Water', *Southern Daily Echo*, 26 April 1946.

29. Barnett, Correlli, *The Lost Victory: British Dreams, British Realities, 1945–19* (London, 1995), p. 228.

30. Ministry of Civil Aviation, *Report of the Flying Boat Base Committee*, MACP No. 13, (London, 1947). Treasury-Ministry of Civil Aviation memos and correspondence are contained within 'Proposed Civil Flying Boat Base', 1945–50, NA HLG/71/373, on which much of this paragraph is based.

31. 'Britain's Marine Southampton Scheme Not Ruled Out', *Southern Daily Echo*, 30 January 1947.

32. J. J. S. Belcher (Treasury) to F. Belcher (MCA), 28 January 1950, HLG/71/373.

33. *British Air Transport*, Cmd 6605, 1945, quoted in Barnett, *The Lost Victory*, p. 228; Morgan, Kenneth O., *Labour in Power 1945–1951* (Oxford, 1984), pp. 102–3. The fact that Christopher Addison was Dominions Secretary was more than merely coincidental.

34. L. Petch (Treasury) to M. T. Flett (MCA), 16 July 1947, HLG/71/373, 'Temporary Flying-Boat Terminal Return to Southampton Next Summer', *Southern Daily Echo*, 30 October 1946. Empty aircraft had to fly 20 'dead' minutes in each direction between Poole and Hythe. The switch to Southampton eliminated this considerable cost, as well as that of maintaining and crewing the launches. At Berth 50, incoming aircraft were winched up to the floating

pontoons, allowing passengers to transfer directly from cabin to terminal building. Once through HM Immigration and Customs, and following a complimentary meal in the restaurant, passengers either collected their cars from the terminal garage or availed themselves of the direct rail link to Waterloo.

35. 'Britain's Flying Boats Return to Their Old Home', *Southern Daily Echo*, 1 April 1948.

36. 'Lord Nathan Opens Premier Air Base at Southampton', *Southern Daily Echo*, 14 April 1948. Note the use of the maritime term 'hull' rather than fuselage.

37. 'Lord Nathan Opens Premier Air Base', *Southern Daily Echo*, 14 April 1948; 'Flying Boats: Expenditure on UK Base at Southampton and Disposal of Bases Overseas Belonging to BOAC and the Ministry of Civil Aviation, 1946–1950', HLG/ T225/372.

38. The return fare, including four nights' hotel accommodation, was 301 pounds. 'Southampton–S. Africa Flying-Boat Service Started Today', *Southern Daily Echo*, 4 May 1948. Most passengers actually flew on South African Airways' Douglas Skymasters rather than the civilian successors of the Lancaster, which BOAC was obliged to fly pending the next generation of homegrown airliners becoming available: Barnett, *The Lost Victory*, p. 238.

39. Rance, *Fast Boats and Flying Boats*, p. 37. In actual fact, the Ministry of Supply owned the 12 Solents in service by 1949, renting them to BOAC.

40. Barnett, *The Lost Victory*, pp. 228–32; Hennessy, Peter, *Never Again: Britain 1945–51* (London, 1992), p. 108; Coster, *Corsairville*, pp. 32–5. With its maximum of 50 passengers, sleeping quarters and dining rooms, the Bristol Brabazon drew heavily on the flying-boat rationale that affluent passengers would always rate comfort above speed and price.

41. Barnett, *The Lost Victory*, p. 238.

42. See, for example, Treasury minute from J. A. Nasmyth to Gorell Barnes, 5 September 1946, HLG/71/373.

43. 'Southampton, Britain's Premier Marine Airport', *Southern Daily Echo*, 22 July 1948. The service ministries were asked whether the SR45 could have a logistical role in Korea, which gives an insight into pessimistic projections of how long the war might last. After the *Princess* was cocooned in 1954, later suggestions included transportation of Saturn V rocket parts for NASA and, even more bizarrely, providing test beds for nuclear reactors. Barnett, *The Lost Victory*, pp. 240–5; Coster, *Corsairville*, p. 33.

44. Edgerton, David, *England and the Aeroplane: An Essay on a Militant and Technological Nation* (London, 1991), pp. 90–1.

45. Ironically, the Comet was originally intended not to kill off the flying boat, but to offer a faster alternative on the stopping route to Australia. Barnett, *The Lost Victory*, pp. 228, 244.

46. Barnett, *The Lost Victory*, p. 243. *Southern Daily Echo*, 12 December 1949. BOAC's sense of tradition and continuity stretched to naming the Stratocruisers after the C-Class Empire flying boats.

47. Rance, *Fast Boats and Flying Boats*, pp. 37, 95.

Chapter 12

1. Despatch from US Consul in Southampton, 27 November 1905, microfilm, University of Southampton Library, T-239.
2. Boyarin, Jonathan, *Storm from Paradise: The Politics of Jewish Memory* (Minneapolis, Minn., 1992), pp. 1–2.
3. Promotional literature for Admiral's Quay, 2003; *Southern Property Advertiser*, 4 November 2004.
4. Promotional literature for Admiral's Quay, 2003.
5. Varley, Telford, *Hampshire* (London, 1909), p. 256.
6. See <http://www.portcities.org.uk>, visited 27 October 2004.
7. Southampton City Council, *Southampton* (Southampton, 1979), pp. 40–1.
8. *Jewish Guardian*, 2 September 1921.
9. Lutyens' original sketch for the Southampton cenotaph is reproduced in Kimber, Sidney, *Thirty-Eight Years of Public Life in Southampton, 1910–1948* (Southampton, 1949), facing p. 49.
10. Southampton Hebrew Congregation minutes, 19 January 1919, Southampton Hebrew Congregation Archives, in the possession of the community.
11. These plaques were originally located in the synagogue in the centre of Southampton, which moved to its current location in the 1960s.
12. Williams, Bill, 'The Anti-Semitism of Tolerance: Middle-Class Manchester and Jews: 1870–1900' in Kidd, A. J. and Roberts, K. W., eds, *City, Class and Culture: Studies of Social Policy and Cultural Production in Victorian Manchester* (Manchester, 1985), p. 94.
13. The description is by the late W. G. Sebald. See the paperback version of Hoare, Philip, *Spike Island: The Memory of a Military Hospital* (London, 2002), inside cover.
14. Hoare, *Spike Island*, p. 339.
15. Holder, John, *Royal Victoria Country Park: The Story of a Great Military Hospital and Royal Victoria Country Park* (Winchester, n.d.), p. 15.
16. Boyarin, *Storm from Paradise*, p. 7.
17. Sandell, Elsie, *Southampton Cavalcade* (Southampton, 1953), p. 20.
18. Sandell, *Southampton Cavalcade*, pp. 17–20.
19. Thomas, Dan, 'The Ocean Village Experience', *Aspire*, 1 (summer 2004), p. 160.
20. *Now in Southampton*, 10 January 1986.
21. Broad, Ian, *The Illustrated Guide to Southampton* (Southampton, 1982), p. 5.
22. Arnott, Alastair, *Maritime Southampton* (Derby, 2002), p. 15.
23. Pinch, Steven, 'From Shipping to Shopping? The Transformation of Southampton', *Dolphin* (March 2002), p. 8; Pinch, Steven, 'City Profile: Southampton', *Cities*, 19(19) (2002), pp. 71–8.
24. Thomas, 'The Ocean Village Experience', p. 160.
25. For Bryant's anti-Semitism and pro-Nazism in the late 1930s and Second World War, see Andrew Roberts, *Eminent Churchillians* (London, 1994), Chapter 6.
26. Bryant, Arthur, 'Preface' in Knowles, Bernard, *Southampton: The English Gateway* (London, 1951), p. 13.

27. Knowles, *Southampton*, p. 248.
28. Perks, Rob, 'The Ellis Island Immigration Museum, New York', *Oral History*, 19(1) (1991), pp. 79–80.
29. Gilkes, Michael, 'The Dark Strangers' in Smith, Lesley, ed., *The Making of Britain: Echoes of Greatness* (Basingstoke, 1988), pp. 143–4.
30. See Patterson, A. Temple, *A History of Southampton 1700–1914* (3 vols, Southampton, 1975), Vol. III, Chapter 9.
31. Especially through the Wilson Line. See the research of Nick Evans reported in *Jewish Chronicle*, 13 July 2001, and in his ongoing Ph.D. research on transmigrancy in Britain.
32. See *Southampton Times*, 8 November 1893, for the official opening and background.
33. Testimony reproduced in Hyslop, Donald, Forsyth, Alastair and Jemima, Sheila, *Titanic Voices* (Southampton, 1994), p. 175.
34. Hyslop et al., *Titanic Voices*, p. 175.
35. Farber family, Manchester Jewish Museum, Oral History collection, J82, J201.
36. For its opening and objectives, see *Manchester Metropolitan News*, 12 April 2002; *Guardian*, 18 June and 1 July 2002; Urbis Museum, Manchester, visited by the author in 2002.
37. Telephone conversation with Enfields Residential letting service, 22 September 2000; adverts for Atlantic Mansions in *Southern Property Advertiser*, 21 September 2000, 25 July 2002; and <http://www.southampton-property.com/let_oceanvillage.html> (viewed 29 July 2002).
38. Boyarin, *Storm from Paradise*, p. 5.
39. Hyslop, Donald and Jemima, Sheila, 'The "Titanic" and Southampton: The Oral Evidence', *Oral History*, 19(1) (1991), p. 41.
40. 'Home Fit for the "New Life" Seekers', *Southern Evening Echo*, 24 February 1989; Leonard, Alan and Baker, Rodney, *A Maritime History of Southampton in Picture Postcards* (Southampton, 1989), p. 38; Boyd-Smith, Peter and Boyd-Smith, Jan, *Southampton in Focus* (Southampton, 1996), p. 27.
41. See his entry in Southampton Hebrew Congregation, Ledger, 1927, Southampton Hebrew Congregation Archives.
42. See Guimond, James, 'The *Titanic* and the Commodification of Catastrophe' in Gray, Peter and Oliver, Kendrick, eds, *The Memory of Catastrophe* (Manchester, 2004), p. 79.
43. See Hyslop et al., *Titanic Voices*, passim; Hyslop and Jemima, 'The "Titanic"', pp. 37–43, especially p. 37; Massey, Anne and Hammond, Mike, '"It Was True! How Can You Laugh?": History and Memory in the Reception of *Titanic* in Britain and Southampton', in Sandler, Kevin and Studlar, Gaylyn, eds, *Titanic: Anatomy of a Blockbuster* (New Brunswick, NJ, 1999), pp. 239–64; Hammond, Mike, '"My Poor Brave Men": Time, Space and Gender in Southampton's Memory of the Titanic', in Bergfelder, Tim and Street, Sarah, eds, *The Titanic in Myth and Memory: Representations in Visual and Literary Culture* (London, 2004), pp. 25–36.
44. Biel, Steven, *Down with the Old Canoe: A Cultural History of the Titanic Disaster* (New York, 1996), p. 6.

45. Biel, *Down with the Old Canoe*, pp. 46–53.

46. Foster, John Wilson, *The Titanic Complex: A Cultural Manifest* (Vancouver, 1997), p. 34.

47. Hyslop and Jemima, 'The "Titanic"', p. 37.

48. Biel, *Down With the Old Canoe*, p. 124.

49. Sam Smith, '"Southampton Water" and Other Objects Made by Sam', Southampton City Art Gallery leaflet, (n.d.).

50. Smith, '"Southampton Water"'.

51. Smith, '"Southampton Water"'.

52. Sher, Anthony, *Middlepost* (London, 1988), p. 21.

53. Kushner, Tony and Knox, Katharine, *Refugees in an Age of Genocide: Global, National and Local Perspectives during the Twentieth Century* (London, 1999), Chapter 3.

54. Letter from Winifred Dominy, who relates how she 'began [her] teaching career with the emigrant children who spoke very little English': *Hampshire: The County Magazine*, 11(8) (June 1971), p. 34; Allan Robinson was a teenager who delivered groceries to Atlantic Park. See his 'Refugees at Atlantic Park, 1920, and North Stoneham, 1937', *Eastleigh and District Local History Society*, Special Paper, 20 (1991); and also letter to Katharine Knox, 1 May 1995 (in author's possession).

55. Letter from Winifred Dominy.

56. It is reproduced in Mann, John Edgar, *The Book of the Stonehams* (Tiverton, 2002), p. 29.

57. Mann, *Book of the Stonehams*, p. 29.

58. Mills, Walter, '100 Years of Carnival', *Eastleigh and District Local History Society*, Occasional Paper, 22 (1987).

59. See the advert for the play in *Eastleigh Weekly News*, 28 December 1923. For a summary of its plot: Joseph Gaer, *The Legend of The Wandering Jew* (New York, 1961), pp. 140–1.

60. For the film's origins, see Charles Chaplin, *My Autobiography* (London, 1964), p. 225.

61. Kushner and Knox, *Refugees in an Age of Genocide*, pp. 83, 89–90.

62. *Jewish Chronicle*, 9 January 1925, 6 February 1925; *Daily Herald*, 7 January 1925, 8 January 1925, for coverage of the hunger strike.

63. *Southern Daily Echo*, 4 June 1924.

64. Kushner and Knox, *Refugees in an Age of Genocide*, p. 94.

65. In the possession of her son, Cyril Orolowitz, and with thanks to him for sending me copies.

66. New, Peter, 'Atlantic Park', *Hampshire: The County Magazine*, 11(6) (April 1971), p. 26.

67. *Eastleigh Weekly News*, 2 October 1931.

68. I have been contacted by relatives of those at Atlantic Park from a variety of countries, all trying to piece together their fragmented and dislocated family histories.

69. See, for example, the headline of the *Daily News*, 7 January 1925: 'Hunger Strike by 700 Jews: Complaints at British Ellis Island', *Southern Daily Echo*, 21 February 2003; and Mann, *The Book of the Stonehams*, p. 27.

70. Samuel, Raphael and Thompson, Paul, eds, *The Myths We Live By* (London, 1990).

71. Kimber, *Thirty-Eight Years*, p. 169.

72. Eastleigh Borough Council Highway and Works Committee, 22 January 1990, 'Naming of Streets Townhill Farm Estate'; Carolyn Dwyer, Principal Engineer, letter to the author, 18 June 1996.

73. Halbwachs, Maurice, *On Collective Memory*, ed. and trans. by Lewis Coser (Chicago, Ill., 1992), p. 52.

74. Eastleigh Borough Council, Highway and Works Committee, 22 January 1990.

75. Robinson, 'Refugees at Atlantic Park', p. 5.

76. *Southern Daily Echo*, 4 June 1924, 14 June 1924; *Eastleigh Weekly News*, 13 February 1925.

77. Eastleigh Borough Council Highway and Works Committee, 22 January 1990.

78. Southampton International Airport, viewers' gallery, December 1994. Subsequently, this small exhibit has been removed.

79. The near full-sized replica was designed and created by a local artist, Alan Manning, and it was unveiled in September 2003 as part of the programme of events, 'History, Heritage and the Hamble Valley' sponsored by Eastleigh Borough Council and the Heritage Lottery Fund. See the *Festival Programme* (Eastleigh, 2003).

80. 'The Development of Eastleigh Airport', n.d. (c. 1989), leaflet in Cope Collection, University of Southampton Library.

81. Anon., *Spitfire: A 60th Anniversary Tribute by the City of Southampton* (Southampton, 2000).

82. *Southern Daily Echo*, 5 June 2000.

83. Taylor, John W. R. and Alward, Maurice, *Spitfire* (Leicester, 1946), p. 7.

84. *Southern Daily Echo*, 10 July 2004.

85. *Southern Daily Echo*, 20 August, 22 August 1942.

86. Beckles, Gordon, *Birth of a Spitfire* (London, 1941), pp. 108, 130.

87. Beckles, *Birth of a Spitfire*, p. 15.

88. Knowles, *Southampton: The English Gateway*, p. 144.

89. Lunn, Ken and Day, Ann, 'Britain as Island: National Identity and the Sea' in Brocklehurst, Helen and Phillips, Robert, eds, *History, Nationhood and the Question of Britain* (Basingstoke, 2004), p. 126.

90. Beckles, *Birth of a Spitfire*, p. 74.

91. For the eccentric tag, see the Southampton Hall of Aviation and *Spitfire: A 60th Anniversary Tribute*.

92. *Observer*, 4 June 2000, in a review of Douglas Murray's biography of Lord Alfred Douglas.

93. Knowles, *Southampton: The English Gateway*, pp. 132–3.

94. Rice, Alan, 'Exploring Inside the Invisible: An Interview with Lubaina Himid', *Wasafiri*, 40 (2003), pp. 20–6.

95. Hoare, *Spike Island*, p. 115.

96. Boyarin, *Storm from Paradise*, p. 4.

97. Boyarin, *Storm from Paradise*, p. 2.

Index

INDEX